T·H·E M·A·I·L· O·R·D·E·R Gourmet

T·H·E
M·A·I·L-
O·R·D·E·R
Gourmet

A Complete Guide
to Buying Fine Foods
by Mail

By Peggy Hardigree

ST. MARTIN'S PRESS   NEW YORK

Design by Mina Greenstein

Library of Congress Cataloging in Publication Data

Hardigree, Peggy Ann, 1945–
    The mail-order gourmet.

    Includes index.
    1. Food—Catalogs. I. Title.
TX354.5.H37 1983   016.6413'0029'473   83-9633
ISBN 0-312-50442-X
ISBN 0-312-50443-8 (pbk.)

CONTENTS

INTRODUCTION VII

A COMPLETE GUIDE TO BUYING
FOOD BY MAIL ix

1. Meat, Game, and Poultry 3
2. Fish and Other Seafood 36
3. Ethnic and Specialty Foods 49
4. Natural Foods 75
5. Cheese 90
6. Baked Goods 111
7. Vegetables, Fruits, and Nuts 127
8. Sweets and Treats 154
9. Coffee and Tea, Herbs and Spices 193
10. Dehydrated Foods 221
11. Cookware and Accessories 230

INDEX 244

All information in this book is up-to-date as of September 1, 1982. However, because of the time it takes for a book to reach consumers after the text is completed, changes in prices and/or product lines are to be expected. Please do not order directly from this book even if prices are given. Always contact the individual company first to ascertain product availability and current price before ordering.

The Mail-Order Gourmet is a resource for use by the general public. Companies are listed at the sole discretion of the author, and no advertising fees are solicited or accepted.

Introduction

Welcome to the largest food store in the world, its aisles lined with the exotic, the unusual, the finest, and, sometimes, the cheapest culinary delights known. Here one can select farmhouse cheeses from Europe or America; country ham and bacon smoked according to old and secret family recipes; freshly roasted, carefully chosen coffees from prime growing areas; aromatic sausages; the finest in produce; the very best fish and seafood; stone-ground flour and meal; herbs and ethnic spices; and giant wheels of tempting cheeses. Even the huge variety of food available in the largest market in the largest city is surpassed by the offerings of this mart. Its shelves are stocked, not just with the ordinary and the expected, but with the extraordinary and the surprising, as well: rosy-pink smoked salmon from the Pacific Northwest; stone crab claws from Florida; sweet and juicy pineapples, fresh from Hawaii; kosher meats from New York; corn-fed, prime beef from Iowa—even a complete New England clambake, seaweed and all.

Many of the offerings are prepared and ready to eat. But those who enjoy the special qualities of home cooking will also find the ingredients needed for preparing the spicy dishes of the

American Southwest, the exotic concoctions of the Orient, and the ethnic dishes that are part of your heritage, no matter what your ancestry. Here, too, you will find offered the cookware needed for preparing these foods.

The quality of these products is seldom matched by those found in local markets, for quality is essential to the survival of the "food store" you are about to enter. The proprietors know their success is dependent upon repeat business and that repeat business is obtained only by offering quality goods at reasonable prices. But they also make it easy for you to sample their wares by offering you the chance to do so without ever leaving the comfort of your home—another reason why food-by-mail is the fastest-growing part of one of the fastest-growing industries in America, the mail-order business.

The Mail-Order Gourmet is a complete guide to ordering food by mail. To prepare it, I contacted—by letter and by telephone—hundreds and hundreds of firms involved in shipping food by mail. I found giant corporations and "mom and pop" operations, family farms and small specialty shops offering freshly baked pastries, carefully aged sausage and cheese, and hundreds of regional delicacies. I sampled food as old as America and food as new as the space age. My goal was to gather what is best representative of the many types of food that can be mail-ordered and the regions and countries from which they come, and to provide readers with information not easily obtained from other sources. If I have achieved this goal it is largely due to the courteous treatment I received from the many sources I contacted.

Like them, I wish you *bon appétit!*

A Complete Guide to Buying Food by Mail

Please read this section before placing any order, requesting the catalog of any firm, or writing even a letter of inquiry. It contains information that will save you time, trouble, money, and the grief caused by undue haste.

Above all, please DON'T try to order directly from this book. The prices that I've given are approximate and are included for you to use as guides. Actual prices may fluctuate with the seasons, with the availability of a particular ingredient, or for a number of other reasons. Always send—or call—for a current price list first.

Catalogs

Most firms listed in this book issue catalogs. Some are merely mimeographed price lists, while others are lavishly produced brochures or booklets containing elaborate descriptions and dozens of tempting color photographs. Many are free, and nearly all are obtainable at nominal cost, usually (but not always) refundable; when the price of the catalog is listed as refundable, this means that the company will credit the cost of the catalog to your first order.

When requesting a catalog, write a complete letter (unless directed otherwise). Specify the type of catalog you want, as some firms may have more than one catalog. Be certain to include your return address in the letter, and mention any enclosures of cash or check, so these will not be overlooked. Date the letter, and be sure to keep a copy for your own records.

If the price of the catalog is less than $1.00, send the amount in coins taped securely between two pieces of cardboard, taping these, in turn, to the bottom of the letter. Write on the cardboard the amount of the enclosure. For catalogs costing more than $1.00, it is best to send a money order, since personal checks take at least two weeks to clear and so cause needless delays.

Some firms may request that you send an "SASE" instead of, or in addition to, a catalog charge. This is a self-addressed, stamped envelope, and you should respond by sending a long business envelope, stamped and legibly addressed to yourself, along with your letter requesting the catalog.

For any of a number of reasons, there may be some delay before you receive your catalog. The supply may be exhausted, you may order at a time when the firm is waiting for its new catalog to be printed, or the catalog may be issued only seasonally. In such instances, it may be months before you receive the catalog you have requested. If you attach a stamped, self-addressed postcard to your letter and ask that it be used to notify you of any delays, most firms will gladly do so. This is especially advisable when you feel you must have the catalog by a certain date.

□

How to Order

Ordering: Most catalogs contain order blanks, but many do not. Always use the order blank if included, as well as any adhesive address labels that may be provided. If no order blank is found in the catalog, print all the pertinent information on a blank sheet of paper. Be very specific about the units (pounds, ounces, dozens, etc.) you are ordering. If the firm has a minimum order requirement, as a small number do, be sure your order meets the minimum requirement. Provide a second choice when the firm asks that you do so. Companies will make substitutions only when you have specifically authorized them to do so.

Some types of food are available only at certain seasons of the year. A few examples include fresh fruit, seafood items, and specialty meats, as well as gift assortments intended for Christmas and other holidays. When a catalog specifies that an item is available only at certain times of the year, or that it must be ordered well in advance of the season, follow the guidelines set forth in the catalog. An out-of-season order may be impossible to fill and can lead to unnecessary confusion.

When ordering perishable food, give some thought to its receipt. Most firms are diligent about meeting the delivery times mentioned in their catalogs, but they cannot provide good service if no one is home to receive their shipment. Perishable goods should not be ordered just prior to your vacation, for example, unless you can arrange for a neighbor to receive and store them.

Delayed Orders: All U.S. companies are required by law to respond to your order within 30 days by either sending it, explaining any delays, or returning your payment. If you have not received your order (or an acceptable explanation for the delay) within 30 days, call or write the company and—providing them with the order number and the items requested—ask for an explanation. If their explanation is not satisfactory, you have the right to cancel your order, and a full refund should be on its way to you within seven days.

Shipping: Food shipped from companies located within the United States will be delivered either by the Postal Service (Parcel Post), United Parcel Service (UPS), or by a private trucking firm. Orders weighing less than 50 pounds can be shipped by Parcel Post or UPS, but there are also some restrictions on oversized packages; consult UPS for these.

UPS: The cost of shipping a package by UPS is determined by where you live, the location of the company shipping the food, and the size and weight of the parcel. UPS has divided the country into 63 sections. Each section has a zoning chart that divides the rest of the country into seven zones. These are then numbered from "Zone 2" to "Zone 8," according to distance and using the first three digits of the zip code as a base.

For example, when shipping a package from New York City, the zone chart lists other New York City addresses (zip code prefix 100) as Zone 2, or the closest zone, and California addresses (zip code prefix 900) as Zone 8, the most distant zone. When a package is shipped from California, the zone numbers are reversed, with the 900 zip code prefix becoming Zone 2 and the 100 zip code prefix serving as Zone 8.

A guide called the "Common Carrier Rate Chart" is needed to translate these zone numbers into shipping costs. This guide lists rates for packages weighing up to 50 pounds, shipped from any zone to any other. The lowest charge, of course, is on a package of 1 pound or less shipped to Zone 2, the highest on 50 pounds shipped to Zone 8. Check with your local UPS office for the current rates.

Along with their catalogs, many firms will send rate charts that allow you to figure shipping costs. Others may simply leave it up to you. When this occurs, your only option is to call the local UPS office and find out what zone you are in in relation to the company. They will provide you with a chart, if you request one, that allows you to figure exact shipping costs. When determining these costs, be sure to allow for the weight of packaging materials.

It is important to keep in mind that UPS cannot deliver to a post office box; they must have a street address in order to deliver goods. If the food is to be delivered to a post office box, it *must* be shipped by Parcel Post.

Parcel Post: Rates for Parcel Post are slightly higher than those for UPS. However, as mentioned above, the UPS option is not available to those who receive mail at a post office box. If you receive your mail at a P.O. box, you should stipulate DELIVERY BY PARCEL POST ONLY; UPS NOT ACCEPTABLE in bold print on the order form; and on your check write, GOODS TO BE SENT BY PARCEL POST ONLY. This assures that your order will be shipped by Parcel Post and not needlessly returned to the shipper.

You should check with the local post office to determine the current rates for Parcel Post, as these are subject to frequent change.

Many companies charge a flat rate for shipping, thus saving you the trouble of figuring costs. When such a flat rate is charged, the food may be shipped by either UPS or Parcel Post, and will be subject to the same limitations.

Truck Shipments: If your order exceeds 50 pounds, or is nonmailable for other reasons, it may be sent by truck, the most expensive method of shipment. A few firms ship only by this method.

Truck charges are based on weight and distance. If the order is heavy and the distance great, these charges can be substantial, and you will want to give them some consideration when ordering. Too, there is usually a minimum charge for shipment by truck (as much as $25 for orders up to 100 pounds) and yet another charge for home delivery. The latter charge can be avoided by picking up the order at the truck terminal, if this is convenient.

For shipments of more than 100 pounds, up to a maximum of 500 pounds, it may be necessary to use the trucks of REA Express. They offer quick service at rates lower than those charged by most truck carriers, and charges can be further reduced by picking up the goods at their terminal.

Truck charges are always collected upon delivery. These must be paid when the carrier arrives, and you must pay with cash or a certified check. Personal checks are not acceptable.

Other Costs: The charges for packing, handling, and insurance are usually nominal and may be included in the shipping charge. When ordering, check the catalog carefully to see if insurance is included, and request it when it is not. Insurance is inexpensive and well worth having, especially on large and costly orders.

If you live in the state where the firm or any of its branches is located and there is a state sales tax, the proper amount should be added to your check when ordering. In many states, however, food is exempt from sales tax. Individual catalogs provide the best guidelines for figuring any sales tax that might apply.

COMMON CARRIER

ANY FRACTION OF A POUND OVER THE WEIGHT SHOWN TAKES THE NEXT HIGHER RATE

WEIGHT NOT TO EXCEED	RATE CHART TO GROUND ZONES						
	2	**3**	**4**	**5**	**6**	**7**	**8**
1 lb.	$1.25	$1.28	$1.32	$1.36	$1.42	$1.48	$1.55
2 "	1.34	1.40	1.47	1.55	1.67	1.79	1.93
3 "	1.43	1.52	1.63	1.75	1.92	2.11	2.32
4 "	1.52	1.64	1.78	1.94	2.18	2.42	2.70
5 "	1.61	1.75	1.93	2.14	2.43	2.74	3.09
6 "	1.70	1.87	2.09	2.33	2.68	3.05	3.47
7 "	1.79	1.99	2.24	2.53	2.94	3.37	3.86
8 "	1.88	2.11	2.40	2.72	3.19	3.68	4.24
9 "	1.97	2.23	2.55	2.92	3.44	4.00	4.63
10 "	2.05	2.34	2.70	3.11	3.69	4.31	5.01
11 "	2.14	2.46	2.86	3.31	3.95	4.63	5.40
12 "	2.23	2.58	3.01	3.50	4.20	4.94	5.78
13 "	2.32	2.70	3.17	3.70	4.45	5.26	6.17
14 "	2.41	2.82	3.32	3.89	4.71	5.57	6.55
15 "	2.50	2.93	3.47	4.09	4.96	5.89	6.94
16 "	2.59	3.05	3.63	4.28	5.21	6.20	7.32
17 "	2.68	3.17	3.78	4.48	5.47	6.52	7.71
18 "	2.77	3.29	3.94	4.67	5.72	6.83	8.09
19 "	2.86	3.41	4.09	4.87	5.97	7.15	8.48
20 "	2.94	3.52	4.24	5.06	6.22	7.46	8.86
21 "	3.03	3.64	4.40	5.26	6.48	7.78	9.25
22 "	3.12	3.76	4.55	5.45	6.73	8.09	9.63
23 "	3.21	3.88	4.71	5.65	6.98	8.41	10.02
24 "	3.30	4.00	4.86	5.84	7.24	8.72	10.40
25 "	3.39	4.11	5.01	6.04	7.49	9.04	10.79
26 "	3.48	4.23	5.17	6.23	7.74	9.35	11.17
27 "	3.57	4.35	5.32	6.43	8.00	9.67	11.56
28 "	3.66	4.47	5.48	6.62	8.25	9.98	11.94
29 "	3.75	4.59	5.63	6.82	8.50	10.30	12.33
30 "	3.83	4.70	5.78	7.01	8.75	10.61	12.71
31 "	3.92	4.82	5.94	7.21	9.01	10.93	13.10
32 "	4.01	4.94	6.09	7.40	9.26	11.24	13.48
33 "	4.10	5.06	6.25	7.60	9.51	11.56	13.87
34 "	4.19	5.18	6.40	7.79	9.77	11.87	14.25
35 "	4.28	5.29	6.55	7.99	10.02	12.19	14.64
36 "	4.37	5.41	6.71	8.18	10.27	12.50	15.02
37 "	4.46	5.53	6.86	8.38	10.53	12.82	15.41
38 "	4.55	5.65	7.02	8.57	10.78	13.13	15.79
39 "	4.64	5.77	7.17	8.77	11.03	13.45	16.18
40 "	4.72	5.88	7.32	8.96	11.28	13.76	16.56
41 "	4.81	6.00	7.48	9.16	11.54	14.08	16.95
42 "	4.90	6.12	7.63	9.35	11.79	14.39	17.33
43 "	4.99	6.24	7.79	9.55	12.04	14.71	17.72
44 "	5.08	6.36	7.94	9.74	12.30	15.02	18.10
45 "	5.17	6.47	8.09	9.94	12.55	15.34	18.49
46 "	5.26	6.59	8.25	10.13	12.80	15.65	18.87
47 "	5.35	6.71	8.40	10.33	13.06	15.97	19.26
48 "	5.44	6.83	8.56	10.52	13.31	16.28	19.64
49 "	5.53	6.95	8.71	10.72	13.56	16.60	20.03
50 "	5.61	7.06	8.86	10.91	13.81	16.91	20.41

ADDITIONAL CHARGES — Common Carrier and Blue Label Air:
For each COD received for collection — $1.50.
For each Address Correction — $1.50.
For each Acknowledgment of Delivery (AOD) — 26 cents.
For each package with a declared value over $100 — 25 cents for each additional $100 or fraction thereof.

0007240 REV. 5-82

UPS ZONE CHART FOR NEW YORK CITY AREA

 UPS United Parcel Service

TERRITORY SERVED	48 CONTINENTAL UNITED STATES		

TO DETERMINE ZONE TAKE FIRST THREE DIGITS OF ZIP CODE TO WHICH PARCEL IS ADDRESSED AND REFER TO CHART BELOW

ZIP CODE PREFIXES	UPS ZONE	ZIP CODE PREFIXES	UPS ZONE	ZIP CODE PREFIXES	UPS ZONE	ZIP CODE PREFIXES	UPS ZONE
010-013	2	200-218	3	410-418	4	654-655	5
014	3	219	2	420-427	5	656-676	6
015-018	2	220-238	3	430-458	4	677-679	7
019	3	239-253	4	460-466	5	680-692	6
020-024	2	254	3	467-468	4	693	7
025-026	3	255-266	4	469	5		
027-029	2	267	3	470	4	700-722	6
030-033	3	268-288	4	471-472	5	723-724	5
034	2	289	5	473	4	725-738	6
035-043	3	290-293	4	474-479	5	739	7
044	4	294	5	480-489	4	740-762	6
045	3	295-297	4	490-491	5	763-770	7
046-049	4	298-299	5	492	4	773	6
050-051	3			493-499	5	774-775	7
052-053	2	300-324	5			776-777	6
054-059	3	325	6	500-503	6	778-797	7
060-089	2	326-329	5	504	5	798-799	8
		330-334	6	505	6		
100-127	2	335-338	5	506-507	5	800-812	7
128-136	3	339	6	508-516	6	813	8
137-139	2	350-364	5	520-539	5	814	7
140-149	3	365-366	6	540	6	815	8
150-154	4	367-374	5	541-549	5	816-820	7
155	3	376	4	550-554	6	821	8
156	4	377-386	5	556-559	5	822-828	7
157-159	3	387	6	560-576	6	829-874	8
160-162	4	388-389	5	577	7	875-877	7
163	3	390-392	6	580-585	6	878-880	8
164-165	4	393	5	586-593	7	881-884	7
166-169	3	394-396	6	594-599	8	890-898	8
170-171	2	397	5				
172-174	3			600-639	5	900-961	8
175-176	2	400-402	5	640-648	6	970-986	8
177	3	403-406	4	650-652	5	988-994	8
178-199	2	407-409	5	653	6		

UPS ZONE CHART FOR LOS ANGELES AREA

 UPS United Parcel Service

TO DETERMINE ZONE, TAKE FIRST THREE DIGITS OF ZIP CODE TO WHICH PARCEL IS ADDRESSED AND REFER TO CHART BELOW

ZIP CODE PREFIXES	UPS ZONE	ZIP CODE PREFIXES	UPS ZONE	ZIP CODE PREFIXES	UPS ZONE
010-089	8	506-507	7	778-789	6
		508-516	6	790-791	5
100-199	8	520-560	7	792	6
		561	6	793-794	5
200-299	8	562-567	7	795-796	6
		570-581	6	797-799	5
300-339	8	582	7		
350-359	7	583-588	6	800-838	5
360-364	8	590-591	5	840-863	4
365-367	7	592-593	6	864	3
368	8	594	5	865	4
369-372	7	595	6	870-871	5
373-379	8	596-599	5	873-874	4
380-384	7			875-884	5
385	8	600-639	7	890-891	3
386-397	7	640-648	6	893-898	4
		650-652	7		
400-402	7	653	6	900-935	2
403-418	8	654-655	7	936-939	3
420-424	7	656-676	6	940-949	4
425-426	8	677	5	950-953	3
427	7	678	6	954-961	4
430-458	8	679	5	970-974	5
460-466	7	680-692	6	975-976	4
467-468	8	693	5	977-986	5
469	7			988-994	5
470	8	700-708	7		
471-472	7	710-711	6		
473	8	712-717	7		
474-479	7	718-719	6		
480-497	8	720-725	7		
498-499	7	726-738	6		
		739	5		
500-504	7	740-775	6		
505	6	776-777	7		

LOCAL ZONE

See separate list for Points in
Los Angeles Local Zone

FIRST-CLASS

```
LETTER RATES:
  1st ounce........................................... 20¢
  Each additional ounce............................... 17¢
```

For Pieces Not Exceeding (oz.)	The Rate Is	For Pieces Not Exceeding (oz.)	The Rate Is
1	$0.20	7	$1.22
2	0.37	8	1.39
3	0.54	9	1.56
4	0.71	10	1.73
5	0.88	11	1.90
6	1.05	12	2.07

FOR PIECES OVER 12 OUNCES SEE FIRST-CLASS ZONE RATED (PRIORITY) MAIL RATES

```
CARD RATES:
  Single postal cards sold by the post
    office.................................   13¢ each.
  Double postal cards sold by the post
    office.................................   26¢ (13¢ each half.)
  Single post cards......................   13¢ each.
  Double post cards (reply-half of
    double post card does not have to bear
    postage when originally mailed)........   26¢ (13¢ each half.)
  Presort rate...........................   Consult Postmaster
  Business reply mail....................   Consult Postmaster
```

SECOND-CLASS
(Newspapers and periodicals with second-class mail privileges.)

For copies mailed by the public, the rate is:

Weight up to and Including

1 ounce	19¢	5 ounces	65¢
2 ounces	35¢	6 ounces	75¢
3 ounces	45¢	7 ounces	85¢
4 ounces	55¢	8 ounces	95¢

Each additional two ounces over 8 ounces, add 10¢.

THIRD CLASS

Circulars, books, catalogs, and other printed matter; merchandise, seeds, cuttings, bulbs, roots, scions, and plants, weighing less than 16 ounces.

0 to 1 oz	$0.20	Over 6 to 8 ozs	0.95
Over 1 to 2 ozs	0.37	Over 8 to 10 ozs	1.05
Over 2 to 3 ozs	0.54	Over 10 to 12 ozs	1.15
Over 3 to 4 ozs	0.71	Over 12 to 14 ozs	1.25
Over 4 to 6 ozs	0.85	Over 14 but less than 16 ozs	1.35

**BULK RATE
CONSULT POSTMASTER**

FIRST-CLASS ZONE RATED (PRIORITY) MAIL

Weight over 12 oz but not exceeding (pounds)	Local 1,2 & 3	Zone 4	Zone 5	Zone 6	Zone 7	Zone 8
1	$2.24	$2.24	$2.24	$2.34	$2.45	$2.58
1.5	2.30	2.42	2.56	2.72	2.87	3.07
2	2.54	2.70	2.88	3.09	3.30	3.57
2.5	2.78	2.98	3.21	3.47	3.73	4.06
3	3.01	3.25	3.53	3.85	4.16	4.56
3.5	3.25	3.53	3.85	4.22	4.59	5.05
4	3.49	3.81	4.18	4.60	5.02	5.55
4.5	3.73	4.09	4.50	4.97	5.45	6.05
5	3.97	4.37	4.83	5.35	5.88	6.54
6	4.44	4.92	5.47	6.10	6.74	7.53
7	4.92	5.48	6.12	6.86	7.60	8.52
8	5.39	6.03	6.77	7.61	8.46	9.51
9	5.87	6.59	7.42	8.36	9.32	10.51
10	6.35	7.15	8.07	9.12	10.18	11.50
11	6.82	7.70	8.71	9.87	11.04	12.49
12	7.30	8.26	9.36	10.62	11.89	13.48
13	7.77	8.81	10.01	11.38	12.75	14.47
14	8.25	9.37	10.66	12.13	13.61	15.46
15	8.73	9.93	11.31	12.88	14.47	16.45
16	9.20	10.48	11.95	13.63	15.33	17.44
17	9.68	11.04	12.60	14.39	16.19	18.43
18	10.15	11.59	13.25	15.14	17.05	19.42
19	10.63	12.15	13.90	15.89	17.91	20.42
20	11.11	12.71	14.55	16.65	18.77	21.41
21	11.58	13.26	15.19	17.40	19.63	22.40
22	12.06	13.82	15.84	18.15	20.48	23.39
23	12.53	14.37	16.49	18.91	21.34	24.38
24	13.01	14.93	17.14	19.66	22.20	25.37
25	13.49	15.49	17.79	20.41	23.06	26.36
26	13.96	16.04	18.43	21.16	23.92	27.35
27	14.44	16.60	19.08	21.92	24.78	28.34
28	14.91	17.15	19.73	22.67	25.64	29.33
29	15.39	17.71	20.38	23.42	26.50	30.33
30	15.87	18.27	21.03	24.18	27.36	31.32
31	16.34	18.82	21.67	24.93	28.22	32.31
32	16.82	19.38	22.32	25.68	29.07	33.30
33	17.29	19.93	22.97	26.44	29.93	34.29
34	17.77	20.49	23.62	27.19	30.79	35.28
35	18.25	21.05	24.27	27.94	31.65	36.27
36	18.72	21.60	24.91	28.69	32.51	37.26
37	19.20	22.16	25.56	29.45	33.37	38.25
38	19.67	22.71	26.21	30.20	34.23	39.24
39	20.15	23.27	26.86	30.95	35.09	40.24
40	20.63	23.83	27.51	31.71	35.95	41.23
41	21.10	24.38	28.15	32.46	36.81	42.22
42	21.58	24.94	28.80	33.21	37.66	43.21
43	22.05	25.49	29.45	33.97	38.52	44.20
44	22.53	26.05	30.10	34.72	39.38	45.19
45	23.01	26.61	30.75	35.47	40.24	46.18
46	23.48	27.16	31.39	36.22	41.10	47.17
47	23.96	27.72	32.04	36.98	41.96	48.16
48	24.43	28.27	32.69	37.73	42.82	49.15
49	24.91	28.83	33.34	38.48	43.68	50.15
50	25.39	29.39	33.99	39.24	44.54	51.14
51	25.86	29.94	34.63	39.99	45.40	52.13
52	26.34	30.50	35.28	40.74	46.25	53.12
53	26.81	31.05	35.93	41.50	47.11	54.11
54	27.29	31.61	36.58	42.25	47.97	55.10
55	27.77	32.17	37.23	43.00	48.83	56.09
56	28.24	32.72	37.87	43.75	49.69	57.08
57	28.72	33.28	38.52	44.51	50.55	58.07
58	29.19	33.83	39.17	45.26	51.41	59.06
59	29.67	34.39	39.82	46.01	52.27	60.06
60	30.15	34.95	40.47	46.77	53.13	61.05
61	30.62	35.50	41.11	47.52	53.99	62.04
62	31.10	36.06	41.76	48.27	54.84	63.03
63	31.57	36.61	42.41	49.03	55.70	64.02
64	32.05	37.17	43.06	49.78	56.56	65.01
65	32.53	37.73	43.71	50.53	57.42	66.00
66	33.00	38.28	44.35	51.28	58.28	66.99
67	33.48	38.84	45.00	52.04	59.14	67.98
68	33.95	39.39	45.65	52.79	60.00	68.97
69	34.43	39.95	46.30	53.54	60.86	69.97
70	34.91	40.51	46.95	54.30	61.72	70.96

Parcels weighing less than 15 pounds, measuring over 84 inches but not exceeding 100 inches in length and girth combined, are chargeable with a minimum rate equal to that for a 15-pound parcel for the zone to which addressed.

ADDITIONAL SERVICES FOR INSURED, CERTIFIED AND REGISTERED MAIL

Restricted Delivery*... $1.00

Return Receipts*
  Requested at time of mailing:
  Showing to whom and when delivered..................... $0.60
  Showing to whom, when, and address where delivered....... $0.70
  Requested after mailing:
  Showing to whom and when delivered.................... $3.75

*Not available for mail insured for $20 or less

COD
Consult Postmaster for fee and conditions of mailing

SPECIAL DELIVERY FEE (In addition to required postage)

Class of Mail	Weight		
	Not more than 2 pounds	More than 2 pounds but not more than 10 pounds	More than 10 pounds
First Class.............	$2.10	$2.35	$3.00
All other classes........	2.35	3.00	3.40

SPECIAL HANDLING Third and Fourth Class Only (In addition to required postage)

10 pounds and less... $0.75

More than 10 pounds... 1.30

MONEY ORDERS   For safe transmission of money

$0.01 to 25.00... $0.75
25.01 to 50.00... 1.10
50.01 to 500.00.. 1.55

SIZE STANDARDS FOR DOMESTIC MAIL

MINIMUM SIZE
Pieces which do not meet the following requirements are prohibited from the mails:
  a. All pieces must be at least .007 of an inch thick, and
  b. All pieces (except keys and identification devices) *which are ¼ inch or less thick* must be:
    (1) Rectangular in shape,
    (2) At least 3½ inches high, and
    (3) At least 5 inches long.
    NOTE: Pieces *greater than ¼ inch thick* can be mailed even if they measure less than 3½ by 5 inches.

NON STANDARD MAIL
All First-Class Mail weighing one ounce or less and all single-piece rate Third-Class mail weighing one ounce or less is nonstandard (and subject to a 9¢ surcharge in addition to the applicable postage and fees) if:
  1. Any of the following dimensions are exceeded:
    Length—11½ inches,
    Height—6 1/8 inches,
    Thickness— ¼ inch, or
  2. The piece has a height to length (aspect) ratio which does not fall between 1 to 1.3 and 1 to 2.5 inclusive. (The aspect ratio is found by dividing the length by the height. If the answer is between 1.3 and 2.5 inclusive, the piece has a standard aspect ratio.)

Weight 1 pound and not exceeding (pounds)	Local	Zones 1 2	Zone 3	Zone 4	Zone 5	Zone 6	Zone 7	Zone 8
2	1.52	1.55	1.61	1.70	1.83	1.99	2.15	2.48
3	1.58	1.63	1.73	1.86	2.06	2.30	2.55	3.05
4	1.65	1.71	1.84	2.02	2.29	2.61	2.94	3.60
5	1.71	1.79	1.96	2.18	2.52	2.92	3.32	4.07
6	1.78	1.87	2.07	2.33	2.74	3.14	3.64	4.54
7	1.84	1.95	2.18	2.49	2.89	3.38	3.95	5.02
8	1.91	2.03	2.30	2.64	3.06	3.63	4.27	5.55
9	1.97	2.11	2.41	2 75	3 25	3.93	4 63	6 08
10	2.04	2.19	2.52	2.87	3.46	4.22	5.00	6.62
11	2.10	2.28	2.60	3.00	3.68	4.51	5.38	7.15
12	2.17	2.36	2.66	3.10	3.89	4.80	5.75	7.69
13	2.21	2.41	2.72	3.19	4.02	4.96	5.95	7.97
14	2.26	2.46	2.78	3.28	4.13	5.12	6.14	8.24
15	2.31	2.51	2.83	3.36	4.25	5.26	6.32	8.48
16	2.35	2.56	2.89	3.44	4.35	5.40	6.49	8.72
17	2.40	2.59	2.94	3.51	4.45	5.53	6.65	8.94
18	2.44	2.64	2.99	3.59	4.55	5.65	6.80	9.15
19	2.48	2.68	3.04	3.66	4.64	5.77	6.94	9.35
20	2.52	2.72	3.10	3.73	4.73	5.89	7.09	9.55
21	2.56	2.76	3.14	3.79	4.82	6.00	7.22	9.73
22	2.60	2.81	3.20	3.86	4.90	6.10	7.35	9.91
23	2.64	2.84	3.26	3.92	4.99	6.21	7.48	10.08
24	2.68	2.93	3.36	4.02	5.07	6.31	7.60	10.24
25	2.72	3.00	3.47	4.15	5.14	6.40	7.75	10.40
26	2.76	3.04	3.56	4.27	5.27	6.58	8.02	10.56
27	2.79	3.08	3.65	4.40	5.44	6.79	8.28	10.71
28	2.83	3.13	3.70	4.47	5.59	7.00	8.53	10.85
29	2.87	3.17	3 75	4.53	5.76	7.17	8.64	10.99
30	2.90	3.21	3.80	4.59	5.84	7.27	8.75	11.13
31	2.97	3.25	3.85	4.65	5.91	7.36	8.86	11.29
32	3.01	3.30	3.90	4.71	5.98	7.44	8.96	11.41
33	3.05	3.34	3.95	4.76	6.05	7.53	9.06	11.53
34	3.08	3.38	4.00	4.82	6.12	7.61	9.16	11.76
35	3.12	3.42	4.04	4.88	6.19	7.69	9.26	12.07
36	3.16	3.44	4.08	4.93	6.25	7.78	9.36	11.88
37	3.20	3.50	4.14	4.98	6.32	7.86	9.45	12.20
38	3.23	3.54	4.18	5.04	6.39	7.93	9.54	12.51
39	3.27	3.58	4.23	5.09	6.45	8.01	9.63	12.82
40	3.31	3.62	4.27	5.14	6.51	8.09	9.72	13.08
41	3.34	3.66	4.32	5.19	6.58	8.16	9.81	13.20
42	3.38	3.70	4.36	5.24	6.64	8.24	9.90	13.31
43	3.42	3.74	4.40	5.29	6.70	8.31	9.98	13.42
44	3.46	3.78	4.45	5.34	6.76	8.38	10.14	13.53
45	3.49	3.81	4.49	5.39	6.82	8.45	10.36	13.64
46	3.53	3.85	4.53	5.44	6.88	8.52	10.58	13.74
47	3.56	3.89	4.58	5.49	6.94	8.66	10.80	13.85
48	3.60	3.93	4.62	5.54	6.99	8.83	11.02	13.95
49	3.64	3.97	4.66	5.59	7.05	9.01	11.24	14.05
50	3.67	4.01	4.71	5.64	7.13	9.18	11.46	14.15
51	3.71	4.04	4.75	5.69	7.27	9.36	11.68	14.25
52	3.74	4.08	4.79	5.79	7.40	9.53	11.90	14.35
53	3.78	4.12	4.83	5.90	7.54	9.71	12.12	14.44
54	3.82	4.16	4.87	6.00	7.67	9.88	12.34	14.54
55	3.85	4.19	4.94	6.11	7.81	10.06	12.56	14.76
56	3.89	4.23	5.02	6.21	7.94	10.23	12.78	15.02
57	3.92	4.27	5.11	6.32	8.08	10.41	13.00	15.28
58	3.96	4.32	5.19	6.42	8.21	10.58	13.22	15.54
59	3.99	4.39	5.28	6.53	8.35	10.76	13.44	15.80
60	4.03	4.46	5.36	6.63	8.48	10.93	13.66	16.06
61	4.06	4.53	5.45	6.74	8.62	11.11	13.88	16.32
62	4.10	4.60	5.53	6.84	8.75	11.28	14.10	16.58
63	4.13	4.67	5.62	6.95	8.89	11.46	14.32	16.84
64	4.17	4.74	5.70	7.05	9.02	11.63	14.54	17.10
65	4.20	4.81	5.79	7.16	9.16	11.81	14.76	17.36
66	4.24	4.88	5.87	7.26	9.29	11.98	14.98	17.62
67	4.27	4.95	5.96	7.37	9.43	12.16	15.20	17.88
68	4.31	5.02	6.04	7.47	9.56	12.33	15.42	18.14
69	4.34	5.09	6.13	7.58	9.70	12.51	15.64	18.40
70	4.38	5.16	6.21	7.68	9.83	12.68	15.86	18.66

NOTE: If Within (Intra-BMC) BMC ZIP Code destinations for your post office are not shown above, consult your local postmaster and write the ZIP Codes in the space provided.

Consult Postmaster for bound printer matter, special fourth-class, and library rates.

Method of Payment: Catalogs tell you the method of payment preferred by each firm, and you will find that most offer you several options. Each method of payment has its own advantages and disadvantages, and you should be aware of these when placing your order.

Personal checks are convenient to you and are accepted by most companies in the mail-order food business. This is the least expensive method of payment for you, as well. The only real drawback is that most firms will not ship your order until the check has cleared, which usually means a delay of at least two weeks. If you are in no hurry to receive your order, this is the best means of payment.

Money orders are handled like cash and will cause no delays in shipment, as long as you are ordering from a firm located within the United States. They are relatively inexpensive—costing about 50 cents for any amount up to $1,000—and available at banks, post offices, and even retail stores. As with a check, payment can be stopped when the need arises.

COD means "cash on delivery," and relatively few companies accept such orders. When they do, payment must be in cash or by certified check. There are always service charges on COD shipments.

Stamps and cash should never be sent through the mails, except in very small amounts for catalog costs.

Credit cards are the most convenient but also the most expensive means of payment. Dozens and dozens of firms accept phone orders charged to Visa, American Express, MasterCard, and other interbank charge cards. This allows for faster delivery and easier billing (you receive just one bill at the end of the month, no matter how many times you order), but keep in mind that you also pay a heavy finance charge on the unpaid balance due the credit card company. Another drawback is that some companies set minimum order amounts on such purchases.

□

Receiving Your Order

Open your order carefully as soon as it is received. Save the shipping carton, wrapping material, and address labels. These may be needed if, for whatever reason, you are dissatisfied and wish to return the goods.

Guarantees and Warranties: The best of all guarantees, and one frequently offered, simply states: "Satisfaction guaranteed or your money back." This means that if you are not pleased with the product, for any reason, you can return it and receive a refund, exchange, or credit. Often such an adjustment will be made with no questions asked.

The return policies of many companies, however, are not that simple. Many require that you obtain permission before returning any goods. This means you must write a letter describing the reason for your dissatisfaction, and wait for a reply from the company, before returning any goods. Others make adjustments only within a certain time limit. Many firms accept returned goods only when sent back in the package in which they were shipped. Some companies charge a small fee for restocking returned goods, and other firms make no refunds at all. For these reasons, you should always read their policy (in the catalog) carefully before ordering, save the original boxes and wrapping materials, and waste no time in letting the company know when you have a complaint. Unless the catalog says otherwise, you will have to pay the cost of shipping returned goods.

The term "warranty" seldom applies to food. A warranty is more likely to cover the life and functions of an item such as an electrical appliance. You will need to understand the functions of a warranty only if you choose to order cookware or appliances from the firms listed in this book who offer such items.

The warranty is usually backed by the manufacturer, not the retailer. Full information about the warranty arrives with the product. A brochure packed with the product details the limits of the warranty, as well as any conditions under which the warranty would be invalidated. A warranty may expire in as little as 60 days, or it may provide lifetime coverage. With goods covered by a warranty you will receive a postcard that must be signed, dated, and mailed to the manufacturer. The warranty does not take effect until the manufacturer receives this card.

Complaints: If you have reason to complain about the company or its products, contact the firm by letter describing the problem and what you would like done about it. If no action results, contact the firm once more. If your second letter brings no satisfactory action, there are three agencies that will take action on your behalf.

The Direct Mail Marketing Association, whose members do nearly three-fourths of all U.S. mail-order business, will not only refer your complaint to the proper state or federal agency but will also apply pressure of its own to see that the problem is resolved. For assistance, write to the Mail Order Action Line, DMMA, 6 East 43rd St., New York, NY 10017.

The Federal Trade Commission investigates cases of fraud and deception, but they act very slowly unless they have received numerous complaints about the same firm. If you feel you have been the victim of fraud, forward all the details to the Bureau of Consumer Protection, Federal Trade Commission, Washington, DC 20580.

The U.S. Postal Service is the most powerful of all agencies handling such complaints, simply because it has the power to withhold mail delivery until problems are acted on. Every complaint received is investigated, and nearly 90 percent are resolved. Problems should be brought to the attention of the Chief Postal Inspector, U.S. Postal Service, Washington, DC 20260.

☐

CHAPTER ONE

MEAT, GAME, AND POULTRY

Firms listed in this section offer the fine cuts of prime beef usually seen only in the finest restaurants; the superbly cured ham, bacon, and sausage of Virgina, Kentucky, Tennessee, Vermont, and other regions; and a wide selection of salamis, bologna, and wursts.

Top-quality steaks and roasts such as filet mignon, prime rib, crown roast of lamb, and aged porterhouse may be ordered individually from the large packing houses, and sides or quarters of naturally raised beef or veal for the freezer are also available from the same sources. Suckling pigs are available for special occasions. Such quality meat is expensive, of course, but it is frequently so much tastier than that offered in the ordinary markets that you may decide it is well worth the extra cost.

A few words need to be said about the old-fashioned hams sold by numerous companies listed in this chapter. Most of these are cured, smoked, and aged according to prized recipes that have been handed down from one generation to the next, and they are offered by producers throughout the South, Northeast, and Midwest. Opinions vary widely from one region to the next as to how a ham should be smoked and cured. One processor

3

may coat the ham with black pepper before it is smoked; another after. Others may use no pepper at all. When corncobs provide the smoke, the resulting flavor is characteristic of one region, while apple, hickory, maple, and other hardwoods are favored by others. Some hams are hot-smoked, while others are cured at lower temperatures. There is disagreement about how long a ham should be aged. All the processes are represented here, and the choice is yours.

Perhaps you prefer buffalo steak, mallard duck, Canadian goose, or even antelope roast. These too are offered by the firms described in this chapter, along with chicken, turkey, and more ordinary poultry. While the prices for the exotic meats are often high, you may feel that the price is justified by the quality and uniqueness.

All perishable meats are packed in dry ice and shipped air freight to your door. Their safe arrival is guaranteed.

□

AMANA SOCIETY MEAT SHOP
Amana, IA 52203
(319) 622-3111
Free catalog. Accepts checks and money orders only.
Full guarantee.

The story of Amana began nearly 250 years ago when a group of Germans seeking religious freedom migrated to America. In this group of hardworking, determined individualists were several master butchers who brought their recipes and trade secrets along. The towering smokehouse built in 1858 by descendants of the original immigrants is still in use today, and in it members of the Society produce smoked hams, bacon, and sausages that enjoy a worldwide reputation for quality.

Amana hams, which may be ordered either bone-in or boneless, are fully cooked by the smoking process. Average weight is 12 to 14 pounds; the price is just under $40.00. Their slab bacon, cured in a thick sugar brine, then smoked to a deep mahogany color, comes in 6- to 8-pound slabs, and costs around $20.00. Canadian bacon sells at just under $30.00 for a 5-pound package. Sausages offered by the Amana Society include knockwurst, bratwurst, ring bologna, and summer sausage. These are sold only as part of the numerous gift assortments found in the catalog. These assortments usually include samples of the ham, bacon, cheese, and other foods, such as German-style mustard, produced by the Amana Society, and they range in price from about $10.00 to $55.00 or so. Shipping charges are additional on all orders.

□

B & B FOOD PRODUCTS, INC.
Route 1
Cadiz, KY 42211
(502) 235-5294
Accepts checks, money orders, MasterCard, and
Visa, but credit card orders must exceed $15.00. All
items are fully guaranteed to be as advertised and to
arrive safely at your door.

Outstanding country hams are the most famous product offered by this firm, which has operated out of Trigg County, Kentucky, for more than 70 years. The company raises its own hogs under sanitary, climate-controlled conditions, feeding them only a special diet of ground corn supplemented with vitamins and minerals. Selected hams are cured in a secret mixture of salt, sugar, and other ingredients, then smoked over a mixture of hickory and sassafras woods. These hams won the Grand Champion Country Ham Award four out of five years at the Kentucky State Fair, and one of the prize-winning hams later sold for the staggering price of $35,150—that's $2,140 a pound. Your own ham costs less than $40.00 for a 12- to 13-pound ham, less than $50.00 for one weighing 17 to 18 pounds, uncooked. Cooked hams are available at slightly higher prices.

Dry-cured, hickory-smoked slab bacon, without which no country breakfast would be complete, was added to the B & B line only after eight years of research satisfied this firm that it was worthy of the honor. A slab weighing 4 to 5 pounds costs about $13.00, with slabs as large as 18 pounds available. Sacks of smoked country pork sausage, which the firm has been selling throughout its 70-year history, are offered at about the same price per pound.

Western boneless strip sirloins (six 11-ounce steaks for about $60.00) and filet mignons (eight 11-ounce steaks for under $65.00) are also offered, and four 10-ounce filets of prime rib, four 6-ounce filet mignons, and four 10-ounce strip sirloins, in one package, cost just over $85.00.

Smoked turkey, a real delicacy, is available at about $30.00 for a bird weighing about 10 pounds, while 5 pounds of smoked turkey breasts cost about $25.00. A package of 16 smoked quail runs a little over $40.00. All prices given by this firm include shipping and insurance charges, so prices will vary slightly according to the place of delivery.

□

BECK SAUSAGE, INC.
South Park Route
Box 2141
Jackson, WY 83001
(307) 733–8343
Free price list and brochure. Accepts checks, money
orders, MasterCard, and Visa. Telephone orders
accepted.

Formerly known as the Jackson Hole Cold Storage Co., this firm has long been an outstanding source of various forms of smoked buffalo meat, a food high in protein but low in cholesterol and saturated fats. The name of the firm was changed about a year ago when it was bought out by John and Gary Beck, a father-and-son team who hold patents on several modern food processes but who cling to tradition in providing the type of meat that fed many a settler in the days of the Old West.

Smoked buffalo tenderloin roast heads the list of cuts offered by the Becks. It arrives at your home fully cooked, and the refrigerated meat can be sliced and served cold for cocktail parties or snacks, or heated and served as the main course. The roast costs about $7.25 for a 1-pound roll, and this price includes delivery.

The Becks also produce Jackson Hole Buffalo Salami, which we tasted and found to be moist and delightfully spiced; Teton Wilderness Salami, which is milder and lightly flavored with sage; and Pioneer Buffalo Salami, which is heavily smoked and mellowed by a secret blend of spices. Their Saloon Salami is flavored with white wine and cheddar cheese; and I found their buffalo jerky, the old trail standby, far superior to any beef jerky I had tried. Prices for these items range from $6.25 a pound upwards, but be sure to obtain the current price list before ordering, as the Becks advise us that their prices are subject to frequent change.

□

BURGER'S SMOKEHOUSE
Highway 87 South
California, MO 65018
(314) 796–3134
Accepts checks, money orders, MasterCard, Visa,
and American Express. All products are fully
guaranteed as long as unsatisfactory goods are
returned within 60 days of purchase.

Like many firms in the mail-order industry, Burger's Smokehouse got its start during the Great Depression, when E. M. Burger and his wife began curing and selling a few hams to help make ends meet. In 1952, when the senior Burger announced that he hoped to cure and sell 1,000 hams that winter, his sanity was questioned, according to family members. But that goal was reached, then surpassed, and today the firm is one of the largest country meat producing firms in the United States, processing and selling more than 200,000 hams annually.

All their hams come from corn-fed hogs and are cured by the original, secret recipe, aged at least one year, and shipped promptly upon receipt of your order. A 14- to 22-pound ham sells for about $2.15 a pound, plus shipping costs. Sliced ham is available at the same price. Boneless, precooked ham sells for about $3.50 a pound, and 2 pounds of sliced country bacon will cost you roughly $5.00. If bought in the slab, the price of the bacon drops to about $2.20 a pound.

Smoked chicken and turkey are recent additions to the Burger line. A plump, broad-breasted turkey, made delightful with the taste and aroma of hickory smoke, sells at about $2.15 per pound for a bird weighing 8 to 12 pounds. The smoked chickens weigh about 2 pounds each, and a pair costs just over $10.00. A 5-pound roll of smoked turkey breast is offered at approximately $16.00.

A complete line of prime steaks is another new addition to the Burger line. These include thick filet mignons, strip sirloins, and several packages combining the two. A package of eight 6-ounce filet mignons will set you back just over $50.00; a package containing ten 10-ounce strip steaks costs about $80.00. If you're a real lover of fine steak, a package of fifty filets and fifty strip steaks can be sent to your door for about $800.00. Numerous gift packages are also available from Burger's, and they offer a limited selection of cheese and snack items.

□

DEER VALLEY FARM
R.D. 1
Guilford, NY 13780
(607) 764–8556
*Free catalog. Accepts checks and money orders; no
credit cards.*

Located in the rolling hills of central New York State, about 40 miles south of Utica, Deer Valley Farm has built up an outstanding reputation as a supplier of organic and natural foods. During its 35 years in the business, it has grown from a small, family-operated venture into a major concern. With the recent addition of a federally inspected meat plant, the company began offering one of the most complete lines of meat in the mail-order industry. All its meats are processed without the use of nitrates.

Trimmed beefsteaks cost a little over $2.00 per pound for chuck or as much as $5.00 per pound for filet mignon. Standing rib roast fetches just under $3.00 per pound. The rolled rib roast is slightly higher, at about $4.00 a pound, but still quite reasonable.

If you prefer veal, prices start at about $3.60 a pound for the roasts and cheaper cuts, ranging upward to as much as $6.00 a pound for the more expensive sweetbreads, calves' liver, and other more costly cuts. In between, there is a full line of veal, including loin and rib chops at about $4.00 per pound.

Not many companies ship lamb through the mail, but this one does. The leg of lamb costs about $3.30 per pound; ground lamb fetches roughly the same price; and the rib or loin chops will set you back a little over $4.00 a pound.

Deer Valley also sells a complete line of pork and pork products. Selections include spare ribs at approximately $1.65 per pound, loin and shoulder roast at about $2.60 per pound, sausage at about $2.20 per pound, and fresh ham at just over $2.00 per pound.

□

EARLY'S HONEY STAND
Rural Route 2
Spring Hill, TN 37174
(615) 486-2230
Free catalog. Accepts checks, money orders,
MasterCard, and Visa; no CODs.

"From the very moment you unpack this sausage, you know it is going to be something special," said Jack Shelton, in an article written for *Bon Appétit* magazine. "I assure you that Early's pork sausage is the best I have found to date, and I have been searching for a long time."

That is an opinion with which I wholeheartedly agree. I find it difficult to say enough, in this limited space, about the outstanding quality of the food shipped out by the Earlys, a family that has been winning praise with its country fare since 1925. Perhaps it is enough to say that when they shipped me a few samples of their finest, it won them a customer for life.

The company began as a roadside honey stand, as its name suggests. Today, however, honey accounts for only a tiny percentage of the business done by this nationally known firm. Smoked ham, sausage, and other pork products are the backbone of their business, though they do offer a limited line of cheese, jams and jellies, and stone-ground meal and flour.

The most famous item is their sausage, made without a speck of the cereals and fillers too commonly found in other sausages, and seasoned with a secret blend of sage, peppers, and other spices. Its taste is further improved by slow smoking over green hickory wood, and it comes to you in an old-fashioned cloth poke, as fine sausage should. A 3-pound poke costs $8.50 and up, depending on the shipping distance.

I'd honestly suggest that you give Early's smoked bacon a try, for it is the best I have tasted in years. Carefully chosen slabs are hand-rubbed with Early's own honey, cured in special sugars, then slowly smoked over hickory coals. It bears little resemblance to most bacon sold in stores. A slab costs a little over $2.00 per pound; the sliced product is only slightly higher.

Hams at Early's are dry salt-cured, then hung for several months in a smokehouse filled with cool hickory smoke. They are a wee bit saltier than most hams, but also far superior to most. They cost under $2.50 per pound, plus postage; and like all other meat products sold by Early's, they should be ordered well in advance, because this is one place where demand almost always exceeds supply.

□

Fin 'n Feather Farm
Route 25
Dundee, IL 60118
(312) 742–5040
Accepts checks, money orders, MasterCard, Visa,
and American Express. Credit card orders accepted,
toll-free, at (800) 942–8176. All products fully
guaranteed.

In business for more than forty years, this company offers one of the most complete and interesting assortments of meat and poultry I encountered during research for this book. Just to browse through their free catalog is an experience in itself.

According to its brochure, this was the first firm in the country to offer smoked pheasant, and that gourmet delight is still available; the 2-pound bird sells for under $20.00. If smoked turkey sounds more to your liking, one weighing about 6 pounds can be ordered for about $25.00; or the company will ship you a hickory-smoked duck, weighing 2¼ to 2¾ pounds, for less than $15.00. A pair of smoked Cornish hens, total weight above 4 pounds, will cost you about $16.00.

The complete line of prime beef includes a 12-pound heart of the rib roast for about $95.00, eight 12-ounce strip steaks for about $80.00, twelve 6-ounce filet mignons for about $70.00, eight 12-ounce Delmonico steaks for less than $60.00, and other assortments too numerous to describe here.

Also offered is a complete line of bacon and sausage, including a 2-pound slab of Canadian bacon for about $14.00 and a 5-pound pack of sliced, hickory-smoked country bacon for under $20.00. A 3½-pound ham, boneless and fully cooked, runs just over $20.00.

Several exciting gift plans are offered, making it possible for you to send a gift that will last for months or throughout the year. One plan, costing about $100.00, offers a smoked turkey at Christmas, a smoked ham at Easter, and a fresh, oven-ready turkey at Thanksgiving. The six-month plan costs about $130.00, and for about $200.00, some lucky person on your list can receive a deliciously edible gift each month for a full year.

□

GASPAR'S SAUSAGE CO., INC.
P.O. Box 436
North Dartmouth, MA 02747
(800) 343–8086; Massachusetts residents phone (toll-free) 998–2012.
Free price list. Accepts checks, money orders, Visa, and MasterCard.

Sausages head the list of New England–style delicacies shipped out by Gaspar's. Among these are a few types I encountered nowhere else in the mail-order industry, such as linquica, a mild sausage that originated in Portugal, and chourica, a hotter sausage with the same origins.

In addition to numerous other sausages, Gaspar's offers a limited selection of Vermont-style cheese, New England condiments such as Yankee mustard, and regional favorites such as salt cod and quince marmalade. Also available are syrups in flavors such as coffee, chocolate, vanilla, and strawberry.

Sausages are offered in 4-, 8-, and 12-pound assortments, the prices ranging from less than $15.00 to as much as $40.00, depending on the size and type you choose. However, if you'd like to try a wide sampling of the fare offered by this firm, you can choose from among several samplers, such as "The Continental." For a little under $25.00, you receive: two 1-pound packages of mild linquica sausage, two 1-pound packages of chourica sausages, 1 pound of quince jam, 1 pound of salted cod, approximately 9 ounces of tinned sardines, spiced, and one 6-ounce box of imported bite-sized sugar cookies from Portugal. Prices include shipping.

□

GOURMET FARE
4545 South Racine Avenue
Chicago, IL 60609
(800) 621-0222
Free catalog. Accepts checks, money orders,
MasterCard, Visa, BankAmericard, and American
Express. All products fully guaranteed.

Since 1932, this firm has offered specially selected prime beef and other meats to its customers—"gourmet meats for exquisite dining," as they describe them on their letterhead—and I assure you that those I have received more than live up to every claim made by the company. This is beautifully marbled, exquisitely flavored steak that you can literally cut with a fork before allowing each treasured bite to melt away in your mouth. We are talking about steak so tender one almost forgets how to chew.

Their filet mignons, cut from the center of carefully aged tenderloins, head the list of offerings. You can sample six 6-ounce filets for under $40.00. Porterhouse steaks, weighing no less than a full pound each, come in boxes of six for under $70.00. Six 8-ounce rib eyes cost about $50.00. For extra special occasions, you might want to serve their 12-pound prime rib roast, which will cost you about $90.00. All these cuts of beef, and many, many others, are, of course, available in larger packages and in several combination packages.

Gourmet Fare also offers a tempting arsenal of pork, veal, and lamb. From among the various cuts of lamb, you might choose to try the 4-pound crown roast at about $70.00, the rib chops at just over $90.00 for sixteen 6-ounce chops, the leg roast, weighing 6 pounds and costing about $50.00. From among their creamy-pink milk-fed Provimi veal, you could select 4 pounds sliced for scallopini at under $70.00, 4 pounds of chops for less than $60.00, or four pounds of diced veal liver for about $36.00. Center-cut pork chops cost roughly $45.00 for two dozen 4-ounce chops. Baby back ribs are offered at about $45.00 for a box of eight 10-ounce cuts.

If quality poultry tempts you, you might try the fresh broad-breasted hen turkey. The 12-pounder sells for about $40.00. Or try the gourmet chicken specialties that arrive at your door ready to be popped into the oven. The Chicken Cordon Bleu—boneless breast of chicken rolled around imported ham and cheese—costs about $30.00 for six 6¾-ounce servings. Romanoff Royall, rich with noodles and cheese sauce, costs approximately the same, as does the famous Chicken Kiev.

If gourmet fare is your weakness, as it is mine, then Gourmet Fare is a company that deserves your attention.

□

GWALTNEY OF SMITHFIELD
P.O. Box 489
Smithfield, VA 23430
Free price list on request. Accepts checks, money orders, Visa, MasterCard, BankAmericard, and American Express. Full guarantee.

Since 1870, the Gwaltney smokehouse has been producing its rightfully famous Smithfield hams, making it the oldest firm in Virginia with a legal right to cure and sell hams under the Smithfield name; under a Commonwealth statute, only hams processed in this county can be termed genuine Smithfields.

Long before the first white settlers came to these shores, the Indians of this region had developed the dry-curing and smoking processes that are used today by Gwaltney and about half a dozen other smokehouses in the county. The process requires about a year to complete, but it brings forth a ham that is to pork as filet mignon is to beef. The hams are so good, as a matter of fact, that as early as 1878 Queen Victoria was having them shipped back to England for service on the royal table—certainly one of the earliest examples of food being "mail-ordered."

Uncooked Smithfields weigh 13 to 15 pounds and cost a little over $40.00. Cooked Smithfields weigh 10 to 12 pounds and cost a little over $50.00. Boneless hams, trimmed and cooked, cost $54.95 and up, depending on weight, with the price just mentioned buying a ham of 9 to 11 pounds.

The firm also offers a cheaper version called the Williamsburg ham, which is aged only about half as long as the Smithfield. An uncooked ham of about 12 pounds costs just over $30.00, and a cooked Williamsburg of about 11 pounds costs about $45.00. A slab of colonial-style smoked bacon costs about $20.00 for 8 to 10 pounds, and there is a shipping charge of $4.00 for each item ordered.

□

HARRINGTON'S
Richmond, VT 05477
(802) 434–3411
Free catalog. Accepts checks, money orders, Visa, MasterCard, American Express, Diners Club, and Carte Blanche. Full guarantee if correct address is provided with order.

"Pork is among the many pleasures of Vermont tables," says Craig Claiborne, food writer for *The New York Times*, "and one of the most admirable of the pork products made here is ham with the Harrington label."

Those famous hams have had the distinction of being served at the White House, as well as being featured on the menus of distinguished hotels, resorts, and restaurants known for their fine food. All hams are carefully selected from very young porkers raised in the corn country of the Midwest, then smoked over a mixture of smoldering maple wood and corncobs, a technique that Harrington's has used for more than a century and one that many gourmets believe produces a ham far superior to those smoked over hickory or other woods. That they are expensive is beyond dispute; the price is over $6.00 per pound, with the hams weighing in at 10 to 13 pounds apiece. Other smoked pork products include slab bacon, Canadian bacon, sausage, and loin chops. For approximately $60.00, there is a sample box that allows you to try half a ham (about 6½ pounds), plus 1 pound each of the slab and Canadian bacon.

Other cob-smoked products from Harrington's include pheasant (around $40.00 for a brace of two), turkey (about $40.00 for a 10-pound hen), and salmon (approximately $60.00 for a side weighing 1¾ pounds). A number of club plans are offered, ranging in price from under $10.00 to approximately $300.00, and the catalog also offers cheese, maple syrup, and several other delicacies native to Vermont.

□

V. W. JOYNER & COMPANY
Main Street
Smithfield, VA 23430
(804) 357–2161
Free brochure on request. Accepts checks, money
orders, Visa, and MasterCard.

Since 1889, the Joyner firm has been producing the famous Smithfield hams, cutting carefully selected hams in a fashion distinctive to this product, peppering them heavily, curing them in a brown sugar mixture, then smoking them over smoldering wood cut from the same groves that were used generations ago. The method is time consuming and costly, but I can give you my personal assurance that it produces a uniquely delicious ham worth every penny of the price.

If you've never tried a Smithfield ham, let me pass along a few personal tips on how it should be handled and prepared. Keep the ham in a cool, dry place until you are ready to cook it. Wash the ham in warm water, then use a stiff brush to scrub away every last trace of the black-pepper coating. Soak the ham in water for 12 to 48 hours. Place the ham in a large kettle and cover it with water, then cook it at a simmer for about 25 minutes per pound, or until the temperature recorded on a meat thermometer inserted into the heaviest part of the meat stands at 156°F. Never, never boil a Smithfield ham. Slicing the meat into wafer-thin slices will enhance its already remarkable flavor.

The uncooked ham sells at about $3.00 per pound, or it can be ordered precooked at about $4.25 a pound. Brown-sugar–cured Virginia bacon, in a 9- to 12-pound slab, sells at a little over $2.00 per pound. A red-eye ham, more suitable for frying and serving at breakfast time than the Smithfield variety, costs approximately $2.60 per pound.

□

IRVING LEVITT CO.
34-36 Newmarket Square
Boston, MA 02118
(617) 442–6700
Free catalog on request. Accepts checks, money orders only; no CODs.

For more than 40 years, this firm has been providing its line of quality meats to some of the most discriminating restaurants and hotels in America, but because of limited advertising it has not been too widely known among the general public. That appears likely to change. *The New York Times* recently published a comparison survey of all the meat-purveying houses in Boston and New York, and Levitt's was given the highest rating of all. Having sampled their gourmet steaks and been delighted, I can hardly disagree with the opinion expressed by the *Times*.

The firm offers a full line of beef, veal, lamb, and pork—nearly every cut one could imagine—and all their beef is graded USDA Prime. I would suggest their Executive Gourmet Selection as a good way to sample their steaks. It contains four 14-ounce strip sirloins and four 8-ounce filet mignons, and will cost you about $90.00. Or you might wish to try their Châteaubriand tenderloin; a pair, total weight about 10 pounds, can be ordered for approximately $130.00. The Châteaubriand can also be ordered as part of the French Silver Service Selection, which means you'll also receive two double-thick lamb chops and a pair of French rib chops, in addition to a single Châteaubriand weighing about 5 pounds. The cost is about $100.00.

The company also offers an uncut prime sirloin roast of 12 to 13 pounds for roughly $130.00. This is the same cut of meat that yields boneless strip sirloins, and you can cut those steaks from it if you wish, or you can roast it entire for what may turn out to be the ultimate in dinner party enjoyment.

Pork loin back ribs, the very best cut for barbecuing, cost about $30.00 for sixteen 6-ounce cuts; and center-cut pork chops sell for about the same price. Sixteen 6-ounce top round veal cutlets can be ordered for $50.00 or so; and an 8-pound smoked ham sells for approximately $30.00.

A roasted duck drenched in orange sauce will cost you less than $20.00 for a 5-pound fowl; or, if you prefer to cook the duck yourself, a fresh Massachusetts duckling of the same size sells for about $15.00. A brace of a dozen squab, about 11 ounces each, sells for about $55.00; and a pair of pheasants can be hard for about $26.00 fresh, $36.00 smoked. Fifteen game hens, boned and stuffed with wild rice, sell for just under $60.00, and a 10-pound leg of venison, a meat that is becoming harder and harder to find, can be shipped to your door at a cost of $70.00 or so.

□

Maison Glass
52 East 58 Street
New York, NY 10022
(212) 755–3316
Catalog price: $5.00.
Accepts checks, money orders, Visa, MasterCard,
American Express, and Diners Club. Charge
accounts invited. Minimum order: $15.00. Full
guarantee.

In 1902, when Ernest Glass left his native Paris to establish his "Maison Française" in New York City, home entertainment had reached an unparalleled level of splendor. Families such as the Astors, Du Ponts, Mellons, Phipps, Vanderbilts, Whitneys, and Rockefellers had mansions that were fully staffed with chefs, butlers, maids, and chauffeurs. Elaborately prepared cuisine was the order of the day, and rare delicacies from various parts of the world were in great demand. Monsieur Glass helped meet the requirements of this turn-of-the-century haute cuisine.

Over the years, tastes and life-styles have changed, but one thing remains constant: People are still interested in fine cuisine. Today, more than 80 years after it first opened its doors, Maison Glass stands apart as one of the finest sources of quality food. I truly believe its quality and selection are without equal in the mail-order industry.

Beautifully marbled boneless sirloin strip steaks (around $80.00 for a box of six 12-ounce steaks), French lamb chops (about $70.00 for eight 7-ounce chops), Smithfield bacon (about $3.00 per pound), Smithfield ham (around $9.00 per pound), sliced prosciutto (about $13.00 per pound), and goose liverwurst (about $13.00 per pound) are just a few of the fine meats you'll find offered here. For something truly elegant, if a bit unusual, you might also try the smoked filet mignon. Brushed with honey, brown sugar, spices and cognac, then smoked over smoldering apple, the filets are available at a cost of around $100.00 for approximately 5 pounds of luscious dining.

If you are more inclined toward game or poultry, be not disheartened. Selections here, all smoked, include: capons (about $6.00 per pound), mallards (around $7.00 per pound), geese (about $6.50 per pound), pheasants (about $7.50 per pound), partridges (about $14.00 per pound), and even wild turkeys (around $9.00 per pound).

Nothing lends more elegance to a luncheon, tea, dinner or cocktail party than a fine pâté or foie gras, and here you can choose from among dozens. Strasbourg foie gras with truffles heads the list, at a cost of well over $30.00 for a 5-ounce tin. Other pâtés, pastes, and spreads include those made from chopped chicken livers (around $3.00 for an 8-ounce tin), crab (about $2.50 for a 3-ounce jar), lobster (about $3.50 for a 3-ounce jar), smoked rainbow trout (around $3.00 for a 2-ounce tube), and pheasant (around $3.00 for a 2-ounce tin). Beautiful tureens filled with truffled goose liver are also available, the largest holding 8 ounces and selling for just under $100.00, the smallest selling for around $25.00 and holding just 1½ ounces of pâté.

But Maison Glass is much more than a purveyor of meat. If it is edible, elegant, and among the best of its kind, you can almost certainly find it in the catalog of Maison Glass. Consider a few items from their mouth-watering list of seafood.

Their caviars include the simple lumpfish roes that sell for as little as $4.00 for a 4-ounce jar and range upward to the elegant belugas that sell for around $40.00 per ounce, with about a dozen choices in between.

As there should be on any seafood list, this one presents

smoked salmon and trout (from Scotland and Norway), both priced at just over $30.00 per pound. Other smoked fish and seafoods include abalone (about $10.00 per pound), crab legs (around $9.00 for a 3-ounce tin), eel (about $1.00 per ounce), and brook trout ($4.95 each; size not given).

In addition to dozens of kinds of fancy breads and crackers, Maison Glass offers a full selection of international cheeses to serve with them. Prices start at about $4.25 per pound, and a few of the notable choices include a Beaumont from France, an appenzellar from Switzerland, a cheddar from Canada, a gouda from Holland, a skim-milk cheese from Norway, and a Danish camembert, with dozens more from which to choose.

One could go on and on. This company offers page after elaborate page of coffees, teas, spices, relishes and condiments, soups (including the full line of Knorr's soups), vegetables and mushrooms (including the hard-to-obtain cepes, chanterelles, and morels), and confections. For an introduction to the elegance of Maison Glass, consider some of its assortments and gift packages.

Start with The Emperor, a beautiful hamper filled with rare delicacies and priced at approximately $600.00. In the hamper, you'll find a 14-ounce tin of fresh beluga caviar (from the company's private stock), a large tureen of foie gras, a 2-pound tin of assorted roasted nuts, a 2-pound tin of assorted hand-dipped chocolates, 2 quarts of fine brandied fruits, a crock of French *cornichons*, a jar of Niçoise olives, a jar of rare Tasmanian leatherwood honey, a jar of imported Italian mustard, and a tin of Russian tea. This will make for quite a picnic, will it not?

If you're not prepared to spend quite that much, then you might consider an assortment called the Grand Buffet, priced at approximately $325.00. This sumptuous feast includes a country ham, a whole smoked turkey, 2 pounds of smoked Scottish salmon, pumpernickel and rye breads, assorted crackers, capers, a large crock of French green olives, spiced crabapples, ginger pears, French mustard, imported biscuits, a 2-pound wheel of French brie, a 2-pound tin of assorted roasted nuts, and, of course, a box of after-dinner mints.

For approximately $150.00, if you're interested in sampling a number of international delicacies, the catalog features a redwood tub filled with American sturgeon caviar, Niçoise olives, French fruit preserves, mustard fruits, whole roasted chestnuts, giant white asparagus, ratatouille, a tin of French onion soup, herbal jelly, mustard with green peppercorns, petit babas, quail eggs, *cornichons,* and assorted pickled fruits. Other assortments cost as little as $40.00 and as much as $700.00.

To shop at Maison Glass is not inexpensive, admittedly. But, as someone once said, "To cheapen a fine thing is to destroy its beauty."

□

MANCHESTER FARMS
P.O. Box 97
Dalzell, SC 29040
(803) 469-2588
Free catalog on request. Accepts checks, money orders, MasterCard, Visa, and American Express.
Full guarantee.

Manchester Farms was among the first firms to ship quail through the mails, and today their business has grown to such proportions that their plump, juicy birds are found in supermarkets and restaurants all across the nation. Yet mail order continues to be the backbone of their business.

The tiny Pharoah quail are grain-fed to maturity, under government inspection, then made oven-ready and frozen before shipment. Or, if you prefer, you can order hickory-smoked birds that arrive ready to heat and serve. Either way, a box of sixteen quail costs about $45.00. A box containing 40 fresh and 40 smoked quail will be shipped for approximately $170.00. And, if you're looking for an even more unusual appetizer, you might try the pickled quail eggs. A gallon bucket (225 eggs) costs about $60.00.

□

MURRAY'S, INC.
26 South Sixth Street
Minneapolis, MN 55402
Accepts checks and money orders only; no CODs.
Full guarantee.

Murray's Restaurant and Cocktail Lounge, in downtown Minneapolis, is known throughout the Midwest for its soft, glamorous atmosphere—creamy draperies over mirrored walls, pale pink tablecloths, strolling violinists, and piano dinner music. In this romantic atmosphere, customers enjoy some of the most highly regarded steaks in America, steaks so popular that Murray's was literally forced into the mail-order business by customer demand. Steaks shipped through the mail are exactly the same as those served at the restaurant—carefully aged prime beef—and arrive packed in beautiful boxes suitable for giving as gifts.

New York strip steaks are their most popular item. Cut 1¼ inches thick and weighing 12 ounces each, these cost about $90.00 for a box of eight. Filet mignons are cut to the same thickness, weigh 6 ounces apiece, and come in boxes of sixteen for about $85.00; or you can order four of the strip steaks and eight filets, in a combination package called The Royal Duet, for less than $90.00. Gift certificates are also available.

□

COLONEL BILL NEWSOM'S HAMS
127 North Highland Avenue
Princeton, KY 42445
(502) 365-2482
Free price list. Accepts checks and money orders
only; no CODs.

Since Colonial days in Virginia and for nearly 200 years in Kentucky, the Newsom family has been producing dry-cured hams with a rich tangy flavor enhanced by long smoking and many months of aging. Noted gourmet-author James Beard has suggested this as one of the best country hams available today, and the product has received favorable notice in numerous newspapers and magazines, among them *Bon Appétit, Great Recipes,* and *Food and Wine.* It is the only product offered by this firm.

Weight range of the hams is 14 to 17 pounds apiece, with larger hams available by special request. When we checked, the hams were priced at approximately $2.75 per pound, with shipping charges extra. Each ham is gift wrapped, packed, and shipped in an individual box, and with any order you receive a pamphlet loaded with helpful hints on preparing and serving Kentucky country ham, which is a great deal saltier than that to which most people are accustomed.

□

OMAHA STEAKS INTERNATIONAL
4400 South 96 Street
P.O. Box 3300
Omaha, NE 68103
(402) 391–3660 or (800) 228–9055; within Nebraska, call collect 0 (402) 391–3660.
Catalog price $1. New customers receive a ten percent discount on all orders from the catalog. Accepts checks, money orders, Visa, MasterCard, American Express, Diners Club, and Carte Blanche. Credit application available. Unqualified guarantee.

Back in 1897, the Simons (father and son) sailed from Europe to the United States and settled in Nebraska, finding the country ideal for raising the highest quality beef. In 1917, they founded Omaha Steaks, which supplied tender, corn-fed beef to restaurants. As years went by, the general public began clamoring to buy the flavorful beef for home use. In 1952, Omaha Steaks obliged by initiating a mail-order business and today the firm prides itself not only on its quality meats but on its commitment to shopping convenience and dependable service.

A look at the 20-page, full-color catalog will make your mouth water. There are filet mignons in a variety of sizes. A package of six 6-ounce filets, each about 1¼ inch thick, plus seasoned butter sauce and cooking instructions, costs about $49. Or, you can order their "Best Buy" on the 6-ounce filets: 24 for about $129. There are boneless strip sirloins in several sizes; four 9-ounce ones are about $44. Top sirloin steaks, filets of prime rib (rib eye steaks), Porterhouse and T-bone steaks are also available. A package of two 16-ounce T-bone steaks costs about $33. Less expensive, but still juicy and flavorful are the ranch steaks and the minute steaks. Heart of Prime Rib roast costs about $62 for a four-pound roast or $67 for a precooked one.

If you hanker for surf and turf combinations, four 6-ounce filet mignons and 2 pounds of Alaskan king crab legs are about $60. Four 8-ounce filets with four 6-ounce lobster tails are about $90. Omaha Steaks also offers the crab and lobster separately, as well as salmon steaks, shrimp, scrod, trout, bay scallops and the rare abalone. Pork, lamb, and veal selections are offered, as are smoked meat (2 pounds of Canadian-style bacon is about $23), chicken, quail (eight quail are about $52) and Cornish game hens. To round out your mail-order dinner, there is a limited but luscious-looking selection of hors d'oeuvres and desserts. All of these are certified as kosher.

Omaha Steaks prides itself on its shipping system. All foods, frozen at the peak of flavor, are vacuum wrapped, then packed with dry ice in a sturdy, reusable picnic cooler before being placed in the outer shipping carton. Also included with your order is the company's cookbook, which has helpful storage and serving hints as well as a number of recipes by James Beard. Satisfaction is guaranteed or Omaha Steaks will either replace your order or refund your money.

☐

OZARK MOUNTAIN SMOKEHOUSE
P.O. Box 37
Farmington AR 72730
(800) 643–3437
Free catalog on request. Accepts checks, money
orders, Visa, Interbank, and MasterCard. Safe
arrival guaranteed, but Christmas orders must be
received before December 10.

The smoked meat and poultry products offered by this family-owned firm are sold at several stores throughout the South and are produced on a farm that has been in the family for genera-tions. The homestead itself has become a popular tourist attrac-tion, and visitors are taken on a tour of the smokehouse, where they can see meats being cured by methods older than America itself.

Hams and bacon are cured with salt and sugar for a briny flavor, then slowly smoked over a mixture of hickory and sassafras

coals. The owners say this method produces a ham that needs so
soaking or simmering. Hams can be ordered uncooked or cooked
and boneless, all between $50.00 and $65.00, depending on the
size and style you select. A 9-pound slab of cured bacon costs
$35.00 or so, and 4 pounds of Canadian bacon costs just under
$30.00.

Smoked turkeys are available either whole or boneless. The
whole turkey costs just over $30.00 for an 8-pound hen, and the
boneless mixture of white and dark meat sells at about $35.00 for
a roll of about 5 pounds. Smoked chickens cost about $7.00 per
pound, and hickory-smoked salami costs about the same. Numerous gift packages are offered, and most products arrive packed in
an attractive muslin calendar bag.

□

Pfaelzer Brothers
4501 West District Boulevard
Chicago, IL 60632
(800) 621–0226; within Illinois, call collect (312) 927–7100.
Catalog price: $2.00 (catalog includes a coupon
worth $5.00 toward any purchase). Accepts checks,
money orders, Visa, BankAmericard, MasterCard,
American Express, and Diners Club. Credit
application available. Full guarantee.

Nearly 60 years ago, three brothers named Pfaelzer began selling
meat from a horse-drawn wagon that traveled the streets of Chicago. From that small beginning has evolved a multimillion-
dollar firm that is now a division of Armour and Company and
whose name is almost synonymous with the direct-mail marketing of gourmet quality meat. Just a glance at their beautifully
illustrated catalog is enough to set your mouth to watering.

Consider their Beef Wellington. Tenderloin of beef is laden
with onions and mushrooms sautéed in sauterne and brandy,
then wrapped in golden puff pastry and frozen. It arrives at your
home with a pouch of Madeira wine sauce, ready to be baked and
served. Four 10-ounce servings of this noble entree cost about
$60.00, which is no more than you'd expect to pay in a decent

restaurant and less than you'd be willing to pay once you've experienced it.

Many other entrées arrive ready to pop into the oven and eat. Among them, you will find listed Chicken à la Kiev (chicken breasts stuffed with seasoned butter); Chicken Cordon Bleu (chicken breasts stuffed with bacon and cheese); Chicken Marco Polo (chicken breasts stuffed with broccoli); and Chicken Romanoff (chicken breasts stuffed with noodles, sour cream, and cheddar cheese sauce). You'll pay about $45.00 for four 8-ounce portions of any version of the stuffed chicken breasts; or, for about the same price, you can select four 12-ounce Rock Cornish game hens stuffed with mushrooms and wild rice. A 5-pound roast duck, which arrives fully cooked and sealed in a pouch of orange-sherry sauce is offered at just over $20.00; but, if you prefer wild duck to the domestic and also prefer to do your own cooking, you might choose to order their Wild Game Assortment (about $90.00). In addition to two 2-pound mallards, you'll receive two pheasants of the same size, two 2-pound buffalo steaks, and an 8-ounce accompaniment of long-grain Canadian wild rice.

Suckling pig is one of the more popular items for holidays and other festive occasions. This dish once graced only royal tables, but Pfaelzer Brothers will ship a 14- to 19-pound suckling to you for about $90.00. Or, if turkey and ham are more in line with your holiday preference, they will send you a 10-pound hen turkey for about $40.00, a 20-pound tom for just under $50.00, or a 10-pound ham, trimmed and fully cooked, for about $50.00.

But it is for their luscious assortment of fresh meats that this firm is most widely known, and their selection is among the largest in the industry. The least expensive package—about $65.00—is their Blue Ribbon Assortment. It includes four 6-ounce filet mignons, four 8-ounce chopped sirloin patties, and two 12-ounce boneless strip steaks. Several other assortments are offered for less than $80.00. Typical is the Gourmet Steak Assortment, which includes four 8-ounce filet mignons and four 10-ounce boneless strip steaks. But, if you really want to splurge on beef, you could try their Assortment "59," which brings you a full loin of grain-fed beef expertly carved into 65 mouth-watering steaks and patties, and one 4-pound rolled sirloin tip roast. It sells for just under $330.00.

Lamb, pork, and milk-fed veal are, of course, also available. For about $60.00 you can choose eight 8-ounce French lamb chops, a 6-pound boneless leg of lamb, or a 4-pound crown of lamb rib roast, with other cuts of lamb available at only slightly higher prices. For about $45.00, you can order sixteen 5-ounce center-cut pork chops, eight 10-ounce pork spareribs, or a 4-pound pork loin roast. A 7-pound crown pork rib roast costs slightly less than $60.00. Several packages of milk-fed veal are offered at between $60 and $80. These include two dozen 4-ounce top round veal slices, sixteen 6-ounce top round veal cutlets, and a 4-pound boneless loin roast.

This fine old company has expanded its line to include cheese, jams and jellies, and nearly every type of food described in this catalog, but often their selection is limited. One part of their line, however, needs to be mentioned here, and that is their Food-of-the-Month plan, a gift that will surely cause recipients to realize you are thinking of them throughout the year.

The full 12-month plan costs about $750.00. The person you select will receive gifts such as a ham, a turkey, half a dozen lobster tails, steaks or steak assortments, prepared chicken dishes, lamb chops, or corned beef brisket. Twelve gifts are shipped on selected holidays. Gift plans covering shorter periods of time are available for prices that go as low as $340.95 for the 4-month plan.

□

SCHALLER & WEBER, INC.
22-35 46 Street
Long Island City, NY 11105
(212) 721–5480
Free price list. Accepts checks and money orders only; no CODs. Minimum order $20.00.

Schaller and Weber claims to be "the only American sausage and processed meats manufacturer to consistently receive the coveted Gold Medals of Honor awarded at International Exhibitions in Holland, Austria, and Germany." Established in 1937, their products are found in leading specialty food outlets throughout the country.

Among the cold cuts offered are ham bologna, tongue

bologna, Bavarian bierwurst, Wuerzburger (Bavarian-style head-cheese), cooked salami, and teawurst, a smoked spread with a touch of paprika. The cold cuts are priced between $3.30 and $3.60 per pound, though prices are always subject to change. At prices ranging from $3.30 to around $5.00 per pound are such cold meats as goose liverwurst, touristenwurst (salami-style ring sausage), landjager (a salami snack stick), and blockwurst (a salami without garlic).

A number of very interesting smoked meat and poultry items can be found here. Prime among these is a Westphalian ham, which is a mild, dry-cured type of ham that originated in the Black Forest of Germany. These sell for well over $6.00 per pound, with bacon, cured by the same process, selling for about half as much. For truly special occasions, you might want to try their smoked breast of goose; priced at approximately $15.00 a pound, this is a gourmet delight sold by only a handful of companies in the United States.

□

SIGNATURE PRIME
143 South Water Market
Chicago, IL 60608
(800) 621–0397
Free catalog on request. Accepts checks, money orders, Visa, and MasterCard. Full guarantee.

Prime beefsteaks and roasts make up the bulk of the Signature Prime line, and the various combination bundles run $50.00 and upwards. A typical package holds six 10-ounce boneless strip sirloins and six 6-ounce filet mignons, and sells for about $70.00. Another pack holds seven dozen steaks of various types, and will cost you about $335.00.

Thinking of throwing a luau? Signature Prime offers a 21-pound (average weight) whole suckling pig that is ideal for spit-roasting, at a cost of just over $60.00. The complete line of veal includes ten 10-ounce veal porterhouse steaks for about $75.00; and the full line of lamb has offerings such as an 8-pound crown roast at about $140.00.

In addition to a line of domestic fowl that includes turkey (less than $45.00 for a 10-pound hen), boneless breast of chicken (just over $50.00 for twelve 10-ounce pieces), and Rock Cornish game hens (just over $40.00 for six 20-ounce hens), Signature also sells several kinds of wild fowl. Twelve pheasants (16 to 18 ounces apiece) sell for about $80.00. Six 14-ounce squab will set you back roughly $60.00. A 5-pound Long Island duck runs about $100.00, and a dozen partridges (14 ounces apiece) are priced about the same as the duck.

Nearly any kind or cut of wild game can be ordered from Signature Prime. Varieties include Canadian brown bear, antelope, venison from Wisconsin white-tailed deer, imported New Zealand wild goat, and South American llama. Due to the seasonal nature of wild game, both the prices and availability change on a short-term basis. Wild game prices are quoted on request, and you should always check the current prices before ordering wild game from this company.

□

THE SMITHFIELD HAM & PRODUCTS CO., INC.
Smithfield, VA 23430

Free catalog on request. Accepts checks, money orders, Visa, MasterCard, BankAmericard, American Express, Diners Club, and Carte Blanche. Full guarantee.

One reason for the unique flavor of Smithfield hams is the fact that the meat is cut from porkers raised on a diet of peanuts, and this company is one of the few that continues to feed its hogs in the traditional way. After butchering, the hams are dry cured, heavily spiced, then smoked over a mixture of oak, hickory, and applewood coals—a secret process that has been used for at least 300 years. Each ham is then aged for one to two years to develop its unique, stimulating flavor. An uncooked ham of 10 to 12 pounds sells for under $40.00, and a cooked ham of about the same weight will cost you $50.00 or so.

This firm also offers a somewhat less expensive version of this renowned ham. Sold as the James River Brand Virginia ham, these are dry cured, pepper coated, hickory smoked, and aged for 3 to 4 months. Uncooked and ready to be baked, broiled, or

fried, these hams weigh 11 to 13 pounds apiece and sell for about
$30.00. There is a $3.00 shipping charge for each ham shipped.
Amber Brand Smithfield bacon is cured by much the same
method used in curing the hams. Vacuum sealed and gift boxed,
it is sold in 3- to 4-pound slabs for about $8.00, or in 8- to 10-
pound slabs for just under $20.00. Add a $2.00 shipping charge
for each slab ordered.

The firm also offers and produces deviled Smithfield ham, a
spicy concoction that makes an interesting appetizer. Six 7-ounce
jars cost about $15.00. Chicken Brunswick stew, pork barbecue,
beef stew, barbecue sauce, and turkey barbecue—all rich with
the unique Smithfield flavor—are also available, but only in various gift assortments ($14.95 to $22.95) and only in addition to an
order for ham or bacon.

□

STOCKYARDS PACKING COMPANY, INC.
340 North Oakley Boulevard
Chicago, IL 60602
(800) 621–1119
*Free catalog on request. Accepts checks and money
orders only; no CODs. Full guarantee. Free delivery
within 400 miles of Chicago.*

Since 1893, when the Chicago stockyards were the meat center
of the nation, this family business has been engaged in supplying
fine cuts of meat to famous restaurants and clubs. While most
other companies in this line have been swallowed up by the giant
conglomerates, Stockyards remains a family business and fully in-
tends to stay that way, according to a letter I received from a
fourth-generation member of the family that established this
firm. He sums it up by saying, "Our family pride is part of every
order we ship."

Considering the fact that all meat is U.S. Prime, which is
becoming somewhat difficult to find in many areas, prices here
are more than reasonable. A pack of eight 5-ounce tenderloins,
for example, costs about $40.00; or six 16-ounce T-bones will ar-
rive for less than $60.00. Rib eyes, strip steaks, filet mignons,
and all other favored steaks are available at comparable prices.

The various rib and sirloin roasts cost $60.00 to $75.00, depending on the weight and cut ordered, and there are dozens from which you may choose.

Many beef specialties not sold by other firms are found here. Five pounds of oxtail, cut for soup or braising, costs about $25.00; the same amount of cubed stewing beef costs about $30.00; and ten 8-ounce packs of skewered beef kabobs, complete with green peppers and onions, sells for about $40.00. Chopped beef, in various forms, sells at about $5.00 per pound; and there are prepared dishes such as Beef Wellington, which costs about $55.00 for six 7-ounce portions. Eight serving portions of pepper steak costs roughly $35.00; and eight large portions of prepared beef stew costs approximately the same.

Prepared poultry dishes such as chicken Kiev and chicken à la king are available at about $30.00 for six 7-ounce servings, or you can order six boneless chicken breasts stuffed with wild rice at about the same cost. A 5-pound capon fetches $20.00, and six 16-ounce Rock Cornish game hens sell for $25.00.

The lamb includes a boned leg, weight 7 pounds, for approximately $40.00, a 4-pound crown roast for just over $50.00, and 5 pounds of skewered lamb kabobs, complete with green pepper and onion, for less than $50.00. The milk-fed veal offerings include a 5-pound boneless leg roast for about $80.00, 5 pounds of thin-sliced scallops for use in scallopini and other dishes, at a cost of around $85.00; or two 4-pound rib roasts for less than $70.00. Discounts are given on volume orders for any item offered by this fine old company.

□

TROPHY STEAKS
3548 North Kostner Avenue
Chicago, IL 60641
(312) 282–2900
Free catalog on request. Accepts checks, money orders, Visa, BankAmericard, MasterCard, and American Express. Credit applications sent on request.

Established more than 50 years ago, this company has for the past six years been a division of the much larger Bruss Company, one of the oldest of the Chicago meat packers. But one thing about Trophy Steaks has not changed, according to Charles Hunter, president of the division: "We remain dedicated to offering highest quality meat and gourmet items that are prepared to fine restaurant specifications. We have a high rate of repeat customers, which causes us to feel that we are on the right track." You can, if you wish, pamper the entire family with their full loin of prime beef. For a little over $200.00, you'll receive: twelve 12-ounce sirloin strip steaks, twelve 8-ounce sirloin butt steaks, ten 6-ounce filet mignons, one 4-pound bottom sirloin roast, and twelve 6-ounce ground sirloin patties. If you're not ready to spend that much on your first order, the steak packages sold by this firm start at less than $40.00 for six 6-ounce filet mignons and go as high as $93.00 for a bundle of eight 14-ounce sirloin strip steaks. In between, you'll find such offerings as the Surf and Turf (three 6-ounce filet mignons and three 8-ounce lobster tails) for about $55.00, a 4-pound Châteaubriand for slightly more than $50.00, and four 16-ounce T-bones for about the same price.

For $600.00 or so, you can send a gift that will delight the recipient month after month, for a full year. Each month will bring gift boxes holding items such as lamb chops, filet mignons, corned beef brisket, Rock Cornish game hens stuffed with wild rice, Châteaubriand, eye of rib roast, or a hen turkey. A six-month plan costs about $310.00, and the three-month plan, $160 or so. Ask about the Golden Trophy Monthly Plans.

□

FRED USINGER, INC.
1030 North Third Street
Milwaukee, WI 53203
(414) 276-9100
Free price list on request. Accepts checks and money
order only; no CODs. Minimum order: 5 pounds.

Sausage, sausage, sausage—that's what this firm is all about. For more than 80 years a Milwaukee institution, the old *Saturday Evening Post* once referred to Usinger's as "the Tiffany of sausage makers," and its customers have included such celebrities as Teddy Roosevelt, Alfred Lunt, Jack Carson, Tony Curtis, news-

caster H. V. Kaltenborn, and Liberace. Usinger's supplies fine
restaurants across the United States, but limits production to
about 5 million pounds annually. Still, if it is known as sausage,
you can order it from Usinger's—and at reasonable prices.

For a little over $2.00 a pound you can choose from among
half a dozen types of blood sausage, including Thueringer, pepper blood, and tongue blood. Half a dozen types of liver sausage,
including Braunschweiger, goose liver, and Hildesheimer, are offered at less than $3.00 per pound. As for sausage to be cooked—
such as ring bologna, knockwurst, smoked Polish sausage, and
bratwurst—about three dozen kinds are offered at prices ranging
from $2.39 to $3.09 per pound. Salami, all-beef summer sausage,
Genoa salami, pepperoni, and Thueringer summer sausage range
in price from $3.09 to $4.09 per pound, and a garlicky Land-
jaeger sells at just under $5.00 per pound.

Too, Usinger's offers an extensive line of fine luncheon meats.
Most expensive among these is a roast pork loaf at a little over
$5.00 per pound. Corned cooked beef loaf is in the same price
range. But for just $2.59 or so per pound, you can choose from
among German-style head cheese, jellied sulze, long bologna,
old-fashioned loaf, luncheon loaf, or half a dozen other kinds.
Dozens of other types are available at prices no higher than you
would expect to pay in your local market. There is a shipping
charge of 80 cents on each order, and you will be charged 25
cents for each pound of dry ice used in shipping perishable
items.

□

VEAL FROM PROMARCO
P.O. Box 508
Watertown, WI 53094
(800) 558–9560
Free brochure and price list on request. Accepts
checks and money orders only.

While nearly all other purveyors of meat tend to specialize in
beef or ham, with fine veal offered almost as a second thought,
here the approach is the exact opposite, and veal is the only meat
considered worth selling. All items offered are made from veal
fed only the famous Provimi milk formula.

The deluxe cube steaks are one of the most popular offerings. Lean, boneless pieces of veal are portioned to 4 ounces, then run through a tenderizer. Virtually free of fat and gristle, these cost about $36.00 for a 6-pound (24-steak) box. Ground veal steaks, also in 4-ounce portions, cost just over $20.00 for the 6-pound box.

If you're interested in trying something new for breakfast, you can order 6 pounds (twenty-four 4-ounce portions) of veal breakfast patties for under $25.00; and, for luncheon or the buffet, 6 pounds (twenty-four 4-ounce patties) of veal bratwurst can be yours.

Veal leg slices, cut from the round, sirloin, and butt, are excellent timber for such famous gourmet dishes as Veal Paprika, Veal Marsala, or Veal Sicilienne. A 6-pound box costs less than $60.00. If veal liver is more to your liking, 6 pounds of thinly sliced meat will set you back about $33.00. And for a really unusual addition to the buffet, you might try putting out their veal meatballs, which arrive with packets of dehydrated mushroom sauce for you to prepare and pour over them. The meatballs come in 5-pound boxes at a cost of about $20.00.

□

WEAVER'S FAMOUS LEBANON BOLOGNA, INC.
P.O. Box 525
Lebanon, PA 17042
Free catalog on request. Accepts checks, money
orders, Visa, MasterCard, and American Express.

In the early 1800s, Pennsylvania Dutch settlers in the fertile valleys of Lebanon County began making a ready-to-eat, semidry sausage that would become famous the world over as Lebanon bologna. The sausage was made by individual farmers who created their own original recipes, blends of herbs, spices, and meats. Near the close of that century, Daniel Weaver became the first to produce Lebanon bologna on a volume basis, and today the recipe for Weaver's product remains a closely guarded family secret, passed along from one generation to the next. The bologna, like the ham, bacon, and all other Weaver meat products, is hung by hand in old-fashioned smokehouses exactly like those used a century ago. The Lebanon bologna can be used as an hors d'oeuvre, canapé, as a delicious filling for sandwiches, for luncheon snacks, and even, according to the Pennsylvania Dutch, for dessert.

The Lebanon bologna sells at a little over $4.00 per pound. Smoked bacon costs under $3.00 per pound, and smoked ham sells at about $3.70 per pound. There is also smoked chipped beef at approximately $7.50 per pound, Canadian bacon at a little over $6.00 per pound, and a sweet version of the bologna at about $5.00 per pound. All these meats are dry-cured and smoked over mixed hardwoods, and a number of gift combinations are offered at prices ranging from about $20.00 to as high as $76.95. All orders are filled in less than two weeks.

□

WOLFERMAN'S
2820 West 53 Street
Fairway, KS 66205
(800) 255–0169
Free catalog. Accepts checks, money orders, Visa,
MasterCard, and American Express. Meat and candy
items available October through April only.

Established in 1888, Wolferman's is in the business of providing, as they put it, "good things to eat." A little of everything is offered in the small but beautifully illustrated catalog, with special emphasis given, I find, to smoked meats and some extremely interesting items for those who love a hearty breakfast.

Smoked ham, bacon, Canadian bacon, and summer sausage make up the list of meats, and there is smoked turkey for those whose preference is poultry. All these can be ordered individually, at competitive prices; or, if you'd like to splurge and order some of each, the firm offers (for around $100.00) a box that includes an 11-pound smoked turkey, a 3-pound ham, 2 pounds each of regular and Canadian bacon, and a 4½-pound beef summer sausage.

A number of special breakfast packages are offered, including one kit for making Eggs Benedict. For a little over $30.00, you receive ten packages of Wolferman's English muffins (40 muffins), 2 pounds of Canadian bacon, and enough mix to make 2 quarts of hollandaise sauce. Other assortments, ranging in price from $30.00 to $75.00, come with ham, bacon, coffee, tea, breakfast biscuits, and assorted jams, jellies, and marmalades. Also offered by Wolferman's are imported Belgian chocolates and molded bars of pure chocolate (both at about $7.50 per pound), and a 2-pound fruitcake that sells for approximately $15.00. Shipping charges are always extra.

□

CHAPTER TWO

FISH AND OTHER SEAFOOD

In this chapter you will find sources that guarantee fresh orders of fish and other seafood delivered to your door, no matter how far from the source your door happens to be located. The range of items includes regional specialties not frequently seen outside local areas, imports from other countries, and hard-to-find domestic varieties. There are the highly prized Chincoteague and bluepoint oysters, just right for eating on the half shell, as well as cherrystone and steamer clams, and mussels for use in true Italian sauces. Shrimp, lobster, and blue and Dungeness crabs can be shipped fresh to your door, and even tiny bay scallops from New England—which are becoming almost impossible to find— are available from firms listed in this chapter.

From salmon to swordfish, from catfish to caviar, whatever the fresh seafood of your choosing, you will find it offered by one or more of the firms listed here. But please don't balk at the frozen products—modern flash-freezing techniques are so effective that little flavor is lost during the process, which begins almost as soon as the fish are taken from the water.

Then there is fish that comes to you smoked, dried, salted, pickled, and marinated. These range from the gently cured, pale-pink smoked Atlantic salmon through herring marinated in wine and cream, dried salt cod, to the zesty smoked whitefish and back to the Pacific salmon that bears remarkably little resemblance to its Eastern cousin.

So, no matter what your preference, no matter how landlocked you may be—this chapter is for the seafood lover in you.

□

JACK AUGUST'S, INC.
5 Bridge Street
Northampton, MA 01060
(413) 584-1197
Free price list. Accepts checks and money orders.

Since 1935, this establishment has been specializing in seafood, and its local reputation for quality is firmly established. The dining room, with its Cape Cod nautical atmosphere, is famous throughout the region, and the fish market next door is perhaps the most complete in the state. However, the company is only now entering the mail-order business, and entering it only because they were almost forced to do so by the growing demand for three of the products sold in their seafood restaurant. These three are their New England clam chowder, their Manhattan clam chowder, and Jack August's fish chowder. All three are made by the same recipe used in the restaurant, and each costs about $30.00 for a case of twenty-four 15-ounce cans, with shipping and insurance charges extra. They hope to offer other items in the near future, so you might find it worthwhile to keep them in mind when you develop a hunger for food with an authentic New England flavor.

□

CAVIARTERIA, INC.
29 East 60 Street
New York, NY 10022
(800) 221-1020
*Free catalog. Accepts checks, money orders, Visa,
MasterCard, and American Express.*

Sevruga, beluga, American sturgeon, lumpfish, and salmon caviars are just a few of the varieties you will find offered and described in the catalog of this company, the largest distributor of caviar in the United States. The caviars are put up in containers that range in size from 2½ ounces to 2 kilos, and cost as little as $10.00 for the smallest jar of salmon roe to as much as $1,850.00 for the largest tin of fine-grained, pearl-grey beluga. Fresh pressed caviar, which is pressed to a pastelike consistency and is said to be a favorite among Russian-born consumers, is also available here, priced at about $35.00 for a 3½-ounce jar or $600.00 for a 2-kilo tin.

If you'd like to enjoy the flavor of the world's most highly regarded caviar without paying the price, you might try ordering some Kamchatka caviar, a brand name under which the firm markets the broken eggs found at the bottom of barrels of its finest beluga caviar. The cost is only a fraction of what you would pay for unbroken eggs, and the claim is that only the texture is different, not the flavor.

Also offered are smoked Scottish, Norwegian, and Nova Scotian salmon, the fish priced at $20.00 to $25.00 per pound, and a number of tinned Scandinavian seafood pâtés, among them pâtés made from smoked salmon, cod roe, smoked herring, and anchovies. The seafood pâtés sell at approximately $6.00 per 10½-ounce tube. For the most elaborate occasions, you might also want to consider their fresh salmon mousse, a delicate smoked salmon mousse with a center of fresh whole grain caviar. Weighing 1 pound, it is priced at about $30.00. All shipping charges are extra here.

□

JOHN HARMON'S STORE
Sugar Hill, NH 03585
(603) 823–8000
Free brochure and price list. Accepts checks and money orders. Full guarantee.

In 1954, John Harmon and his wife left the Madison Avenue rat race for semiretirement in a charming corner of New England, where they soon established a small shop specializing in those hard-to-find, one-of-a-kind items rarely found in city markets. By the time the Harmons passed away, in 1980, the tiny store had developed a national reputation for the cheese, maple syrup, and other items that it shipped through the mails. While the new owners, Bert and Maxine Aldrich, continue to specialize in items that are unique to New England, they have expanded the line to include several items that are of interest to seafood lovers.

Lump crabmeat from the Atlantic blue crab is offered in 10-ounce tins. This connoisseur's item, which is probably the sweetest crabmeat of all, is perfect for salads, casseroles, crab cakes, dips, crêpes and soups. Two tins sell for $10.50, or you could go all out and order ten cans for $40.50.

Smoked Atlantic salmon is seldom found in tins, but you can order two kinds from Harmon's. There is the smoked meat itself, ready to serve, and a delicious salmon pâté, which can be eaten by itself or made into a luscious spread by adding a little mayonnaise. Both types come in 3¾-ounce tins, at a price of $6.50 per tin. Smoked herring fillets, which are imported from Nova Scotia and which sell at $10.50 for four 7-ounce tins, close out the list of seafood offered by this New Hampshire institution.

□

HEGG & HEGG, INC.
801 Marine Drive
Port Angeles, WA 98362
(206) 457–3344
Free brochure on request. Accepts checks and money orders only; no CODs. Delivery guaranteed.

Operating out of an unpretentious building near the shores of Puget Sound, this firm began almost as a weekend hobby for two brothers and went on to establish such a reputation for quality that their smoked seafood products are now shipped throughout the world, and production is rarely high enough to fill the demand. Hegg & Hegg has never had a salesman, yet some of the nation's finest stores—Marshall Field, Neiman-Marcus, Frederick and Nelson are examples—have sought out and stocked their delicacies, and their list of customers is dotted with names such as Shirley Temple Black, Tennessee Ernie Ford, and the late John Wayne.

Items from the smokehouse are most responsible for the

worldwide fame of this company. All smoking is done over native alderwood, a technique used for centuries by Indians of the Pacific Northwest, producing a very delicate smoke flavor. Salmon from the waters of Puget Sound is the most popular smoked item, and a whole smoked fish (about 4 pounds) costs slightly less than $30.00.

Hegg & Hegg also smokes several other types of seafood native to the Pacific Northwest and rarely available in the East. Among these are butter clams, sturgeon, and the tiny shrimp of Puget Sound. A number of sampler packages are offered that make it possible for you to experience a little of each. One I have tried (for about $11.00) includes one ½-ounce size tin each of salmon, butter clams, sturgeon, albacore tuna, and shrimp. The tins come in a round reed box encased with a fishnet and would make a most attractive, as well as tasty, gift. Many other assortments are offered—none costing more than $28.75—and all are beautifully packaged.

Unsmoked foods are also available, if those are more to your liking. Among them is Dungeness crabmeat (three tins with a net weight of 6½ ounces for about $15.00), which is native to this region and difficult to find elsewhere; six 4½-ounce tins of shrimp meat for about the same price; and six 7-ounce tins of albacore tuna, packaged in natural oil, at a cost of $13.00 or so.

This firm has truly earned the worldwide reputation it enjoys.

□

Josephson's Smokehouse and Dock
106 Marine Drive
Astoria, OR 97103
(503) 325–2190
Free catalog on request. Accepts checks, money
orders, Visa, and MasterCard. Full guarantee.

In 1920, an immigrant named Anton Josephson began a small smoked salmon business on the banks of the Columbia River using techniques he brought with him from Scandinavia. Today, Michael and Linda Josephson, third-generation owners of the company he founded, cling proudly to the exacting standards and careful smoking procedures established by their grandfather.

Wax-coated wooden barrels are used to hold the sides of salmon and the brine in which they are cured, and only native alder wood is used in a smoking process that produces one of the best smoked salmons it has been my pleasure to enjoy. Our sample package held a slab that was pink, moist, flavorful, and easily sliced into thin wedges that were seasoned just right and absolutely perfect to use in preparing the many Scandinavian dishes described in the little recipe booklet that is sent with each order. The box in which the salmon arrives is made of Oregon spruce, beautifully silkscreened, and would also make an attractive presentation as a gift.

Smoked salmon and pickled salmon are the specialties here, and a single pound of either costs about $16.00. The price per pound drops as the size of your order is increased, however, and 10 pounds of the smoked or pickled fish will cost you only about $10.00 per pound. Smoked sockeye salmon is also available, at a cost of $30.00 or so for a slab weighing about 1½ pounds.

There are also several types of smoked fish available in packs of three ½-pound tins. A pack of smoked albacore tuna sells for a little over $13.00, and a pack of Coho salmon sells for approximately $17.50. For a price of about $20.00 per three-pack you can select smoked chinook salmon, smoked white sturgeon, or a pack containing one can each of smoked tuna, chinook, and white sturgeon. Some items are only seasonally available, so you should always check with the firm before ordering.

□

LATTA'S OREGON DELICACIES
P.O. Box 1377
Newport, OR 97365
(503) 265-7675
Free catalog. Accepts checks, money orders, Visa, and MasterCard. Full guarantee.

Newport, a unique city on Yaquina Bay, boasts one of the largest commercial fisheries on the West Coast, and its waterfront area is so authentic and interesting that many visiting tourists rate it above Fisherman's Wharf in San Francisco. The fleet of about 650 boats provides a delicious flow of Dungeness crab, giant Pacific oysters, melt-in-your-mouth butter clams, tiny Pacific shrimp, salmon, albacore tuna, and more. All these seafood treats make their way to Latta's, where they are carefully prepared, then packaged in giant clam shells, old-fashioned wicker baskets, wooden crates, and authentic fisherman's netting, and garnished with tiny seashells, starfish, and driftwood. The unique packages are frequently seen in major department stores such as Bloomingdale's, Marshall Fields, and Bon Marché, but the greatest part of Latta's business is done through the mails.

A typical offering is the Oregon Treasure Chest, which sells for about $70.00. This lovely wicker picnic basket comes filled with one ½-pound tin each of smoked sturgeon, smoked Pacific salmon, smoked oysters, albacore tuna, Pacific shrimp, unsmoked Pacific salmon, smoked albacore tuna, and Dungeness crabmeat, set off by a 12-ounce jar of wild blackberry preserves, 4½ ounces of smoked cheese, a ½-pound tin of smoked hazelnuts, and a box of hors d'oeuvre crackers. Any item in the package can be ordered separately, of course, and all are offered at a discount by the case lot.

Two ½-pound tins of Pacific salmon, for example, cost about $9.00, but you can order a case of twenty-four tins for just a little over $50.00. Six ½-pound tins of Dungeness crabmeat cost just under $40.00, but a case of twenty-four tins of the same size costs only $140.00 or so. There is a real savings for volume here, so you might keep Latta's in mind when stocking up for the future—as well as when you have a hankering for those West Coast delicacies that can be so hard to find in other parts of the country.

□

LEGAL SEAFOODS MARKET
237 Hampshire Street
Cambridge, MA 02139
(800) 343–5804; within Massachusetts, call (617) 864–3400.
Free brochure on request. Accepts checks, money
orders, and American Express.

Legal Seafoods may just be the busiest shipper in the mail-order business. Julia Child has long been a faithful patron, and their offerings have been highly touted in such diverse publications as *Forbes Magazine* (". . . an extensive fish menu at reasonable prices"), *The Whole Hub Catalogue* ("Truly a place for fish lovers"), *Travel/Holiday* (". . . the largest and freshest variety of seafood in America"), and *Boston Magazine* (". . . the best seafood in Boston"). As if these testimonials were not enough, their restaurant (located in Boston's Park Plaza hotel) was asked to provide seafood for the inaugural dinner of Ronald Reagan and George Bush in January of 1981.

Here you will find every seafood delight known to man. All are taken directly from the waterfront markets and air-shipped to you as fresh as if you had done the catching yourself. If it is fresh, Legal will have it, and, as this company likes to say, "If it ain't fresh, it ain't Legal."

Lobster prices range from $5.29 per pound for crustaceans of about 1 pound up to $5.99 per pound for the more desirable 1½- to 3-pound specimens. Giants of as much as 7 pounds each are offered, when available, at about $5.50 per pound, and fresh lobster meat costs about $20.00 per pound.

Shrimp ranges in price from about $8.00 for the smallest size offered (26 to 30 per pound) to about $11.00 per pound for the largest (8 to 10 per pound). Peeled and deveined shrimp are slightly higher.

Prime soft-shell crabs, almost impossible to find inland, go for about $1.75 apiece. Alaskan jumbo king crab legs are offered at about $9.00 per pound, or you can buy 6 ounces of the shelled crabmeat for just over $7.00. Snow crab claws sell at about $6.00 per pound.

Fresh oysters head the list of shellfish, with large selects selling at about $3.50 a dozen, in the shell, or approximately $6.00 per pint when opened. Frying clams sell at about $6.00 per pint, and both cherrystones and littlenecks cost about $3.50 per dozen. A bushel of either costs approximately $60.00. Large sea scallops sell at about $6.00 per pound, while the tiny bay scallops cost a dollar less per pound, and the very rare Cape Cod scallops are a dollar higher. Blue mussels, which have become increasingly popular in recent years, cost just $1.00 or so per pound; and you can satisfy your taste for the exotic by ordering a whole octopus at about $3.00 per pound.

Fresh fish prices fluctuate wildly and are determined at the

New England fish pier auction each morning. To determine the current prices and place your order, you should call Legal at their toll-free number. The following prices were being charged on the day I did just that.

A few of the fish being offered at less than $3.00 per pound included mackerel, whitefish, pollock, silver hake, haddock, cod, flounder, grey and lemon sole, bluefish, sea trout, monkfish, and smelt.

At a cost of less than $4.00 per pound, on this day, one could order scrod, perch, striped bass, sea bass, red snapper or mako shark. These prices were for whole fish, with the fillets a good deal higher.

Boneless swordfish, yellowfin tuna fillets, halibut steak, and salmon steaks, when I checked, were being offered at $6.99 per pound, and fresh rainbow trout fillets were going for $4.29 per pound, which was cheaper than in the local markets.

Legal also ships salt- and smoked-cured fish. Prices on these fluctuate less than on the fresh fish. When I checked they were offering salt cod, salt herring, and finnan haddie, that old New England favorite, at $4.29 per pound; smoked rainbow trout at $4.99 per pound; and smoked whitefish at $5.99 per pound. Smoked Irish salmon, which many consider the finest smoked fish in the world, was being offered at $17.99 per pound.

Finally, if you'd like to boast about the source of your seafood, the firm offers a T-shirt (at $5.95) that allows you to do so. "I got scrod in Boston," it declares, "at Legal Seafoods." Their seafood, I assure you, is far more tasteful than their shirts.

□

MURRAY'S STURGEON SHOP
2429 Broadway
New York, NY 10024
(212) 724–2650
Free price list. Accepts checks and money orders only. Minimum order: $25.00. Guarantees next day delivery.

If breakfast at home on Sunday is incomplete without bagels and all that goes with them, try some of the moist and elegant Nova

Scotia salmon, sliced with a skill that would do credit to any surgeon, shipped out by Murray's Sturgeon Shop—an outfit that is, according to Craig Claiborne of *The New York Times*, "One of the great outlets for smoked fish in Manhattan . . . and perhaps the finest in the city."

Murray's had been one of the best-kept secrets in New York until its discovery by the *Times*, but today it is probably the best-known purveyor of deli items in the city, especially famous for its wide selections of smoked fish and caviar.

Only Atlantic salmon (about $24.00 per pound) is offered, and this is narrowed down even further to include only salmon from the waters of Nova Scotia. Lox, the milder version of the same fish, sells at about $18.00 per pound. Smoked lake sturgeon costs $26.00 or so per pound, but you can buy smoked whitefish ("poor man's sturgeon"), which, in my opinion, is at least as good as the costlier fish, for about $6.95 per pound. There is also kippered salmon at approximately $16.00 per pound, smoked sable at under $10.00 per pound, smoked brook trout at just over $8.00 per pound, and smoked butterfish, when available, at $7.95 per pound. Especially good is the pickled salmon in cream sauce, which you can order at about $18.00 per pound. Specify whether you want the fish whole or sliced.

Caviars include giant-grain Beluga malossol, small-grain Sevruga malossol, Romanoff Imperial Beluga, and four types of salmon and American sturgeon caviar. There is also a complete inventory of domestic and imported canned fish including salmon, tuna, sardines, mackerel, brook trout, herring, anchovies, sprats, mussels, clams, shrimp, lobster, and shad roe. On both the canned fish and the caviar, Murray's sends no prices, asking instead that you inquire about current rates before ordering.

□

NELSON CRAB, INC.
Tokeland, WA 98590
(206) 267–2911
Free brochure and price list, plus annual newsletter.
Accepts checks and money orders only; no CODs.
Call to check availability of items before ordering.
Full guarantee.

Since 1940, Nelson Crab has been shipping to other parts of the world the many seafood delicacies that are unique to the rugged coast and icy waters of the Pacific Northwest—items such as giant geoduck clams, Dungeness crab, Pacific oysters and shrimp, razor clams, smoked sturgeon, and coho and blueback salmon. As we were working on this book, however, they were put temporarily out of business by a disastrous fire that destroyed their smokehouse and processing plant. They inform me that they expect to be back in full operation prior to publication of this guide, however, but be sure to request their current prices before ordering.

All items from Nelson can be ordered either by the case or as part of the various gift assortments they offer. Dungeness crabmeat (about $19.50), albacore tuna (about $10.95), smoked king salmon (about $17.50), Dungeness crab legs (about $21.75), smoked sturgeon (about $14.95), Pacific shrimp (about $10.75), smoked oysters (about $12.75), albacore tuna (about $10.95), and minced razor clams (about $15.10) are offered in cases of six 6½-ounce cans. Six 7½-ounce cans of blueback salmon cost about $13.00 and six cans, of the same size, of geoduck clams, which are found only along this coast and which are used to make a clam chowder that has long been one of my personal favorites, sell for about $7.00. Six 3¼-ounce tins of smoked sturgeon will cost you $8.50 or so. Nelson's is one of the very few sources for smoked Dungeness crab legs—a true gourmet delicacy—and a case of six 3¼-ounce tins sells for just under $15.00.

Assortments are beautifully packaged and range in price from $8.75 to $35.70. For about $9.00 you get one tin each of blueback salmon, albacore tuna, Pacific shrimp, and minced geoduck clams, packed in an attractive fishnet bag. At the other end of the price range (about $36.00), you get twelve 6½-ounce tins of savory seafood delicacies packed in a reusable plastic serving tray. This consists of two tins each of Dungeness crabmeat, minced geoduck clams, smoked sturgeon, smoked salmon, Pacific shrimp, and albacore tuna. Shipping and insurance charges are extra on all orders.

□

WISCONSIN FISHING COMPANY
P.O. Box 965
Green Bay, WI 54305
(414) 437-3582
Free price list. Accepts checks, money orders, Visa, and MasterCard. Shipments via bus express shipping service carry a full guarantee; Parcel Post shipments are made only at the buyer's risk.

Established in 1899, this firm began by supplying the freshwater fish taken from the icy waters of Wisconsin to markets as distant as New York and Chicago. Local demand soon forced them into the retail business, and by the 1920s growing interest in their finny products had drawn them into the mail-order field. As time passed, the firm began buying the catch from fishing fleets in more distant waters, and today, they stock and sell more than 200 different sizes and types of fish, shipping on a regular basis to about 32,000 customers from Maine to California. Through them you can enjoy seafood from all parts of the world: shrimp from Brazil, Malaysia, or the Gulf of Mexico; slipper lobster from Taiwan; frogs' legs from India or Japan; rock lobster from Peru; pollock from Cape Cod . . . the list goes on and on.

If it is edible and comes from the water, you can almost certainly buy it from Wisconsin Fishing, and it will arrive no more than 48 hours after your order is received.

Like lobster and lobster tails? Half a dozen sizes and types are offered at prices ranging from $4.25 to $13.00 per pound. Shrimp? The dozen or so varieties offered cost as little as $3.45 or as much as $7.95 per pound. Smoked fish? Whiting sells at about $1.95 per pound; carp costs about $1.60 per pound; lake chubs, about $2.75 per pound; and bluefin herring sells at approximately $2.10 per pound.

If it is fresh-dressed fish you are looking for, there is walleye pike, lake perch, lake smelt, lake trout, whitefish, pink Alaska salmon, and channel catfish—all selling at less than $2.00 per pound. Halibut steaks will cost you $3.10 or so per pound, and swordfish steaks are selling at just under $4.00 per pound. Fillets of any fish are available at a slightly higher cost, and the same is true of fish prebreaded and ready to cook.

Clams can be ordered stuffed (about $3.40 per dozen) or

frozen (about $2.10 per pound); and there is frozen whole Dungeness crab at less than $2.00 per pound, scallops at $6.50 or so per pound, frogs' legs at about $2.95 per pound; and jumbo shrimp stuffed with crabmeat at about $3.60 per pound. Breaded flounder stuffed with crabmeat sells for less than $3.00 per pound, a price that is remarkably low.

Here, too, you will find all the condiments to go with the seafood of your choice. Breading mix, batter mix, and Southern-style frying meal cost about 65 cents per pound, and a case of twelve 8-ounce jars of tartar sauce or cocktail sauce sells for about $11.00. Breaded mushrooms cost $1.50 or so per pound, and breaded cheese curds, which are something of a tradition in Wisconsin, help round out what may well be the most complete line of seafood in the food-by-mail industry.

☐

ETHNIC AND SPECIALTY FOODS

The companies described in this chapter offer wares that will be of special interest to those with a preference for the exotic viands of the world, and those who delight in preparing the cuisines of faraway lands. Importers throughout the United States make available foods from every corner of the globe, and many producers within the country cling to the traditional methods of preparation that are a part of our American heritage. They provide access to such culinary wonders as French pâtés, *cornichons,* and brandied fruits; British potted meats, biscuits, and shortbreads; Italian olive oil, Parmesan cheese, and flour for pasta; Mexican chilies such as ancho, chipotle, and jalapeños; and cookies and chocolates from Holland that arrive in colorful canisters. Here you will find the ingredients for making Indian curries, Hungarian goulash, true Oriental dishes, or even a Scandinavian cold table—and you will find companies ready and waiting to ship nearly any ethnic dish to you already prepared.

Our own Pennsylvania Dutch, Creole, Mexican-American, Polish, Italian, Hungarian, and English specialty shops offer a mélange of foods that are, in their own way, every bit as authentic and as exciting as those sold by the importers. The food they offer you can be duplicated in no other part of the world, and to read their catalogs is to more fully understand the richness and diversity of our American cuisine.

□

CASA MONEO
210 West 14 Street
New York, NY 10011
(212) 929–1644
Free price list. Accepts checks and money orders only. Minimum order: $25.00. There is a handling charge of $3.50 on all orders.

Those looking for authentic Hispanic foods and ingredients need look no further than the price list put out by Casa Moneo. If it is commonly eaten in Spain, Mexico, Central and South America, or the Caribbean, it is available here.

Meat products include *morcilla para* (blood sausage), hot chorizos (a smoked sausage), serrano ham, and sliced Genoa salami. The seafood list offers clams, cockles, mussels, oysters, squid, octopus, sardines, and lobster meat, as well as at least a dozen versions of paella, the hearty seafood stew often considered the national dish of Spain.

All the famous and essential sauces are found here including green chili, salsa fresca, mild and hot enchilada, salsa brava, and many, many more. Chilies, jalapeños, and other peppers can be ordered whole, sliced, roasted and peeled, pickled, or any other way you might want them. Beans come dried, packed in water, or cooked in a number of authentic ways, including refried, and at least a dozen varieties are offered. Various rice, wheat, oat, and corn flours, many of them essential to this cuisine, are available, and there are dozens of varieties of imported cooking oils. Prices were being brought up to date when I contacted this firm, but those prices I did see appeared very reasonable, and the company assures me they will remain the same.

□

CHICO-SAN, INC.
1264 Humboldt Avenue
P.O. Box 1004
Chico, CA 95927
(916) 891–6271
*Free catalog on request. Accepts checks and money
orders only. Minimum order: $10.00. Free newsletter
with order. Prices do not include shipping charges.*

If you are just venturing into the preparation of Oriental food, it might be a good idea to order Chico-San's cookbook, *The Macrobiotic Kitchen* by Cornelia Aihara, which sells for $9.95. It holds over 500 detailed recipes for soups, sauces, tempura, vegetables and sea vegetables, breads, noodles, fish and shellfish, snacks, and desserts. The recipes are basically Japanese, but flavored with influences of China, Southeast Asia, France, and even Russia. After reading it, you should be better prepared to use the ingredients offered in the Chico-San catalog. Bear in mind also that at least half of the items are certified organically grown.

Seaweeds have been used in the Orient for centuries, and Chico-San offers the five most popular varieties of this nutritious vegetable. Selling at about $3.00 for a 2½-ounce package are *wakame* (curly dulse), *kombu, hijiki, kanten, nori,* and *sushi nori*.

Authentic Japanese black beans sell at about $2.60 per pound, and Azuki beans cost about $5.00 per pound. Organically grown California short-grain brown rice costs about 70 cents per pound, and sweet brown rice costs about the same.

Chico-San also offers a full line of condiments that are prepeared to its own specifications in Japan. There is natural soy sauce at a little over $2.00 for 12 ounces; barley-miso sauce at about $2.50–3.50 for 16 ounces; and rice malt vinegar at about $2.75 for 7 ounces. *Kuzu* (wild arrowroot) costs about $3.70 for a 3-ounce packet; and dark sesame oil costs around $8.00 for a 12-ounce bottle.

From among the Oriental treats that are already prepared and ready to eat, I'd suggest you try the *umeboshi,* or salt plums. This uniquely Japanese fruit is cured in salt for several months, yet, when the salt is washed away, it retains an elusive sweetness that makes it ideal for serving with the Oriental teas offered by Chico-San and other companies described in this catalog. The plums cost about $4.60 for an 8½-ounce container.

Rice syrup candies, another interesting snack from the Orient, are made from rice and a syrup derived from rice and barley malt. They come in two flavors: taffy and caramel, which has bits of almonds, raisins, coconut, and oats. Wrapped in the shape of old-fashioned candy kisses, they cost 80 cents for a bag of 16, in cases of 12 bags.

□

CHINA BOWL TRADING COMPANY, INC.
80 Fifth Avenue
New York, NY 10011
(212) 255–2935
Free brochure and price list. Accepts checks and
money orders only; no CODs. Minimum order $7.50.

Here you will find a complete line of imported Chinese specialty foods that permit authentic Chinese dishes to be prepared easily at home, and if you wish you can even order bamboo chopsticks (four pairs for about 30 cents) with which to eat them. The chopsticks come with a set of directions and an interesting little booklet about chopstick etiquette.

Exotic spices and herbs are essential to the true Chinese cuisine, and here you will find many types that may not be available in local markets. Package sizes range from 1 ounce to about 2½ ounces, depending on the type of spice inside, and most sell at about $1.00 per package. The list includes fermented black beans, which are not only used to make the salty, tangy black bean sauce called for in so many Chinese recipes, but are also useful as flavoring for other sauces; Szechuan peppercorns, mildly hot wild peppers that add zest to many Szechuan and Hunan dishes; star anise, a licorice-flavored herb that is exquisite in most braised beef and poultry dishes; fiery hot Chinese curry powder; and piquant dried coriander, or Chinese parsley, to name just a few.

Dried mushrooms also come by the ounce. Black mushrooms, the most popular type used in Chinese cooking, cost about $2.70 per jar. Tree ears, an unusual type of mushroom with a very rich flavor, cost around $1.65 per jar. Bell-shaped, beige-colored straw mushrooms cost $2.90 per jar; and oyster mushrooms, a personal favorite I have rarely seen in stores, cost $1.90 or so per jar. For about $8.00 you can order a crystal mushroom jar that makes a nice gift for the household chef or, if you prefer, an unusual terrarium.

The Chinese vegetable mix is formulated for use in Moo Shu Pork and other stir-fried dishes, but the combination of tiger-lily buds and three types of mushrooms makes an interesting dish in itself. A 1-ounce jar of the dried mix sells at about $1.75. Miniature shrimp are also found in many Chinese dishes, but they make an unusual and exciting appetizer with no additives whatsoever. A 2-ounce jar of the salty little crustaceans sells for $1.75 or so. Tree chestnuts, with their smoky flavor and firm texture, also double as appetizer or as ingredient in braised dishes, and a 4-ounce jar sells for about $1.40.

Noodles sell at about $1.25 for a 8-ounce package, and you can select nearly any type called for in Oriental cooking. There are the classic wheat-flour noodles, rice sticks, sweet rice noodles, cellophane noodles, and, of course, the dried spicy beancurd noodles that lend a subtle flavor and good color to so many stir-frys, soups and vegetable dishes. With the noodles, you will need the proper sauce, and China Bowl is able to provide nearly any sauce or flavoring you might desire, as long as its origins are Chinese. Oyster, plum, hot mustard, fish, hoisin, sweet and sour, Chinese barbecue, and two types of soy sauce are found on the list, as well as such flavorings as hot oil, sesame oil, chili paste with garlic, white or red rice vinegar, and Chinese cooking wine. Most sauces are in 6-ounce jars, and prices start at $1.10 per jar, with the most expensive sauces selling at about $2.00 per jar.

Coconut candy, a taffylike sweet made from South China coconuts and cane sugar, is a treat for all age groups; and with your end-of-the-meal tea, you will want to serve the traditional crisp fortune cookies containing predictions or wise sayings. Both sweets come in boxes of twelve at a price of about $1.10 per box.

□

JOHN F. COPE COMPANY, INC.
5984 Main Street
East Petersburg, PA 17520
Free price list on request. Accepts checks and money orders only; no CODs.

Dried sweet corn is a distinctively American food that has been in use since well before the Pilgrims landed, and it has long been a favored delicacy among the Pennsylvania Dutch, who originally dried the corn in the sun and, later, on wood- and coal-burning stoves. With the development of the canning process early in this century, most American farmers dropped this traditional method of food preservation in favor of the more modern methods. In the Pennsylvania Dutch country around Lancaster County, however, a few of the more conservative households retained the old processing methods because they preferred the special toasted flavor of dried sweet corn. Some of these farmers began to sell the corn that was in excess of their family needs, and soon dried sweet corn was considered a dish peculiar to this area, where it is served as a traditional Christmas and Thanksgiving dish.

By 1900, a Lancaster County farmer named John F. Cope had already established the first commercial dried sweet corn operation in the country, and today the fourth generation of his family sells the famous product to visitors to the Pennsylvania Dutch area and distributes it throughout the world.

With each order of corn, you receive a recipe booklet filled with dozens of authentic recipes for using this old-fashioned product. The dried sweet corn comes in 10-ounce packages, three packages to the box, and costs about $7.00 per box, depending on the destination. Discounts are given for larger orders. Wet-pack dried sweet corn, which retains the distinctive flavor, but is ready to heat and serve, is available in cans at a slightly higher price. Or you can order the dried corn in old-fashioned gift tins that make beautiful canisters; three 20-ounce tins sell for about $17.50.

The Cope family grows its own corn, and the crop includes some of the finest popcorn we have tasted. Three 15-ounce jars cost around $4.75, or it can be bought in three 32-ounce gift tins at a cost of approximately $9.00. The sweet corn and the popcorn, in their distinctive tins, are also offered in a number of combination packages that would make unusual and attractive gifts at Christmas.

□

CREOLE DELICACIES COMPANY, INC.
533 St. Ann Street
P.O. Box 51042
New Orleans, LA 70116
Free catalog. Accepts checks, money orders, Visa,
American Express, MasterCard, and BankAmericard.
Full guarantee on all except foreign orders.

Just to open a package from Creole Delicacies is like a visit to the French Quarter of New Orleans, for you are quickly surrounded by the pungent aromas that are familiar to all who have visited that area. The promise held out by those scents is quickly fulfilled when you sample the food inside.

Now in its twenty-eighth year, Creole Delicacies began as a small gourmet shop on historic Jackson Square in the heart of New Orleans' French Quarter and quickly built an international reputation for quality. All items are beautifully packaged, and all are representative of the best in the Creole cuisine.

Coffee with chicory is so closely linked to New Orleans that no Creole meal would be complete without it, and that is available at about $5.50 per pound; or you can buy pure roasted chicory to add to your own coffee at about $3.50 per pound. To go with the coffee, you can make your own French Market–style doughnuts from a mix that sells for about $5.95 for a 32-ounce box.

Offered are some of the most famous soups served in the French Quarter, all in 10-ounce cans, and selling at around $15.00 for six cans, mixed any way you choose. These include shrimp Creole, shrimp gumbo, turtle soup, and crayfish bisque.

Condiments and sauces range from mildly spicy to fiery hot. These include Creole seasoning, Creole mustard, hot pepper jelly, and Tabasco sauce, all at less than $2.50 per 8-ounce jar. In addition, there are various spice combinations specially concocted for use in favorite Creole dishes, all selling at about $1.00 per 2-ounce package. Also offered is remoulade sauce, which generations of New Orleans chefs have used to add a spicy, piquant flavor to seafood salads and cocktails; three 10-ounce jars sell for just under $12.00.

Offered only at Christmas are a 10- to 12-pound smoked turkey for under $35.00 and Southern-style hickory-smoked ham

(14- to 16 pounds) for about $40.00. Also during that season you can order a gift box of 24 Louisiana navel oranges for under $25.00. Not edible, but an unusual gift for a child, is a handmade "Mammy" doll, 11 inches tall, for about $12.00.

Preserves made from traditional Southern recipes are put up in 10-ounce jars. The offerings include strawberry, blackberry, pear, peach, watermelon rind, and orange marmalade. Three jars of any type, or any combination, cost about $10.00. Or, instead, you can choose three jars of wine jelly for the same price. Pure Louisiana cane syrup, cooked in an open kettle, is also offered at just under $8.00 for three 12-ounce tins.

Chewy pralines are a Cajun classic, and those offered by Creole Delicacies are hand-poured caramel filled with crunchy pecans. They are offered in several flavors, and sell at about $10.00 for a box of 15 large pralines. Good as these are, I found that I personally prefer their Pralines d'Orleans Sauce, which sells at about $14.00 for three 10-ounce jars. With this sauce in hand, you can easily top off a meal with the same praline parfait served in the finest New Orleans restaurants; and the thick sauce, loaded with crunchy pecans, also makes an excellent topping for cakes, pancakes and waffles—it is a true Creole delicacy.

□

Mrs. De Wildt
R.D. 3
Bangor, PA 18013
Free price list. Accepts checks and money orders only.

For more than 30 years, Mrs. De Wildt has been supplying mail-order customers with all the spices and ingredients needed for authentic Indonesian cookery. On her list are dozens of items you will find it nearly impossible to obtain elsewhere, and the list has recently been expanded to include items from several other countries as well as Indonesia, but that distinctively spicy cuisine remains the heart of it all.

The *rijsttafel*, or "rice table," is the famous Indonesian meal that consists of nine separate dishes. There is a spiced vegetable dish, a meat, seafood or vegetable dish, a chicken dish, hot beef, another chicken or beef dish, a lamb dish, yet another chicken or beef dish, pork in a sweetened soy sauce, and a dish that combines vegetables, pork, shrimp, and mushrooms. Each dish has its own meaningful name, of course, and a taste that is uniquely Indonesian. Mrs. De Wildt offers nine complete instant spice mixtures that enable any cook to prepare an authentic rice table in the home kitchen. The spice packs cost about $1.60 each; of course, you must provide the shrimp, chicken, beef, pork, or whatever.

If you are just becoming interested in Indonesian cookery, the Starter Chef's package offered by Mrs. De Wildt might be of interest to you. It comes with a recipe booklet and small starter packages of chili pastes, sweet soy sauce, shrimp wafers, and the basic spices and spice mixtures called for in many of the most popular Indonesian dishes. The package costs a little less than $30.00. After that, you might try the Nasi Goreng package, which, for under $20.00, brings you all the exotic spices, sauces, and seasonings needed to prepare an Indonesian-style fried rice dinner, including the tea and a dessert called Lyohee.

After trying these starter packages and gaining a little familiarity with the cuisine, you may be tempted to start your dishes from scratch. Then you will need such exotic ingredients as hot chili paste (Mrs. De Wildt offers half a dozen types at about $1.75 per ounce); spiced peanut paste (around $2.25 for 4 ounces); Java soy sauce (around $4.00 a pint); and *atjar tjampur,* a spiced vegetable chutney (about $2.50 for 12 ounces). Just to list the spices, herbs, sauces, and seasonings sold here would require pages.

Other Indonesian delicacies come ready to serve, or nearly so. *Krupak udang,* shrimp-tapioca wafers, are considered a must with Indonesian rice dishes, and those from Mrs. De Wildt are ready to fry and serve. A 14-ounce package costs about $4.00. Then there is *ikan terie,* tiny dried fish, ready to eat, in a 7-ounce jar at a cost of just under $5.00; and *serundeng,* fried spiced coconut with peanuts, at about $4.00 for a 14-ounce jar. *Udang kering,* or dried shrimp, costs $2.00 or so for a 3-ounce bag.

The origins of Indonesian food can be traced to many other lands, especially China and Holland, and these origins are clearly reflected in the offerings of Mrs. De Wildt. The list of Chinese delicacies and ingredients includes bamboo shoots (about $1.50 for a 12-ounce tin), lychees in syrup (about $2.20 for a 20-ounce tin), mango slices in syrup ($2.00 or so for a 15-ounce tin), and toasted coconut chips (approximately $1.75 for 3½ ounces).

The list of imports from Holland is far more extensive, and includes some of that country's most famous products. Cheeses include Edam, soft Gouda, Belegen Gouda, and Leyden cumin, or Komijnekaas, all at about $3.50 per pound. Baked goods include *roggebrood,* a dark rye bread, at about $1.50 for a 1½-pound loaf; *ontbijkoek,* a rye honey cake, at about $1.60 for a 14-ounce loaf; and *stroopwaeils,* or Gouda syrup waffles, at $6.75 or so for a 1-pound package. The extensive list of Dutch chocolates includes *magelslag,* known as "chocolate hail" to many, at about $1.95 for a 7-ounce box; *gestampe muisjes,* candy-coated aniseed, at $1.10 or so for a 7-ounce package; and chocolate initials at approximately $1.35 for a 2¼-ounce box.

Foods imported from other countries that have all contributed to the Indonesian cuisine include cod-liver pieces from West Germany (about $1.50 for a 4-ounce tin); pickled mussels from Denmark (about $1.75 for a 6½-ounce jar); Bombay ducks, a dried fish for toasting or frying, from India ($3.30 for 2 ounces); bean-curd cakes from Japan ($1.95 or so for an 11-ounce tin); dark shrimp jelly from Malaysia (approximately $6.00 for a 5-ounce jar); and *rufina patis,* an anchovy sauce, from the Philippines ($1.35 or so for an 8-ounce bottle).

Those with a desire to sample the food of faraway places will find Mrs. De Wildt's the ideal starting place.

□

FERRARA FOODS & CONFECTIONS, INC.
195-201 Grand Street
New York, NY 10013
(212) 226–6150
Free brochure and price list on request. Accepts
checks and money orders only. There is a $10.00
delivery charge on all orders of less than $150.00.

Established in 1892, in the heart of Little Italy, Caffe A. Ferrara began as the first and only *pasticceria* in the United States. The pastry shop and confectionery is still there, and those specialties remain the heart of the business, but today the business is nationwide and the company sells a full line of Italian specialty foods. The only problem here, for the average buyer, is that all goods must be ordered by the case. For those wishing to stock up at reasonable prices, however, such bulk orders can be an advantage, so this source is one that should not be too quickly dismissed.

Pasta comes in cases of twenty 1-pound packages, and the average cost per case is about $16.00. Varieties include fettuccelle, two kinds of linguine, capellini, fidelini, spaghettini, spaghetti, ziti, rigatoni, cannaroni rigati, tufoli, fusilli, pennoni, penne, penne rigati, gnocchi, rotelli, tubetti, and tripolini, as well as spinach noodles, bow ties, and special cuts for lasagna. To go with any or all, there is a choice of white or red clam sauce, offered in cases of twelve 10½-ounce cans, at about $11.00 per case.

Other "back of the stove" offerings come in cases of twelve 16-ounce cans, and they include minestrone (under $12.00 per case), *ceci*, or chick-peas (about $15.00 per case), macaroni and beans (around $11.00 per case), stuffed cabbages (about $30.00 per case), ravioli with beef (just over $16.00 per case), stuffed green peppers (less than $30.00 per case), and red Madrilen consommé (under $10.00 per case).

Soup comes in cases of twelve 13-ounce cans, and there are more than two dozen varieties from which to choose, not all of them Italian in origin. These range in price from about $8.00 per case to $15.00 per case, and some of the more interesting offerings are cream of artichoke, black bean, crab bisque and crab soup Maryland, gazpacho, lentil soup, both shrimp and lobster bisque, Philadelphia-style snapper soup, Senegalese, and vichyssoise. One good way to sample them all would be to order the 36-can assortment, offered at less than $40.00.

□

GAZIN'S
P.O. Box 19221
New Orleans, LA 70179
(504) 482–0302
*Free catalog. Accepts checks, money orders, Visa,
and MasterCard. Minimum of $10.00 on credit card
orders. Full guarantee.*

Among those areas of the world where a combination of cultures, climate, and produce have created a distinctive cuisine, few hold more interest for the gourmet than New Orleans. There, blessed with a mild climate, rich, abundant land, and bountiful seafood, generations of inspired cooks have created one of the most distinguished cuisines in America. Firmly based on the traditional cuisine of the early French settlers, the Creole cooking of the region has been strongly influenced by the Spaniards, Africans, Italians, and American Indians, resulting in a cuisine quite unlike any other.

The folks at Gazin's appear to have put together the best of Louisiana recipes, food specialties, and gourmet cooking tools to make it easy for you to enjoy that delectable Creole cuisine in your own home. If the mention of New Orleans sets your mouth to watering, you will not want to be without this remarkable little catalog.

Offered here are many famous regional soups such as seafood gumbo, crayfish bisque, shrimp Creole, and turtle, all in cases of twelve 1-ounce cans, all priced between $17.50 and $22.95 per case. Offered, too, are many of the zesty sauces that are so essential to the Creole cuisine, flavorful concoctions such as Vieux Carré barbecue sauce, Creole sauce and Creole mustard, and, perhaps the most famous of all, remoulade sauce, as it is served in the finest New Orleans restaurants. These are put together in various combinations, all priced at less than $12.00. For even greater zest, the company offers such condiments as hot pepper and mint pepper jellies.

Browsing through the catalog, you'll find an overwhelming variety. For approximately $7.50, there is a kit for making the classic New Orleans "Poor Boy" sandwich; it contains two loaves of New Orleans French bread, old-fashioned smoked sausage, and a jar of Creole mustard, all packed in an attractive gift basket. Of course there is coffee laced with chicory, as well as pecan-flavored wild rice, red beans with sausage, and sweets that include pralines and bourbon-laced dessert cakes.

About one-fourth of the catalog is devoted to cookware and kitchen aids, including many items that would be especially useful in preparing and serving Creole-style dishes. There is, among these, a 2-gallon aluminum steamer with two inserts designed specifically for steaming seafood and vegetable combinations; and a stacked steamer that can be used four ways: as a strainer, 5-quart covered pot, single or double steamer. These are both priced under $30.00 apiece, while a 12-quart gumbo pot, said to be especially good for the slow simmering that gives this dish its rich flavor, sells for around $35.00. A traditional French omelet pan with sloping sides, a silverstone interior, and a diameter of 10 inches costs around $25.00. If it is essential to the proper preparation of Creole cuisine, odds are good you'll find it here.

New Orleans merchants have long given their customers what they call *lagniappe*, and Gazin's continues that tradition. The term means a little something extra, and if you order at Gazin's costs more than $25.00, your *lagniappe* will be a special gift package of Creole delicacies.

□

LE JARDIN DU GOURMET
West Danville, VT 05873
Free catalog on request. Accepts checks and money orders only.

Most of the business done by this small firm is in seeds and herbs—especially the exotic varieties—but it offers, in addition, a very, very interesting list of French and Italian imports, and—what's more—it offers them at prices that are very difficult to match in local markets and specialty shops.

Soups from France include mushroom, onion, and vichyssoise, all at about $1.20 for a can that, when diluted, makes 30 ounces of soup. Escargot from the same country costs around $3.65 for a tin of 18 snails; and, while you are ordering those, you might want to pick up a ceramic serving dish, designed especially for escargot, at a cost of about $3.50, and a package of escargot seasoning for about 45 cents.

White truffles, imported from Italy, sell at under $14.00 for a 1-ounce tin; or you can order a 2½-ounce tin of foie gras with truffles for less than $10.00. Half a dozen other types of pâté are offered at comparable prices. To go with the pâté you might want caviar, and although those offered here are domestic, the prices are very reasonable, starting at $4.75 for a 2-ounce jar.

Quenelles, a form of dumpling, are a highly favored food in France, and here you can choose from among several varieties. You will find listed pike dumplings in brine (slightly over $2.00 for a 9-ounce tin); pike dumplings in shrimp sauce (about $3.00 for a 15-ounce tin); and veal dumplings in brine (around $2.60 for a 14-ounce tin).

Exotic vegetables and vegetable dishes are a specialty here, and a few sample offerings include stuffed vine leaves in olive oil (around $1.75 for a 14-ounce tin); hearts of palm (approximately $1.85 for a 14-ounce tin); dry green *flageolets* (about $2.55 for 16 ounces); and pickled English walnuts (around $2.00 for a 9-ounce jar). Then there are three types of mushrooms considered nearly essential to the French cuisine: morels, chanterelles, and *cèpes.* None of the three can be cultivated—all must be obtained from hunters who find them in the wild—so they are very expensive. The *cèpes* sell at about $6.45 for an 8-ounce tin; the chanterelles at about $7.95 for 8 ounces; and the morels at approximately $6.25 per ounce, dried.

This is not really the best of sources for sweets and desserts, but they do offer a few items that might be of interest when you have a craving for such goodies. *Marrons glacés,* the famous candied chestnuts of France, are offered at about $8.40 for an 8-ounce tin; or you can order *crème de marrons,* a dessert topping made of chestnuts, vanilla, and sugar, at around $1.10 for an 8½-ounce tin. But probably the most interesting dessert offered here is the Irish-style whiskey-flavored fruitcake. The 1¾-pound cake comes in a lithographed tin, and, at about $6.75, it is one of the real bargains I encountered during my excursion through the world of mail-order food.

□

PACIFIC TRADER
Central Square
Chatham, NY 12037
(518) 392-2125.
*Free catalog. Accepts checks, money orders, Visa,
and MasterCard.*

This importer carries just about everything needed to cook authentic Chinese, Indonesian, Japanese, Korean, or Middle Eastern meals. There is an impressive list of prepared dishes, and a long list of hard-to-find ingredients.

There are, of course, Oriental vegetables such as bamboo shoots, bean sprouts, straw mushrooms, and bean curd; and plenty of sea vegetables such as dulse, arame (a shredded seaweed), and Hiziki (a noodlelike sea vegetable usually cooked with rice). Instant soups include teriyaki, pork char siu, aka miso, and shiro miso. Any type of rice, flour, noodle, or bean needed for this type cooking is listed, and so are all the famous sauces that go with or over them.

Among the prepared foods, you'll find such exotic delicacies as stuffed pickled eggplant (just under $3.00 for a 16-ounce tin), dolma (vine leaves stuffed with rice; around $2.50 for a 13-ounce tin), and pilaf, the seasoned grain and noodle staple of the Middle East (around $1.25 for 8 ounces). In addition to fortune cookies, there are snacks and candies such as *botan ame* (rice candy), haw flakes (Chinese wafer candy), banana chips, ginger folds, rice cakes, and even a sweet bean jelly. Snacks come in various weights, none priced higher than $2.00. Shipping charges are extra.

□

PAPRIKAS WEISS IMPORTER
1546 Second Avenue
New York, NY 10028
(212) 288-6117
*Annual subscription to catalog costs $1.00. Accepts
checks, money orders, Visa, and MasterCard;
telephone orders accepted, but no collect calls.*

The Paprikas Weiss story is the story of the American dream come true.

Isadore Weiss had been an apprentice *fueszeres* (spiceman) in Hungary, later opening his own small shop outside Budapest. But upon his arrival in this country late in the last century, he found the only available job was as janitor in a drugstore. He was still on that job when his wife angrily complained that she was unable to cook his favorite dishes properly because the paprika available here was so inferior. Weiss wrote to a friend in Hungary and had him ship a 20-pound bag of paprika—the first Hungarian paprika imported into the United States—and a dynasty was born.

That bag of paprika vanished almost overnight, borrowed one cup at a time by the Hungarian neighbors, and Isadore Weiss knew he was onto a good thing. After obtaining a small loan, he began selling paprika door to door from a bag on his back, and soon the neighborhood children could be heard yelling, "Here comes Paprikas Weiss (Weiss with the paprika)." By 1910, he had opened his own store, and was rightfully called "the most famous Hungarian in the United States" because he was the only source for several spices and foods without which most Hungarians would prefer not to live. His food was reaching every Hungarian community in our country and being discovered by folks from every ethnic group.

Today Paprikas Weiss remains the largest importer of Hungarian paprika, selling more than 200,000 pounds of that pungent spice annually, and its gourmet shop is a New York institution that attracts visitors from all over the world. Ed Weiss, the grandson of Isadore and present head of the corporation, is a recognized expert not only on spices but on gourmet foods of every type, and clients of Paprikas Weiss include such famed restaurants as the Four Seasons, the 21 Club, and the Magic Pan.

Ed Weiss says he is "in the business of selling pleasant memories," and such memories abound in the food shop that has somehow managed to maintain its character as a neighborhood store with an ethnic flavor. Still located on Second Avenue and 80 Street, only a block from its original site, it holds a tempting, aromatic clutter of coffee, tea, spices, and food from every corner of the world. Caviar and marzipan vie with pungent salamis and fresh baked goods for the attention of the customer. Mr. Weiss has resisted all suggestions that he replace the floor-to-ceiling wooden shelving or add fancy chrome and modern lighting, for this is, as he says, "a place of memories."

In addition to all the coffees and teas, herbs and spices that you will find mentioned elsewhere in this book, the mail-order division of Paprikas Weiss makes available throughout the world many of the exotic delights found in the famous shop on Second Avenue. The accent is on the Hungarian, but nearly every country on earth is represented in their catalog.

Their *tel szalami* (winter sausage) has been described by one food writer as "a medley of subtle succulent flavors." Made by a recipe that has been closely guarded for generations, it comes from Hungary and sells at around $9.00 per pound. Scout sausage, which is a tantalizing combination of beef and pork seasoned with fiery paprika, sells at around $7.98 per pound; for about the same price you can order either *sibiu salami*, a Romanian product flavored with white pepper, or Paprikas Weiss' own pork sausage, their best-selling meat product, mildly smoked and flavored with sweet paprika. If ham is more to your liking, they offer genuine Budapest ham, boneless, skinless, and ready to eat, at about $5.00 per pound.

For those truly elegant moments, they offer genuine Strasbourg foie gras. With truffles, the 2½-ounce tin sells for around $24.00; *foie gras au naturel*, pure goose liver without the truffles, costs about $30.00 for a 7-ounce tin. Half a dozen more goose liver products are available at comparable prices.

A number of meat and fish delicacies imported from Hungary and Romania are offered at around $3.00 for a 14-ounce tin. These include beef and pork goulash; fish à la paprika, which is carp in highly seasoned sour cream; fish salad; fish à la Bakony, which combines carp and mushrooms in sour cream; and beef meatballs with gravy.

From Poland there is wild boar goulash in juniper sauce, the 14½-ounce tin selling for about $5.00. Plump sardines, packed in pure olive oil, are imported from Portugal and cost around $2.00 for a 3¾-ounce tin. Shad roe, which is often impossible to obtain in local markets, sells for about $13.00 per 7½-ounce can. Four 4-ounce tins of smoked oysters or baby clams cost about $3.00 each.

Polish sauerkraut, made from white cabbage, costs approximately $4.00 for a 33-ounce jar. Red cabbage combined with sweet apples, another Polish product, costs around $3.00 for a 16-ounce jar; or, for about the same price, you can order a 15-ounce jar of pickled baby beets, another product of Poland.

Dried French morels, the mushrooms so essential to the production of many gourmet-quality gravies, sauces, and soups, cost about $20.00 per ounce—or $275.00 per pound.

The cheese offering is limited but interesting. At $5.98 or so per pound, you can choose either Ostyepka, which is a lightly smoked, very creamy sheep cheese, or Bryndza, a soft white cheese imported from Czechoslovakia. Monastery cheese, a semisoft cheese made by the Trappists in Austria, costs about $10.00 for a 2-pound loaf. A 12-ounce Liptauer cheese ball, soft cheddar flavored with Dutch caraway and Hungarian paprika, closes out the cheese list at approximately $5.00.

To add to your enjoyment of all this ethnic food, as well as to help you properly use all the exotic spices, herbs, and ingredients you will find here, the firm also sells a number of ethnic cookbooks covering almost every cuisine imaginable. Heading the list (and holding an honored place on my own kitchen bookshelf), is Ed Weiss's own *Hungarian Cookery*, a collection of antique Hungarian recipes that sells for $9.95 or is sent to you free with any order of $50.00 or more, an amount that is easy to spend after a few glances at the fascinating catalog of Paprikas Weiss.

□

PENNSYLVANIA DUTCH COMPANY, INC.
P.O. Box 128
Mount Holly Springs, PA 17065
*Free price list. Accepts checks, money orders, Visa,
and MasterCard. Minimum order: $10.00. Prices
include shipping charges on orders east of the
Mississippi; on orders west of the Mississippi, add 10
percent to prices indicated.*

Together with a line of old-fashioned sweets and treats, the Pennsylvania Dutch Company offers numerous authentic delicacies that will be familiar to all who have visited the rolling hills around Lancaster County. This is the heart of the Amish farmland, and all these foods are prepared by methods that have been used for generations.

Scrapple is a traditional staple to these people. A delicious combination of pork, pork stock, cornmeal, and special seasonings, the scrapple is sliced, and fried in hot oil, then served with catsup, maple syrup, honey, molasses, applesauce, or apple butter, usually beside scrambled eggs at breakfast. The 15-ounce tin of scrapple costs around $2.50. If apple butter is your choice for serving with it, this company sells a type that has been made the same way—cooked in a wooden barrel with a copper lid and coil, with no sugar added—since 1734. An 18-ounce jar of the apple butter sells at $2.95 or so. If you want pancakes or waffles alongside the scrapple, you might try making them with the special pancake flour listed here. A special blend of wheat, buckwheat, and rye flours, it is still milled by water power and costs approximately $2.75 for a 26-ounce bag.

For other meals and other moods, you will find such items as sweet and sour dressing, made sweet with maple syrup and sour with vinegar, and essential for preparing many of the most famous of the Pennsylvania Dutch dishes, at around $2.45 for an 8-ounce jar; bacon dressing, made with cider vinegar and bits of smoked bacon, to serve over salads or hot vegetables, at around $2.75 for a 6-ounce jar; chow-chow, a delicious combination of spicy pickled celery, green and wax beans, cauliflower, carrots, corn, red peppers, and red kidney beans, at about $2.75 for a 15-ounce jar; and old-fashioned corn relish, a delicious concoction of half a dozen vegetables, at approximately $2.75 for a 13-ounce jar. Nearly all these are made from recipes brought to this country in the 1700s, and *I* believe you will find them as welcome today as they were back then.

□

RAY'S BRAND PRODUCTS, INC.
1920-22-24 South Thirteenth Street
Springfield, IL 62705
Free price list. Always check current prices before ordering, as they are subject to frequent change. Accepts checks and money orders only. Minimum order: 6 cans.

In 1922, in a room behind a small grocery store, Ray De Frates used a large copper kettle to produce a batch of all-meat chili with beans, which he packed in glass jars and sold to his grocery customers. That chili became so popular that the grocery business was soon put aside, and today the chili is packed in cans and shipped to all parts of the country in response to the demands of customers, who literally forced Ray's into the mail-order business. The copper kettle used to make that first batch of chili remains on display in the main office of the company, and Ray De Frates' nephew, now head of the firm, continues to make the chili exactly as it was made sixty years ago.

According to Bill De Frates,

What makes this chili unique is the fact that there has never been a filler of any kind added to the product—no cereal, flour, starches, etc. We do not use heart meat, tripe, or other meat by-products. We use only choice beef from the rib section of the steers. This meat is always at least fifty percent lean; some fat is allowed because we feel that a little fat is needed in the best chili.

Sample cans I received proved excellent, not as fiery hot as some I have tasted, but all the better for that. For the average taste, this just may be some of the best chili around.

The original-recipe all-meat chili comes in 19½-ounce cans. Six cans, when we checked, were selling for around $11.00. Ray's also offers chili with beans and chili-mac, both in 20-ounce cans, six cans of either type (or any mixture of the two) selling for a little over $9.00. All orders are shipped within three days of their receipt.

□

H. ROTH & SON
1577 First Avenue
New York, NY 10028
(212) 734–1111
Free catalog. Accepts checks, money orders, COD
orders, Visa, MasterCard, Diners Club, American
Express, and Carte Blanche. There is a $2.00
handling charge on orders of less than $10.00.

Located in New York's Yorkville section and famous for its Hungarian specialties, the shop of H. Roth & Son is crammed full of imported delicacies from around the world. Here you can order red and green lentils, black turtle beans, peas (whole or split, yellow or green), and French *flageolets*. There are flours such as buckwheat, chestnut, chick-pea, and a special blend for strudel. Or, if you prefer, you can order the strudel dough already prepared, in sheets. Nuts for baking or for snacking come shelled whole or ground, and include such varieties as hazelnuts, black walnuts, and Brazil nuts.

Among the Hungarian specialties are egg drops *(tarhonya)*, a potato substitute that is browned in shortening, then simmered until tender in chicken broth or water; spaetzle noodles, and prune butter *(lekvar)*, a thick puree used as a filling for strudel. Also sold are apple, plum, and apricot butters. To these can be added several flavors of Hungarian jam, including the very popular sour cherry and honey from faraway places such as Israel and Brazil.

The very complete list of herbs and spices includes a special blend for goulash, Hungarian paprika, and poppy seeds for making the famous Hungarian poppy seed cake. Other baking items include paste food coloring, almond paste, multicolored sugar crystals, and candied rose petals. H. Roth & Son is also an excellent source for Brazilian, Chinese, and Indonesian imported foods, as well as for dried and candied fruits, but always obtain a current price list before placing an order here, as their prices tend to fluctuate wildly.

□

SINAI KOSHER FOOD CORP.
1000 West Pershing Road
Chicago, IL 60609
(312) 927–2810.
Free brochure on request. Accepts checks and money
orders. Always check current prices before ordering.
Minimum order: 500 pounds.

For over 70 years, Sinai has made and packaged sausage under strict rabbinical supervision. As a result of the worldwide reputation it built in the sausage business, it is hardly surprising that its customers requested Sinai to supply other cuts of meat they wanted and needed. The Jewish housewife, like any other, wants a full selection of meats she can place in the home freezer and have ready for use at any time. But the service needed has been lacking in many Jewish communities. Sinai is helping change all that.

Richard Lowenstein, vice-president of the firm, explains,

We provide a unique service to kosher meat customers. Because our products cannot be sent without refrigeration, we ask our customers to get a group together so that we can ship by freezer trucks, which require a minimum order of five hundred pounds. [In other words, if you order only fifty pounds, you still have to pay the freight for five hundred pounds.] We put up each family's order individually and ship it to one designated place—either one person's home, or perhaps to a synagogue. Quite a few synagogues' women's clubs use this as a project for their members. We prepay the freight and charge each family for its share.

We offer a varied selection—much more than any local kosher butcher could provide. All our meats are of the very highest quality, very closely trimmed, soaked, salted, deveined (kosher made) and frozen, ready to cook.

Because meat prices fluctuate so widely at various times throughout the year, Sinai requested that I quote no prices in this book and that you always check with them before ordering.

It was sausage that made this company famous throughout the world, and all those kosher products remain available. On the list of all-beef deli meats you will find salami and salami sticks; frankfurters and cocktail franks; smoked sausage; knockwurst and bologna; Polish, liver, and breakfast sausages; sausage rolls and sausage links; and many low-fat sausages. The list also includes stuffed kishke (or derma).

Sliced meats include corned beef, beef pastrami, tongue, breakfast beef strips, bologna, and smoked beef salami. All these, like the sausages above, are put up in convenient-sized packages, usually 1 pound or less to the package.

Kosher beef of every cut and in every form is available here. Roasts include chuck, shoulder, rib, rib eye, and a rolled pot roast, as well as the brisket of beef. Steaks include cubed, chuck, rib and rib eye, shoulder, and more. Ground beef is available in bulk or in patties. The list also includes beef liver, tongue, and short ribs.

Lamb rib chops, shoulder steaks, shoulder roast, and stewing pieces make up the full list of lamb offered, but the list of veal is far longer, including roasts, chops, and cutlets, as well as ground and stewing veal.

Kosher poultry can be even more difficult to find, but here you will find everything to fill your poultry needs. Fryers can be ordered whole or cut up; or you can select packages of chicken legs, wings, breasts, or livers, as well as stewing and roasting hens. Hen and tom turkeys are available, as well as Long Island ducks and Cornish hens. There is even unrendered chicken fat to round out your cooking needs.

If, like too many Jewish shoppers, you have had problems finding locally the meat and poultry items you need, Sinai Kosher food will prove a blessing.

□

SULTAN'S DELIGHT, INC.
25 Croton Avenue
Staten Island, NY 10301
(212) 720–1557
*Free catalog. Accepts checks, money orders, Visa,
and MasterCard. Minimum order: $15.00.*

Due to the political situation in the Middle East, foods and spices from that part of the world have become increasingly expensive and difficult to find. So it is refreshing to discover a source that not only offers these foods at remarkably low prices, but also offers to help locate for its customers any items they may be unable to buy elsewhere.

Among the ready-to-serve delicacies listed are stuffed vine leaves, lentil pilaf, artichoke bottoms, and zucchini stuffed with meat and rice. Cheeses include *halabiyey* (braided cheese), feta, Syrian, and half a dozen other Middle Eastern favorites. About a dozen types of bread dough (including filo, marcouk, zaatar, and chapati) can be shipped under refrigeration, and the firm also ships out fresh pastries such as pistachio-filled baklava, *harrissa* (honey cake), and *swarat-il-sit* (or bird's nest cake). Candies include *molabbas* (sugar-coated almonds), *succar nabat* (rock candy), and packs of Greek chewing gum. A number of dried and candied fruits (prunes, figs, dates, raisins, etc.) are shipped, and the firm also offers a number of fruit syrups, juices, and preserves, among them such rarities as date molasses, tamarind syrup, and pomegranate juice. Other beverages include imported and herbal teas, and two blends of Turkish coffee.

Prices on everything offered here were more than reasonable when I checked, but they are likely to fluctuate wildly because of the unrest in the Middle East, so I am quoting no prices here but ask that you check those yourself.

□

TIA MIA
P.O. Box 685
4501 Anapra Road
Sunland Park, NM 88063
Free catalog. Accepts checks, money orders, Visa,
and MasterCard; no CODs. Full guarantee.

The catalog of this company comes in the form of a little newsletter loaded with interesting facts about their Mexican-American specialties, recipes for using their ingredients, and suggestions for serving their prepared items.

Their most popular item, according to the firm, is Tia Mia Chilesalsa Special, a specially prepared base for *chile con queso* (green chili with cheese). This is a full-flavored blending of green and red chilies, jalapeños, tomatillos, tomatoes, onions, garlic and coriander. You simply heat it and add your own cheese, then serve it over hamburger or chopped steak, fried eggs, over grits, or in any of several more ways you will find described in the Tia Mia catalog. Six 10-ounce cans sell for about $13.00.

The green and red chilies that go into the Chilesalsa Special are, like all the other ingredients used by this firm, selected, picked, and prepared under close supervision of the owners, and all their specialties are created from authentic old family recipes. They are not like the foods sold in fast-food operations and in supermarkets, nor should you expect them to be.

Their *caldillo*, for example, after you have added your own beef or chicken, makes an authentic Mexican stew unlike anything known to most Americans. *Caldillo* is a melding of various chilies, tomatoes, onions, coriander (Chinese parsley or cilantro), garlic and hominy. It makes a complete meal when served over tortillas or crusty slices of garlic bread. It is available with either red or green chilies as the base, and the two 28-ounce cans of either type sell for around $10.00.

If you prefer to prepare your own Mexican-American dishes, Tia Mia also sells many of the ingredients, sauces, and seasonings you will need to get started. Two 26-ounce cans of green chilies, for example, sell for about $9.00. Or you can order six 3½-ounce tins of jalapeños for just under $8.00. *Pico de gallo verde*—which translates as "beak of the rooster" and is a thick sauce commonly added to tacos, refried beans, or scrambled eggs—costs about $10.00 for four 7½-ounce cans. Other useful sauces, selling at about the same price, include Salsa Ranchera, essential to making ranch-style eggs; and Salsa Tipica, which is a mildly spicy sauce for tacos.

To add a little Mexican atmosphere to your kitchen, as well as some useful ingredients to your larder, you might order (for about $40.00) an authentic *ristera*—a 3-foot-long strand of plump red chilies that you can hang as a decoration and use as needed. To hang beside the *ristera,* there is (for about $30.00) an equally long rope of braided Mexican garlic bulbs. You might also add to the Mexican atmosphere by setting out a handwoven tortilla basket holding 3 pounds of roasted peanuts seasoned with red chili. The full basket sells for a little over $20.00.

The jalapeño pepper plays a prominent role in Mexican-American cookery, and that role is clearly reflected in the products offered by Tia Mia. Fiery hot jalapeño mustard sells at about $6.00 for a 5-ounce jar; or you can order a 5-ounce jar of dried jalapeño flakes for about the same price. Jalapeño pepper jelly—a hot, sweet, and tangy concoction that is a unique complement to lamb, Cornish hen, or ham—is put up in attractive reusable glass storage jars and shipped in a hand-woven tortilla basket. The basket holds two 10-ounce jars of jelly—one red and one green—and sells for under $20.00.

Handwoven tortilla baskets such as these serve as containers for the half a dozen or so gift selections sent out by Tia Maria, and they are attractive enough to warrant your attention when gift shopping. Selections range in price from $16.00 to $35.00. An example is the Mexican Tang-O selection at about $31.00, which I have tried and believe to be well worth the price. The baskets holds one 10½-ounce jar of red jalapeño jelly, one 10½-ounce jar of green jalapeño jelly, a 9-ounce jar of jalapeño mustard, and a 5-ounce jar of dried jalapeño flakes. The basket and jars will find many uses around my house, and the quality of the contents was such that Tia Mia can add my family to their list of satisfied customers.

CHAPTER FOUR

NATURAL FOODS

While nearly every town and city today has at least one health-food store, most of us do not have access to the farmers who produce naturally grown foods, nor are we always able to find everything we need on local counters. By ordering through the mail, however, one can order directly from producers of naturally grown grains, fruits, and vegetables; from one farmer, you can even order organically raised beef, veal, and lamb. Natural vitamins and food supplements are offered by the companies listed here, and, if you wish, you can even order natural cosmetics. Here you will find unusual items such as seaweed and carob, and you will also find foods for those with special dietary requirements and allergies.

Although we have listed specific health-food sources in this chapter, you will find that many of the companies listed in other chapters produce their food without harmful additives, and companies listed there should not be overlooked when shopping for healthful food.

□

BARTH'S OF LONG ISLAND
270 West Merrick Road
Valley Stream, NY 11582
Free catalog. Accepts checks and money orders only;
no CODs. Add 85 cents delivery charge to all
orders.

Barth's catalog is about 100 pages of natural foods, food supplements and vitamins, including many of its own brand products. There are dried instant soups in a number of varieties such as beef, chicken, onion, pea, carrot, and celery, and all are made without any additives (4-ounce jars, at $1.95 or so, make 20 servings). Among the other food selections are an oat cereal with wheat germ and prunes (around $1.70 for a ⅛-pound box); a seed, fruit, and nut mixture consisting of shelled sunflower and pumpkin seeds, raisins, almonds, cashews, dates, and sesame seeds (approximately $4.65 per 14-ounce can); rare tupelo honey for those on restricted diets (under $4.00 per 1-pound jar); sunflower kernels (under $3.00 per pound); wheat germ flakes (about $2.65 for a 1-pound can); and honey molasses drops (about $3.85 for 13 ounces) that are said to be loaded with natural energy.

Herb teas are put up in packages of 32 tea bags, all selling at less than $2.00 per package. The teas include camomile, peppermint, alfalfa mint, rose hip, and Roseamint, a blend of peppermint, strawberry leaves, and rose hips. Ginseng tea is available at approximately $3.50 for 32 tea bags.

All-natural preserves include rose hip, apricot, strawberry, wild blueberry, black cherry, red raspberry, and red currant. Average price is about $2.50 for a 12-ounce jar.

Barth's offers a number of appliances to help you prepare natural foods and beverages at home. There is a stainless-steel automatic kitchen center (around $200.00) that serves as mixer and dough mixer, grinder, liquefier, blender, soup and salad maker, grater, pulverizer, and even as an ice chopper and ice-cream freezer. An instant juicer sells for about $120.00; an electric food grinder for converting nuts and seeds into meal costs approximately $25.00; and a home grain mill, nonelectric, sells at less than $30.00.

Health and beauty aids from Barth's are as natural as their foods, made with such goodies as aloe vera, cocoa butter, avocado, and essence of cucumber and strawberry. They offer, for example, three bath-size bars of rose water and glycerine soap, said to be especially good for dry, chapped skin, for around $4.00; and an 8-ounce bottle of jojoba-oil shampoo and conditioner, made from the oil of a bush native to the American Southwest, for around $6.00. More than a dozen aloe vera beauty products are offered, including a 4-ounce bottle of hand and body lotion for about $3.50.

For more than thirty years, Barth's has built their business on the belief that nature holds the key to health and better living, and, if you share that belief, theirs is one catalog you can hardly do without.

□

BETTER FOODS, INC.
200 North Washington Street
Greencastle, PA 17225
Catalog: $1.00. Accepts checks and money orders
only; no CODs. Minimum ordrer: $15.00.

The catalog sent out by Better Foods is one of the most complete in the natural foods industry. In addition to all the basic foods—whole grains, legumes, nuts, fruits, juices, and herbs—and many items made without harmful additives—oils, baked goods, pasta, soups, and seaonings—there is a large selection of vegetarian entrées and a good selection of natural vitamins and cosmetics. But the catalog does much more than merely list these foods; it completely describes their ingredients and nutritive values and is loaded with tips and recipes for preparing and serving them. The catalog itself—for $1.00—is probably one of the best buys in the mail-order industry.

All their baked goods are made from natural ingredients such as whole grains, raw sugar or honey, milk, soy, and unsulphured molasses. Breads sell at around 75 cents for a 1-pound loaf, and the selection includes wheat and soy, unbleached white flour and soy, whole-grain rye, and whole-grain wheat. For about the same price, you can also order banana bread, date and nut loaf, or sticky buns. At least a dozen kind of cookies are offered (at about 89 cents per dozen), including carob chip, bran-raisin, and sugarless oatmeal.

For baking your own goodies at home, there is dark buck-wheat flour (about $1.30 per 2-pound bag); rye flour (about 80 cents per 2-pound bag); and unbleached white flour with wheat germ (about $4.70 for 5 pounds); as well as dozens of prepared mixes and special baking ingredients.

Pastas are made from either whole wheat or a combination of semolina, soy, and Jerusalem artichoke; sell at about $1.39 for a 12-ounce bag; and include macaroni, spaghetti, linguine and lasagna. To go with these, you can order (at about $2.39 per pound) pure vegetable-enzyme cheeses such as white or yellow cheddar, Colby longhorn, mozzarella, provolone, Swiss or Muenster. Add to them, from among the dozens of meat substitutes, some nonmeat meat balls (under $2.00 for 19 ounces), some diced or sliced chicken substitute (about $1.60 for 13 ounces), chili (around $1.40 for 20 ounces), or any of a number of meat substitutes found here, and you have all the makings of an authentic but meatless Italian dinner.

It need not be Italian, as long as it is natural and healthful. There are prepared foods such as beefless beef stew (about 90 cents for a 12-ounce can), sauerkraut (around $1.60 per quart), vegetarian chicken pie (about 89 cents for an 8-ounce pie), vegetarian turkey substitute (around $2.00 for twelve 8-ounce slices), and dozens of dehydrated soups at 98 cents or so for a package of 3 ounces.

Juices range from apple (about $1.30 per quart) to vegetable cocktail (63 cents per quart), with about two dozen choices in between, including grape (a little over $2.00 per quart) and grapefruit, orange, and papaya (all about $1.70 per quart).

Natural sweeteners start with pure Vermont maple syrup (around $10.00 per quart) and go from there to include honey (about $1.45 per pound), blackstrap molasses (around $1.90 per pint), fructose granules (about $1.10 per pound), and numerous others. There are also many prepared natural sweets such as honey-drop candy (approximately $1.60 for an 8-ounce bag), carob chips (about $1.40 for a 12-ounce bag) and high-protein chocolate bars (about $3.15 for eight 2-ounce bars). You can even choose from about a dozen flavors (cherry, grape, lemon, raspberry, etc.) of pure vegetable gelatins at 55 cents or so per 2-ounce package.

Although this company does offer one of the largest selections in its field, there are certain points you should keep in mind when ordering from them. The first is that they ship by UPS only, which means no deliveries to post office boxes. They also insist that you sign an agreement allowing UPS to deliver to a neighbor if you are not home when the parcel arrives. And finally, they assume no responsibility for spoilage or lost shipments.

□

DAISYFRESH DAIRY CULTURES
P.O. Box 36
Santa Cruz, CA 95063
Free price list and brochure. Accepts checks and money orders only. All prices include delivery.

A family business that has been supplying dairy cultures direct to about 1,400 dairy stores since 1972, Dairyfresh offers its wholesale prices direct to you at home. You save as much as 47 percent by bypassing the retailer.

Four different cultures are offered: Bulgarian yogurt, Swiss acidophilus, Irish country buttermilk, and Danish sour cream. Each comes with complete instructions for making the finished product at home, as well as with a booklet of recipes for using it. Cost is about $2.50 for a packet that should keep the average family supplied with yogurt (or whatever) for about a month. Price per packet is lower on larger orders. For example, 12 packets of any culture can be ordered for around $22.00, a savings of approximately $8.00.

Since the correct temperature is essential to success in making yogurt or other dairy cultures, Dairyfresh offers (for about $3.00) a professional dairy thermometer. They also offer (for $2.95) a yogurt manual that includes 160 different yogurt recipes. Both will be shipped to you free of cost if your initial order for the dairy cultures is $6.00 or more.

□

DEER VALLEY FARM
R.D. 1
Guilford, NY 13780
(607) 764–8556
*Free catalog. Accepts checks and money orders only;
no CODs.*

Deer Valley Farm has been devoted to organic farming since
1947, constantly building up their soil with liberal applications of
manure, straw, leaves, rock phosphate, kelp, compost, and other
natural soil builders. Such care has made Deer Valley one of the
most successful organic farms in all of the United States.

With a few rare exceptions, all the items listed in their catalog
are grown on the New York farm, and even those exceptions are
guaranteed to be grown or made with absolutely no harmful
chemicals, sprays, preservatives, or additives.

Completely natural baked items include such delicacies as
wheat or rice wafers (around $1.20 for 5 ounces), toasted soy
snacks (about $1.25 per pound), cheese sticks (about $1.40 for 10
ounces), fig bars (about $1.07 for 14 ounces), whole-wheat bread
(about $1.00 for a 1-pound, 2-ounce loaf), French or Italian bread
(about $1.00 for a 1-pound loaf), and whole-wheat angel cake,
made without baking powder (under $2.00 for a 17-ounce cake).

There are a number of dairy products and milk substitutes in
the catalog, including Tiger Milk, produced according to the formula made famous by Adelle Davis, selling at around $4.50 for a
12-ounce container. Butter made on the farm from fresh cultured
cream sells at around $2.65 per pound. Whey costs about $5.00
for 10 pounds. Unpasteurized natural cheese, all produced in
Wisconsin and New York, sells at an average price of about $3.10
per pound, and the varieties include three types of Swiss, three
types of cheddar, and bricks of Muenster.

At around $1.75 per pound, the farm offers about half a dozen
varieties of honey, including basswood, buckwheat, clover, and
orange blossom; rare types of honey, such as tupelo, are available
at slightly higher prices. About as many varieties of molasses are
offered, prices starting at around $2.60 per quart.

Organic nuts and seeds of every variety are sold here, including such standards as peanuts (a little over $2.00 per pound);
pistachios (about $5.65 per pound); pecans (around $2.70 per

pound); and cashews (approximately $3.30 per pound, in pieces, slightly higher whole)—and harder-to-find varieties such as filberts ($4.50 per pound); pine nuts ($7.95 per pound); and macadamias ($10.50 or so per pound).

In addition to pages of grains, herbs and herb products, vitamins, and food supplements, Deer Valley also sells many tools that would be useful in growing your own organic food and a number of appliances that would be useful in preparing either what you grow or what you buy. There is, for example, an electric flour mill at around $190.00, a hand-operated baby-food grinder at $7.50 or so, and an electric yogurt maker for approximately $25.00.

Perhaps the most important thing about Deer Valley Farm— at least to nonvegetarians seeking the most healthful food they can buy—is that this is the only readily available source for a full line of naturally raised beef, pork, lamb, and poultry. More information about those products is given in the chapter dealing with meat, poultry, and game. And, by the way, if you are ever in central New York State, the folks at Deer Valley invite you to drop by for a visit and use their facilities for an outing.

□

ENER-G FOODS, INC.
6901 Fox Avenue
P.O. Box 24723
Seattle, WA 98124
(206) 767–6660
*Free price list on request. Send no payment with
your order. All orders are shipped, then billed.*

During World War II, when German invaders confiscated all the grains in Holland, a strange event occurred. A number of Dutch people who had been sickly for years suddenly began to feel well again. This event caused two Dutch doctors to begin the research that led to the discovery of an ailment called celiac sprue, an intolerance to gluten, a sticky elastic protein found in wheat, rye, oats, and barley, but not in rice and corn. It was later found that many, many other people are mildly allergic to this same gluten. Other folks are allergic to milk or eggs, and Ener-G Foods was created to fill the special dietary needs of people with these and other medical problems. The list of foods they offer is so long that only a sampling can be given here.

Among the wheat-free, glutenless baked products are white and brown rice breads (about $1.30 per 8-ounce loaf); rice hamburger buns and rice muffins (about $1.60 per package of six); rice–caraway seed cookies, rice carob cookies, rice chocolate cookies, and rice–peanut butter cookies (all at around $2.70 per package of 18); and corn hazelnut cookies (about $2.50 for a package of 12). There are also numerous wheat-free mixes for baking glutenless breads and cookies at home, the average price being about $1.40 for a 16-ounce package.

Wheat-free pastas range in price from $1.49 for 12-ounce packages of spaghetti and elbow or shell macaroni to around $2.50 for 12-ounce packages of anellini and rigatini, or about $2.85 for 12-ounce boxes of tagliatelle. All are made from a base of cornstarch and tapioca.

For those allergic to eggs, there is an egg replacer at $3.00 or so per 18-ounce package, and, unlike many other egg substitutes, this one contains no egg white. If milk creates a problem, the company offers Nutquik, a powdered milk substitute made from ground almonds, at about $3.00 per 16-ounce package, and Soyquik, a substitute made from pure soy powder, at $1.40 or so per 15-ounce package. Milk and egg substitutes must be ordered by the case, 12 packages to each case.

□

LEON R. HORSTED
Route 2
Waunakee, WI 53597
Price list: 15 cents plus SASE.

Doing business from the family farm just a few miles outside the small Wisconsin town of Waunakee, the Horsteds send their price list out in the form of a delightful little mimeographed newsletter that is loaded with poems, recipes, and information about natural foods. Many of the items are donated by their customers. But it is the items on the list—many of them grown by the Horsteds, some bought from other sources—that will be of greatest interest to those seeking natural foods.

Flour made from organically grown grains range in price from 35 to 90 cents per pound, and includes barley, buckwheat, corn, millet, rice, soybean, and wheat. Wheat germ sells at about 50 cents per pound, and hulled sunflower kernels sell at $1.20 or so per pound.

At approximately $3.15 per pound there is either Colby or cheddar cheese, both produced on a Wisconsin farm that uses only organic methods, and other nearby farmers produce pure maple syrup that sells at roughly $2.75 per pint; buckwheat honey that sells at about 85 cents per pound; and raw, cold-pressed sunflower oil that goes at around $2.40 per quart.

From other sources there are tree-ripened, organically grown black olives at around $1.60 per pound, a 1-ounce carob bar for about 20 cents, sea salt at about 35 cents per pound, and sea kelp at about $2.00 for 3 ounces. And if you are interested in growing your own organic garden, for 85 cents plus shipping the Horsteds will send you an 8-pound bag of mineralized plant-grade compost fertilizer.

□

INTERNATIONAL YOGURT COMPANY
628 North Doheny Drive
Los Angeles, CA 90069
Free price list on request. Full guarantee.

In business for more than forty years, International Yogurt is very likely the largest mail-order supplier of yogurt cultures and related products. All their products are made by the Rosell Bacteriological Institute of Montreal, which was founded in a Trappist monastery, and they have been pioneers in introducing new and better lactic cultures to the general public.

Cultures cost around $2.50 for a package that should keep you supplied for about a month. Types include yogurt, buttermilk, sour cream, and a special culture for making fresh cheese in your own home. Available at the same price is a culture for making kefir, which, in case you have never tasted it, is a thickened milk that looks somewhat like buttermilk but tastes a little like yogurt. Also available at the same price is a culture for making sweet acidophilus milk, especially good for those with digestive problems.

To help you work successfully with these cultures at home, there are items such as a 2-quart yogurt incubator (around $25.00), a floating dairy thermometer (about $3.50), and *The Complete Book of Yogurt* by S. N. Henrick ($6.95). If you want the benefits of yogurt without the trouble of making it, concentrated yogurt tablets are available (about $5.00, package size not given), as well as ready-to-eat kefir grains (about $6.50, package size not given). And if you're *really* into yogurt, the company offers a number of cosmetic and beauty aid items made from a yogurt base, such as a 6-ounce bottle of yogurt shampoo for about $4.95, and a yogurt face and body power for around $4.50.

□

JAFFE BROTHERS
P.O. Box 636
Valley Center, CA 92082
(714) 749–1133
Free catalog on request. Accepts checks and money orders; no CODs.

Now in its thirty-third year in business, this company began in a humble little building that could easily fit into a corner of the giant warehouse presently needed to stock the vast amounts of organically grown foods that are shipped all over the United States and to faraway countries such as Thailand, Japan, France, England, and the Netherlands.

Nearly all the food sold by Jaffe Bros. originates from growers with whom the company has collaborated for a period of time and who are willing to sign declarations attesting to the organic cultivation of their crops. After all these years, and after stupendous growth, Jaffe Bros. remains a family business, ". . . conducted without fanfare, dedicated to providing unsulphured, unfumigated food products grown by organic or natural means thereby relieving customers of the worry of filling their stomachs with food laden with poisons," according to a letter I received from Sid Jaffe, co-owner of the firm.

One minor problem here, for the average buyer, is that in order to reduce both the cost of the food and the cost of shipping, all items are sold in bulk.

Dried organic fruits are a specialty here. If the price seems high at first glance, consider that it takes about 8 pounds of the fresh fruit to make 1 pound of the dried product. All come in 5-pound boxes, and they include apples (about $11.50 per box), apricots (about $17.50 per box), black mission figs (around $7.00 per box), peaches (about $9.00 per box), and half a dozen other choices at comparable prices. Organic tropical dried fruits are put up in 20-pound boxes, and include papaya and pineapple (both at about $43.00 per box), as well as whole bananas (under $30.00 per box).

Shelled nuts, also in 5-pound boxes, include almonds (about $11.00 per box), peanuts (around $6.25 per box), cashew pieces (about $11.50 per box), whole cashews (about $18.75 per box), pecan halves (approximately $20.50 per box), walnut halves ($12.75 or so per box), and macadamias (a little over $25.00 per box).

Organic grains and grain products include yellow cornmeal (about $1.90 for 5 pounds), millet (around $2.30 for 5 pounds), rolled oats ($2.00 or so for 5 pounds), wheat berries (about $1.85 for 5 pounds), rye flour (around $2.25 for 5 pounds), and buckwheat groats (approximately $4.75 for 5 pounds), plus half a dozen more selections at comparable prices.

Legumes on the list, all in 5-pound packages, include green split peas (about $3.25), soy beans (around $2.25), mung beans (about $5.35), and lentils (approximately $4.75).

Seven types of seeds, all potent sources of raw protein, vitamins, and minerals, are offered in 5-pound packages. They are sunflower (about $5.50), hulled sesame (about $4.85), flax (around $2.35), alfalfa (approximately $9.50), pumpkin (about $13.25), and chia ($13.50 or so).

Carob powder, made from pods picked from naturally grown carob trees, can be ordered either raw or toasted at a cost of about $4.00 for 5 pounds; and bee pollen, the only food source known to contain all twenty-two elements that make up the living functioning tissue of the human body, costs around $13.25 for a 2-pound package.

Jaffe Bros. offers several gift selections, among them (for about $14.50) a Tropical Gift Mailer that consists of a 16-ounce package of dried pineapple, a 16-ounce package of black mission figs, a 16-ounce package of date-coconut confection, an 8-ounce package of dried papaya, and an 8-ounce package of dried whole bananas. Or, if you'd like to let those on your list make their own selections, you can send your gift list to Jaffe Bros., along with the amounts you wish to spend on each one, and the company will send each person on the list a "letter of credit" in the amount you stipulate. It's an excellent way to send excellent food to those you love.

□

Shiloh Farms, Inc.
Sulphur Springs, AR 72768
(501) 298–3297
Free catalog. Accepts checks and money orders only;
no CODs. No minimum order, but there is a $5.00
service charge on orders of less than $25.00.

If you are a regular customer of the health-food stores, you almost certainly have had some experience with the products of Shiloh Farms, for they presently supply more than 400 food and health items to well over 1,000 retail stores in all parts of the United States. What you may not know is that they also run a very large mail-order operation, and many of their goods (though not all) can be ordered directly from the Shiloh Farms warehouse, often at incredible savings. Among the items which cannot be shipped directly to the consumer are meats, poultry, juices, and frozen products, but that still leaves hundreds of items that will be of interest to those seeking natural foods.

To mention just a few of the many items that can be ordered through the mail, there are carrots by the 25-pound bag (about $9.50) and oranges by the bushel (about $17.00); several varieties of dates and date confections, shredded coconut and coconut candies; dried fruits such as apples, bananas, and pears; raw shelled nuts of every type; raw sweetening agents such as honey, molasses, and maple syrup; and numerous sources of vegetable protein. In the colder months only, you can order cheddar, Colby, and Swiss cheeses (about $3.00 per pound), as well as Alpahorn, a combination of Colby, cheddar and longhorn, at about the same price.

The bulk of Shiloh Farms business is in grains, seeds, flours, and baked goods. Many of these are the products of Arrowhead Mills, which sells only to retailers and does not ship through the mails. They include raw, unprocessed bran, rice flour, barley and soybean grits, flax meal, and chia seeds, the latter famous among the Indians of the Southwest as a source of quick energy, and more than 40 types of baked goods. Those baked goods include sourdough rye bread, corn-soy muffins, banana loaf, whole-wheat hamburger buns, sesame seed cookies, and even whole-wheat or white pizzas. As for prices, all items are priced far below what you would expect to pay in your local health-food store, but Shiloh Farms does ask that you call them and check their current prices before ordering, as their prices fluctuate with the seasons. When calling, be sure to ask about their discounts, which are 20 percent and more on orders of $200.00 and up.

□

WALNUT ACRES
Penns Creek, PA 17862
(717) 837-0601
Free catalog on request. Accepts checks, money
orders, Visa, and MasterCard. A handling charge of
$1.00 is added to all orders.

Paul and Betty Keene, owners of Walnut Acres, insist that they never really intended to become farmers; it just happened that way. However it happened, their 360-acre farm, in a lovely little valley complete with a clear mountain stream, has developed into one of the largest and most famous suppliers of organic foods in America, described in the *Last Whole Earth Catalog* as "the best, most reputable source in the United States. A place with foods like you've never tasted."

When it began more than thirty-six years ago, the Keenes were nearly destitute, living in unheated quarters without modern lighting or plumbing and with two horses providing the only power for the farm work. Today the farm is much more modern and the Keenes are far from destitute, but all their crops continue to be grown by the organic methods they learned, in part, while studying with the famous J. I. Rodale, and their land remains untouched by chemicals or poisonous sprays. Though no public transportation comes closer than 20 miles to Penns Creek, the fame of Walnut Acres is such that the Keenes are visited daily by people from almost every state in the Union, drawn there by their reputation for outstanding natural food.

The 39-page catalog lists food in nearly every category, always including a number of special offers and items on which prices have been reduced for quick sale. Among the specials in my copy were numerous herb teas that had been reduced about 50 cents per 4-ounce package to an average price of about $1.50, green beans at 30 cents per 1-pound tin, whole rose hips at $1.76 per pound, tapioca flour at 73 cents per pound, apple-boysenberry or apple-pomegranate juice at $1.50 per quart; and vegetable-nut soup mix at $1.75 for an 8-ounce tin. On nearly all these specials, further price reductions are offered when quantities are bought.

The body of the catalog offers a rainbow of health-food selections, those mentioned here simply picked at random. For making your own healthful juice at home, there are fresh carrots at about $6.00 for 15 pounds. There are eight varieties of granola, ranging in price from about $1.00 per pound to about $1.65 per pound, depending on the type you choose. More than a dozen hot cereals, all at well below $1.00 per pound, are offered.

In addition to all the grains, flours, legumes, and vegetarian items one normally expects to find in the catalog of a health-food specialist, Walnut Acres offers what few others do: meat, fish, and poultry products made without preservatives and additives. These are made chiefly from livestock raised on the Walnut Acres homestead; when other sources are used, the Keenes see to it that their standards of purity are maintained.

All their beef and chicken is raised on grass and ground feed, with no commercial feed mixes, no hormones, no force feeding. It is then prepared according to the farm's own recipes and sold in 1-pound cans. A few of the canned items include beans and franks (about $1.50 per can), beef stew (under $2.00 per can), braised beef hash (under $2.50 per can), chicken stew (about $1.65 per can), and pure ground beef (around $3.60 per can).

Fish and seafood items are carefully chosen to avoid those that come from possibly polluted waters. For example, they offer (for about $2.60 a jar) 5-ounce jars of boneless salmon fillets, the fish taken from remote, unpolluted Alaskan waters. Their fish chowder (about $1.30 for a 1-pound can) is made from fish taken off the unpolluted Icelandic coast; their clam chowder (about $1.40 for a 1-pound can), like all their other clam concoctions, is made using only deep-sea clams, far less likely to be contaminated than those from inshore waters.

The list is so complete that here you will even find vegetarian meals for the family dog—including completely organic doggie biscuits at about $2.19 per pound. If only because of such diversity, I believe the catalog of Walnut Acres should be in the hands of all who are committed to healthful eating.

□

CHAPTER FIVE

CHEESE

In the catalogs of well over half the companies mentioned in this book, you will find cheese of one or more varieties offered for sale, and in other chapters I have mentioned some that are of special interest. In this chapter, however, I wish to introduce you to those firms that specialize in bringing you the very finest cheese available, whether imported or domestic.

Included here are a number of cheese-producing factories. Some are family operations that offer just a few varieties. Others are full-line operations that ship out such diverse varieties as Stilton, Limburger, brick, blue, Colby, Muenster, Swiss, cheddar, and types you may be encountering for the first time. Still others specialize in their own spreads, cheese balls, smoked and blended varieties.

Importers make available fine cheeses from around the world. From them you can obtain the very best products made in Switzerland, France, Italy, England, or almost any other country you care to name. But all these countries contributed to the art of cheesemaking in America, and so you will find that nearly all their most famous varieties can be duplicated by domestic cheesemakers, often at far lower prices.

You will notice a preponderance of companies offering cheddar, which is not only an indication of how popular this variety is
in America, but also of how easily it may be shipped and stored.
In addition to such easily handled and well-known types, you will
find delicate varieties such as fine Bries, Gruyère, Port Salut,
Danish Havarti, and even a delicate ewe's milk cheese from
Spain, making this chapter, I believe, an especially helpful one
for those who do not have ready access to a well-stocked cheese
shop.

□

CHEESE JUNCTION
1 West Ridgewood Avenue
Ridgewood, NJ 07450
(800) 631–0353
*Free catalog. Accepts checks, money orders, Visa,
MasterCard, and American Express. Minimum credit
card order $15.00. Full guarantee.*

A dazzling array of international cheeses, gourmet coffees and
selected gift items fills the pages of the catalog of this firm. Be it
a block or wheel of cheddar from New York, a Wensleydale from
England, a Limburger from Germany, or a butter cheese from
Sweden, cheese lovers are almost certain to find it among the
more than 100 varieties described here. In addition to such favorites as Colby, Swiss, Monterey Jack, Brie, Camembert, Edam
and Gouda, you'll find dozens of varieties that are less well
known in this country. From France, for example, there is Pont
l'Evêque, a cheese somewhat similar to Brie, and boursalt, a soft
creamy cheese with a pink rind that is ripened in the caves of
France. From Holland comes leyden, a firm textured skim-milk
cheese flavored with caraway and cumin; and from Germany
there is bruder basil, a semisoft cheese that is lightly smoked. In
addition, there are pages of cheese spreads and cheese logs, and
even packaged cheese fondues.
    Prices here are remarkably low. Most cheddars, when I
checked, were selling at prices between $4.00 and $5.00 a
pound, and even an imported Brie could be had for less than
$4.00 per pound. Further savings are realized when an entire
wheel or block of cheese is purchased.

Mocha java, Hawaiian kona, Guatemalan Antigua, and blends from Turkey, France, Italy and Scandinavia are among the gourmet coffees listed. These, too, are remarkably low in price, with even the rare, highly desirable Hawaiian kona selling for just a little over $5.00 per pound. Also available, for around $10.00 apiece, are three coffee samplers, each holding ¼ pound each of half a dozen different coffees. With any order of $18.00 or more, you receive a free gift with a retail value of $4.00.

□

CHEESE 'N' MORE, INC.
Route 5
Merrill, WI 54452
Free catalog on request. Accepts checks and money
orders. There is a $3.50 charge for special packaging
during the summer months. Full guarantee.

Located in the very heart of the most famous cheese-producing area in America, just a few miles north of Wausau and a stone's throw from the Wisconsin River, this mail-order enterprise began as a small retail store that specialized in selling cheese produced in the region. The retail operation was so successful that imported cheeses were soon made available, and the operation was moved into a building that has become something of a tourist attraction: a mock wheel of cheddar with a wedge cut out for an entrance. Inside this unique building, visitors can browse among more than 100 varieties of cheese, as well as fine wines and other gourmet delicacies. These visitors began requesting mail-order service, and Cheese 'N' More responded by making available one of the best selections of any dealer shipping cheese through the mails.

Not every variety sold in the shop is available by mail, but you can choose from among their best-selling varieties, imported as well as domestic. Just those produced in the Dairy State make this a source worth considering.

Colby, which was first made at, and derives its name from, the nearby town of Colby, Wisconsin, is the most popular variety sold here. Excellent with fruit or in cooked dishes, it is offered at around $2.39 per pound. Among the other Wisconsin cheeses are four types of cheddar (ranging in price from $2.29 to $3.09 per pound); baby Swiss (about $2.29 per pound); Swiss (about $3.00 per pound); beer cheese (about $2.60 per pound); Port Salut (around $3.25 per pound); orange-rind Muenster and brick (both at about $2.60 per pound).

Domestic Rondelé, a smooth creamy cheese, tops the list of specialty cheeses and cheese spreads. It can be had seasoned with pepper, with French onion, or with garlic and herbs, in 4-ounce packages at about $1.30 per package. In 16-ounce packages, at a cost of around $2.50 each, there are such spreads as sharp cheddar, port wine, brandy- and bacon-flavored, and spreadable Swiss.

Among the imported cheeses are Edam ($3.70 or so per pound) and Gouda ($3.30 or so per pound) from Holland, Danish Havarti (about $3.30 per pound), Gruyère ($4.20 or so per pound) and Emmenthal (about $3.60 per pound) from Switzerland, Port Salut (around $3.79 per pound) from France, and (at about $3.79 per pound) Jarlsberg, from Norway.

A number of attractively packaged gift selections are available, all of them interesting and none costing more than $34.95. An example is the Northern Delight, selling at well under $20.00. It includes a 12-ounce all-beef summer sausage, a 7-ounce smoked Gouda, a 7-ounce baby Gouda, and 8 ounces each of sharp cheddar, mild cheddar, medium Colby, and mild brick cheeses. In view of today's cheese prices, the price asked for this package seems more than reasonable.

□

CROWLEY CHEESE
Healdville, VT 05147
Free brochure. Accepts checks and money orders only.

When the Crowley family first settled in Healdville following the American Revolution, they, like other farmers, made cheese as a means of preserving the food value of whole milk. By 1824, they were making cheese for their neighbors, and finally, in 1882, the present cheese factory was built. It is believed to be the oldest cheese factory in the Western hemisphere and has been designated a National Historic Site. Visitors to the factory can see cheese being made almost exactly as it was during colonial times, using tools that have been preserved and handed down through the generations. The output is a mere 750 pounds daily, and demand always exceeds supply, for Crowley cheese has become famous throughout the world.

Gourmet magazine referred to this cheese as "excellent." Bon Appétit said of it: ". . . superior, rich in both flavor and texture," and Yankee magazine warned that "If a cheese connoisseur gets hooked on it, then no other cheese will quite satisfy him."

This is a Colby-type cheese, quite unlike the cheddars produced by most other Vermont cheese factories, but also unlike the Colby cheeses made in Wisconsin, where the variety originated. It is shipped out in 2½-pound wheels (about $13.00) or 5-pound wheels (about $23.00), and can be returned within 15 days for a full refund if you are ever dissatisfied. My own sample from Crowley was so tasty that I am willing to bet this option is almost never exercised.

□

Danny's Cheese Shops
South Moger Avenue
Mount Kisco, NY 10549
(914) 666–5655
Free catalog on request. Accepts checks, money orders, Visa, MasterCard, BankAmericard, and American Express. Delivery in perfect condition guaranteed.

About 15 years ago, at the ripe old age of 19, Danny Lieberman opened a small shop in Mount Kisco, New York, that soon became locally famous for the quality of the cheese, smoked fish, and other gourmet items that passed through its doors. Soon that reputation may spread nationwide; with about half a dozen shops now functioning from New York to Florida, Lieberman is in the process of setting up franchise stores across the nation. Like his original shop, these stores will offer more than 300 varieties of cheese—each personally selected by Danny Lieberman—and a full line of gourmet items. In them you will find cheese from

CHEESE 95

Austria, France, Switzerland, Denmark, Italy, Spain, Greece, and the United States, as well as Danny's own secret-recipe cheese balls, pistachio logs, spreads, and what he believes to be the finest Brie and smoked cheese available anywhere. Nearly everything sold in the stores can be mail-ordered, but Danny takes a unique approach to the mail-order business.

Because cheese prices tend to fluctuate wildly, and also because Danny believes that the key is to mail cheese in exactly the right state of underripeness and allow it to ripen on the way to its destination, you must call to check prices and place your order. Is it worth the price of a call? Let Danny Lieberman tell you about that:

> Danny's will not be undersold. For example, we have been running a special sale on French Brie at $1.99 per pound while the chain stores were selling the same at $4.00 per pound; Camembert we offered at 89 cents as compared to $2.29 in the chains. We can do this because we buy in such large quantities; more than 7,000 pounds of French Brie per week, for example. . . . The reason our mailers are so good is that they are made up the night before being mailed, with fresh-cut cheeses, unlike the pre-packs offered by most other companies in the mail-order business. Another reason they are so popular is that they can be made to suit the
> vidual tastes of the recipient.

Danny's also offers a Cheese-of-the-Month Club plan, with each monthly selection made by Danny himself. The club plans can begin in any month. The 3-month plan costs $49.95, the 5-month plan $79.95, the 8-month plan $99.95, and the 12-month plan $149.95. As soon as your order is received, a letter will be sent in your name telling the recipient what cheesely pleasures will be forthcoming, and each monthly box will be beautifully gift packaged.

□

EICHTEN'S HIDDEN ACRES CHEESE FARM
County Road 82
Center City, MN 55012
(612) 257–4752
Free price list. Accepts checks and money orders.

Just 6 short years ago, Joe and Mary Eichten began producing cheese on their Minnesota farmstead, using only the rich fresh milk from their own dairy herd. Since that beginning, they have repeatedly won Grand Champion honors at the Minnesota State Fair for their baby Swiss and Gouda cheeses. These are just two of the varieties they offer to their mail-order customers.

Prices range from around $2.50 per pound to approximately $4.25 per pound. Offered at those prices are half a dozen varieties of the Gouda, Muenster, Colby, baby Swiss, provolone, and several types of cheddar. Offered at comparable prices are a number of cheeses not made by the Eichtens, including blue, brick, mozzarella, Parmesan, and Havarti.

To go with their cheeses, the Eichtens offer a number of sausages, among them Lebanon bologna, German hard salami, pepperoni, dried beef, and two kinds of summer sausage. These cost as little as $3.50 per pound or as much as $5.70, depending on the type and amount you order. Shipping charges are extra.

□

FIGI'S, INC.
Marshfield, WI 54449
(715) 387–1771
Free catalog. Accepts checks, money orders,
MasterCard, Visa, and American Express; no CODs.
Full guarantee.

Figi's, where the motto is "gifts in good taste," is a giant in the mail-order business, sending out more than 20 million catalogs annually and offering nearly 300 food items, among them dozens of cheese selections and gift boxes in which cheese plays a major role.

One interesting offer is their stoneware crock filled with Kave Kure cheese spread. The spread is a blend of sharp and mellow cheddars, and the old-fashioned brown glazed stoneware crock can be personalized with your holiday message, company logo, or whatever. The crock, holding 12 ounces of cheese, sells for about $6.95.

Another Christmastime attention-getter is their cheese bells, aged cheddar cut into ½-pound bells. Two bells with a 12-ounce smoked beef sausage cost around $12.95. Then there is the Cheese Nibbler, selling for $5.95 or so; it holds 3¼ ounces of ripe cheddar, 2 ounces each of brick and cheddar with caraway, and 2 ounces each of Colby and Edam. Cheese logs are another popular item, and Figi's offers a box of four varieties (cheddar rolled in paprika; onion cheddar rolled in parsley flakes; smoked cheddar rolled in walnuts; and Swiss rolled in almonds), each weighing 6 ounces, for about $30.00. A box of four cheese balls, with a net weight of 20 ounces, one ball each in the same varieties as the cheese logs, sells for around $7.50. Or to sample almost the full line of cheese snacks offered here, you could order the Cheese Case, which sells for about $17.00; it holds twenty-four 2-ounce foil-wrapped cuts of cheese, including two each of brick, caraway, cheddar, Colby, Edam, Monterey Jack, mozzarella, onion, pepper, salami, sharp cheddar, and Muenster. Like the dozen or so other cheese assortments found in the Figi's catalog, this one holds nothing rare or exotic, but it would be an excellent choice as a holiday gift or simply for year-round snacking and entertaining.

☐

HERKIMER FAMILY TREASURE HOUSE
Upper Otsego Street
Route 51
Ilion, NY 13357
(315) 895-7832
Free price list. Accepts checks and money orders only; no CODs. No shipments during June, July, and August.

When you write to this tiny company located in the Mohawk Valley of New York State, don't expect to receive a fancy catalog or brochure. Instead, look for a personal reply from the owner,

Norma Basloe, who handles all inquiries herself and who sends out some of the finest cheddar made in all New York.

Her philosophy, she says, is:

> . . . to provide as many services as possible and take the best possible care of the customer. If this means that we do not extend the advantage of credit cards and charging, it also means that we can continue to provide the handling of all other services at the lowest possible cost. Most of our customers have never visited the Mohawk Valley. They have become familiar with our products through the receipt of gifts or having had the opportunity to taste Herkimer cheese on some occasion. Our entire mailing list is composed of those who have bought previously from us or who have inquired directly. It is not my desire to expand the list, but to ensure that we continue to keep our customers satisfied with the products and our quality of service.

With a philosophy like that is it any wonder I suggest you give this company a try?

The philosophy would be worthless if the quality of the products were not up to par, but I assure you that their excellent cheddar rivals any we tasted.

A 3-pound wheel of the black-waxed cheddar will set you back about $15.75, or you can get a 5-pound wheel of the same for approximately $23.50. A 2½-pound block goes for about $14.00. The cheddar is also available as part of the half-dozen or so gift assortments sent out by Herkimer, where it is usually put in alongside their cheese logs or cheese balls, which are not sold separately.

The cheese balls and logs, which are not made from cheddar but from cold-pack processed cheese, are made in small quantities and come in flavors such as port wine, garlic, almond, and horseradish. The horseradish flavor I found to be quite good and unlike any other I had tasted, for it is made with old-fashioned root-cellar horseradish, which, in turn, is made with beets.

The most popular gift assortment, according to the company, is their Standby Gift Pack, which sells for under $15.00. It includes three 7-ounce cheese balls with almonds (one garlic, one port wine, and one horseradish), and two 6-ounce sticks of Old Herkimer cheddar.

All prices given here are for destinations east of the Mississippi River; prices are slightly higher in the West.

□

KOLB–LENA CHEESE COMPANY
301 West Railroad Street
Lena, IL 61048
Free brochure. Accepts checks and money orders
only; no telephone orders or CODs. Order during
summer months only at your own risk.

"Samples of our cheeses are being mailed to you, because your taste buds can tell you more about them than we could possibly say on paper," says a letter I received from Christopher Lee, the marketing director of Kolb–Lena—and I want to thank him here, in public, for sending me some of the most delicious cheese I have ever tasted. I urge you to give this company a try.

Nestled among the rolling green hills of northern Illinois, Lena lies in the midst of America's dairyland, where the very best milk is close at hand for cheesemaking, and the Kolb family has been putting that milk to good use for 65 years and four generations. About a dozen varieties are produced in their Lena factory, and these are served in some of the finest restaurants in America. It is possible you have already sampled their Delico brand cheeses, which are sold through a limited number of delis and gourmet shops, and if so, I believe you will agree with me about the high quality of their products.

Their list includes most of the standard varieties you would expect from a major supplier. There is a 2½-pound loaf of cheddar for about $11.00, a 5-pound loaf of Monterey Jack for about $18.00, a 2¾-pound brick cheese for about $10.95; and 2 pounds of Brie for under $11.00. Discounts are given on all volume orders. For example, they offer four 5-pound wheels of Swiss for about $67.00, a considerable savings over most supermarket prices. That is a lot of cheese, but there is no reason three or four families could not share the order.

The firm also produces a number of cheeses with which you

may not be familiar, as well as a few favorites that are so good I want to take the time here to call them to your attention.

Feta, which may be the ancestor of all other cheeses, is a sinfully pleasant cheese. This semisoft cheese is ripened in its own juices and is often used in Greek cooking. While it is most frequently used in this country as a topping for salads, it is also excellent over spaghetti, in omelets, or with grapes and other fruits. A 3-pound wedge costs about $12.50.

Rexoli is a soft, moist cheese somewhat similar to feta, but with a light taste of yeast that makes it an excellent choice for serving with fruit or red wine. A dozen 2½-ounce rounds sell for approximately $9.75.

Old Heidelberg is a mild cheese similar to Liederkranz, though it is more aromatic and soft enough to be spread like butter. Usually served as an appetizer, it costs around $9.85 for half a dozen 4-ounce packages.

Sno-Belle is a specialty cheese made only by this factory, a semisoft cheese that tastes like a blend of Camembert and Port Salut. Like Camembert, the white culture on the surface is progressively ripening the cheese and enhancing its flavor, and it will have extra appeal for those who prefer an exotic type of cheese. A 2¼-pound wheel sells for approximately $13.75, about the same price asked by this company for their Brie and Camembert.

Numerous cheese spreads such as herb, seafood, and taco-flavored round out the list, and all are priced to compete with your local markets. Though summer orders are discouraged and are accepted only at your own risk, for an extra charge of $2.25 such orders can be specially packed in ice and should reach you in good condition.

□

NAUVOO CHEESE COMPANY
Nauvoo, IL 62354
(217) 453-2214
*Free catalog. Accepts checks, money orders,
MasterCard, and BankAmericard. No shipments
made during June, July, and August.*

Some historians say that blue cheese was created when a shepherd boy left his lunch of bread and curds in a limestone cave in southwestern France and later retrieved it to find that the curds had formed a veined cheese. Be that as it may, there is one place in this country where a blue cheese, made from cow's milk, is carefully aged in limestone caves, and that is in the tiny town of Nauvoo, illinois.

Blue cheese is the specialty here, and it comes in a number of shapes, sizes, and forms. There is a 6¾-pound wheel for around $30.00 and a 3¼-pound wheel for about $18.50. A box of four 6-ounce wedges costs around $11.75, eight 4-ounce wedges sell for under $16.00, and twelve 4-ounce wedges cost approximately $20.75.

Pre-crumbled blue cheese, suitable for use in salads and party dips and over fruit, comes in 1-pound containers for about $8.50, and there are 20-ounce stoneware crocks of blue cheese spread for about $11.50 each. A blue cheese recipe book is sent out with each order, and it is filled with new and exciting uses for this old favorite.

□

PLYMOUTH CHEESE CORPORATION
Box 1
Plymouth, VT 05056
Free price list. Accepts checks and money orders only; no CODs.

Started by the father of President Calvin Coolidge and now operated by his only surviving son, John, the Plymouth Cheese Corporation is believed to be the only plant remaining in the world that produces granular curd cheese by hand in the old Vermont manner.

"We make old-fashioned American rat trap store cheese. And we are the only purists left in the business, I think," says John Coolidge when asked about his operation in this snug little hamlet nestled on the eastern slope of the Green Mountains. "We still use the method common to the early Vermont cheese-makers, breaking the curds down by hand rather than with automatic grinders."

Though it may be small in comparison to other cheese factories, Plymouth manages to sell about 70 tons of cheese each year, half of this to the more than 50,000 tourists who visit the village each year, half by mail order. Perhaps that says something about the quality of the product.

Mild and medium-sharp versions of the cheese are offered, as well as cheese with sage, caraway, or pimiento. A 3-pound wheel of any type sells for around $10.00, or you can select a 5-pound wheel for about $16.50.

Plymouth Products also ships maple syrup made by their Vermont neighbors (prices go from around $6.25 per pint up to almost $30.00 per gallon), as well as a number of gift packages made up of traditional New England fare. A typical selection (around $11.00) is made up of 2 cans of baked beans, 1 can of brown bread, 1 can of Indian pudding, and 1 jar of pepper relish. John Coolidge, in the typical straightforward New England manner, tells me he may be forced to raise prices later this year, so be sure to check current prices before placing an order.

□

THE SEWARD FAMILY, INC.
East Wallingford, VT 05742
(802) 259-2311
Free brochure. Accepts checks and money orders.

"The best raw-milk Cheddars, besides those of the English farmhouse, are those made by the Seward family of Vermont," says writer Larry Miller in *Food & Wine* magazine. "The Seward cheddars have a milkier, mellower taste than most, and are superb."

Quincy Seward first began producing cheese on his Vermont farm in the mid-1800s, and his son later worked as a cheesemaker in a large cheese factory nearby. The art was lost to this family following World War I, then revived in the 1950s by Roland Seward, the great-grandson of Quincy. Today his all-natural cheddar is shipped to all fifty states and a sizable number of foreign countries. You will find no better source of cheddar, in my opinion.

Unlike the yellow and orange cheddar that has become familiar to most Americans—and which is likely to be crumbly and bitter near the edges—Seward cheddar is deep ivory in color, firm yet creamy, with a bright, clean, almost fruity taste. A single taste will assure that you never again buy the processed cheddars sold in most stores, for the two are so different that one wonders how they share the same name, which is about the only thing they have in common.

All cheddar sold here is aged approximately eleven months, and the most popular size is the 2½-pound block that sells for around $11.50, followed by the 5-pound wheel for about $19.00. Other versions of the same cheddar—sage, caraway, smoked, and extra-sharp—are available only as part of the assortments offered in the brochure. I was lucky enough to receive the Seward Family Chest of Cheese, which sells for $16.95 or so and holds a 9-ounce stick of each version of cheese just mentioned. My only problem was in deciding which version I liked best, and I assure you that I mean to order more so I can decide.

□

Shelburne Farms
Shelburne, VT 05482
(802) 985-3222
Free brochure and price list. Accepts checks, money orders, Visa, and MasterCard.

Located in one of Vermont's most picturesque settings, on the shore of Lake Champlain, with views of bays and coves and the majestic Green and Adirondack mountains, Shelburne Farms claims to be the only Vermont producer of authentic farmhouse cheddar.

"Farmhouse cheddar" is the English term used to describe a cheddar made using only the unpasteurized milk of a single herd of cows. The claim is that using fresh milk from a single herd allows its sweet and nutty taste to come through in the cheese. Shelburne makes its cheese from the milk of a single herd of purebread Brown Swiss cows, and believes that it may be the only cheesemaker in the world doing so.

The cheese is aged 6 to 9 months, the sharpness gradually increasing with age. The result is described as "a delicate but rich cheese that, like a good wine, envelops your palate in a sequence of subtle flavors ending with a savory aftertaste." Each block is dipped in an elegant deep brown wax and handsomely labeled. Cheddar aged to your taste may be reserved by paying in advance at current prices. It will be shipped when mature.

Weights of the bars and blocks range from ½ pound to 5 pounds each. Four of the ½-pound bars sell for around $15.00. Two 1-pound blocks cost about the same. A 2½-pounder sells for around $17.00, and the 5-pound block costs approximately $29.00. Shipping charges are extra.

□

STALLMAN'S BON BREE CHEESE FACTORY
35990 Mapleton Road
Oconomowoc, WI 53066
(414) 474-7142
Free brochure. Accepts checks, money orders, Visa, and MasterCard. Minimum order: 2½ pounds.

The rolling hills of the Kettle Moraine region in southern Wisconsin are remarkably similar to the lower foothills of the Swiss Alps, and that is one reason so many immigrant cheese-makers from the Old Country settled in this area. Here, as in the land they had left, their cheese cellars could be built into a hillside, where temperatures and humidity would remain constant throughout the year, and such cheese cellars once dotted the countryside here. Many have closed now, unable to compete with the huge conglomerates, but in the tiny hamlet of Mapleton, Stallman's—built by a group of farmers in 1896—still ages its cheese in the original stone cellar using techniques that have been handed down through four generations of the Stallman family.

Their specialty is a smooth, creamy Port Salut–type cheese called Bon Bree ("happy cheese"), which was developed here by a Swiss immigrant early in this century. It takes about 10 pounds of the highest-quality milk to make 1 pound of this award-winning cheese, and production is limited to about 600 pounds daily. The cheese is sold semisoft, mild, or aged, all at about $2.55 per pound.

A number of other favorites are available here. Brick, Muenster, Limburger and cheddar all sell for less than $2.65 per pound. 2½- and 5-pound wheels of baby Swiss cost about $3.00

per pound. Imported Jarlsberg Swiss costs around $4.15 per pound; and imported Danish blue sells at $3.90 or so per pound, while a domestic blue costs only $3.10 or so per pound. The list also includes a number of smoked cheeses (provolone, about $3.10 per pound; cheddar, around $3.35 per pound) and cheese spreads (Swiss and almond, pink champagne, brandy, bacon and garlic, pizza pepperoni, all costing around $1.95 for a 12-ounce carton), and with any order you receive a handy guide to the characteristics, usage, and storage of cheese.

□

SUGARBUSH FARM
R.F.D. 2
Woodstock, VT 05091
Free brochure. Accepts checks, money orders, Visa, MasterCard, American Express, and Diners Club. Full guarantee.

Gourmet magazine has called Sugarbush Farm "one of the most dependable places in America to find assertive yet richly mellow cheddar." None of this cheese, however, is produced at Sugarbush. Instead, the owner of the farm, Jack Ayres, does business very much as it is done by French cheese merchants; he buys his cheddar all over New England, tasting and sampling, buying and rejecting as he goes. He then ages, cuts, and wraps his selections himself. A prime cheddar may spend as long as two years in his aging cellars.

"There is really no such thing as a true farmhouse cheese anymore. They're all made in factories," Jack Ayres told me. "It's just that some of the factories look like farmhouses."

However they are made and wherever he finds them, I do know that the selection sent me by Sugarbush Farm ranked right up there with the very best cheeses I sampled. His sage-flavored cheddar, a variation said to be a favorite of Henry VIII, I found to be especially good, unlike so many, in which the cheese flavor is overwhelmed by the taste of sage.

In addition to the sage cheese, Sugarbush offers hickory- and maple-smoked cheddar, sharp cheddar, Green Mountain Jack (a mild, Eastern form of Monterey Jack) and Green Mountain Bleu (a rich, creamy form that is excellent in salads) at about $5.35 per pound, plus a small charge for shipping and handling. The cheeses are put up in foot-long, cracker-sized bars weighing 1 pound each, but half-size bars are also available and you can mix the flavors any way you like when ordering a number of bars.

Cheddar remains the most popular item here, and the medium sharp comes in a 3-pound wheel for around $14.25, while the sharp is offered in a 2-pound block for about $10.50 or a 5-pound block for approximately $22.00. It is also boxed together with other Vermont favorites such as honey, maple syrup, and maple sugar candies in a number of gift selections that range in price from $11.95 to $28.50.

□

THE SWISS CHEESE SHOP
Highway 69 North
P.O. Box 429
Monroe, WI 53566
(608) 325-3493
Free brochure. Accepts checks and money orders only; no CODs.

Established in 1938 on the premise that quality aged cheeses, fully cured to bring out the true flavors of natural cheeses, were not available through regular grocery or supermarket channels, The Swiss Cheese Shop has become something of a local tourist attraction and has slowly built a reputation for quality that causes its products to reach cheese lovers in the most distant parts of the United States.

The home shop near Monroe includes a simulated cheese factory where visitors can see the entire sequence of operations necessary to making Swiss cheese, and this is topped off by a cheese-tasting session that helps visitors determine their personal likes and dislikes before buying. I found very little to dislike about the sampler I received from this firm. The package (about $10.95) contained sharp cheddar, aged Swiss, mild Colby, and a zesty caraway stick, with a net weight of 28 ounces, and each bite supported the statement by Archie Myers, president of the firm, that "our offerings of cheese are among the finest available anywhere."

Most of the brochure is devoted to gift-boxed cheese assortments, with something for every taste and almost every budget; the great majority are priced at less than $20.00 each. When you are looking for a lot of cheese at a reasonable price, though, you might consider sending for The Cheese Lover. With a net weight of 8 pounds and selling for around $32.95, it includes bricks of sharp aged cheddar, aged Swiss, mild Colby, Muenster, and Muenster with caraway.

Almost all the favorite cheeses can be ordered in bulk from this firm, and the prices are comparable to what you pay in your local markets. Cheddar, either sharp or smoked, costs around $9.95 for a 2-pound block. Center-cut Swiss costs about $10.95 for 2 pounds, or about $11.95 when smoked. Cured brick cheese, nearly as strong as Limburger, costs $19.95 or so for a 5-pound brick, and 30 ounces of true Limburger will set you back about $9.95. Port du Salut, a semisoft cheese with a hearty flavor, costs around $11.95 for a 2-pound wedge. Keep in mind that many of the softer cheeses are not shipped during June, July, and August.

□

THE SWISS COLONY
Monroe, WI 53566
(608) 246-2000
Free catalog. Accepts checks, money orders, Visa, MasterCard, BankAmericard, and American Express; no CODs. Telephone orders accepted around the clock. Full guarantee.

In 1926, a young man in Monroe, Wisconsin, in the heart of "Little Switzerland," decided to try selling the area's fine cheeses by mail order. He purchased the very best cheese he could find, carefully handwrapped and packaged each cut—and found the public response exceeded his wildest dreams. His one-man operation grew and grew and grew, and today it is the largest mail-order food gift company in the world, employing about 2,000 workers, sending out millions of 144-page catalogs, and shipping an astounding 20 million pounds of food each year in the four weeks prior to Christmas.

The catalog is loaded with page after page of meats, sausages, pastries, nuts, candies, snack items, and gift assortments. But it all began with cheese, and cheese of nearly every type imaginable still fills dozens of pages in their catalog.

Looking for wheels of cheese? One sampler, The Cheese Crate, includes a 12-ounce aged cheddar, a 10-ounce Swiss, and a 12-ounce Edam, at a cost of about $16.95. Then there is Big Red, a 5-pound wheel of two-year-old cheddar for around $22.95. Or a 2-pound wheel of smoked Swiss loaded with chunks of ham at a cost of about $8.95. Or a 2-pound wheel of Wisconsin Colby for around $9.50. The Queen of Cheeses, a semisoft Brie, imported from France, costs around $13.95 for a 2-pound wheel, and each wheel comes in the wooden box used to import it from France.

The list goes on and on. There is a 5-pound wheel of baby Swiss for around $21.95 (with smaller wheels available at lower prices); a 4-pound wheel of smoked baby Swiss for about $19.95; a ham and cheese wheel, with bits of smoked ham added to a 1-pound blending of Swiss and cheddar cheeses, for approximately $7.45; and, for about $8.95, a 1½-pound wheel that combines your choice of pecans or walnuts with aged cheddar.

The list of cheese in blocks, sticks, and chunks is just as complete. Most varieties can be ordered individually or as part of an assortment. One such assortment (selling for about $24.95, with a net weight of 4½ pounds) holds 38 varieties of cheese, among them such favorites as Colby, cheddar, Gouda, Edam, American, Swiss, and brick, as well as rounds, wedges, and links of cheese flavored with bacon, garlic, sage, caraway, and other seasonings.

Cheese logs and cheese balls fill several pages in the catalog, with something for nearly every taste. Cheese log flavors include cheddar with pecans, cheddar with bacon, port wine with walnuts, and Swiss and cheddar with almonds, four 3-ounce logs of any flavor selling for around $5.95, with larger logs available. An even larger variety of cheese balls is offered, including a box holding forty 1-ounce miniatures in an assortment of flavors such as onion and chive, port wine with paprika, and cheddar with almonds, a gourmet's delight at about $17.95.

Cheese spreads to suit nearly every taste are listed, many of them put up in stoneware crocks that would make ideal gifts for the hard-to-please. For around $9.95, one assortment includes one 3½-ounce crock each of sharp cheddar, cheddar with bacon, and Swiss with almonds. Half a dozen other spreads are available at comparable prices.

Six different Cheese-of-the-Month plans are offered by Swiss Colony, ranging in price from as little as $38.50 for a basic 6-month plan to as much as $120.00 for the most elaborate 12-month plan. Upon receipt of your order, the company sends a beautiful gift card announcing future shipments, and each shipment also carries your personal greeting—an excellent way to spread your affection over the calendar.

□

THE WISCONSIN CHEESEMAN
P.O. Box 1
Madison, WI 53701
*Free catalog. Accepts checks, money orders, Visa,
MasterCard, and American Express. Delivery in
perfect condition guaranteed.*

Operating out of a mock Swiss chalet in the heart of the most famous cheese-producing region in the United States, this family-owned company has for the past 35 years offered one of the most complete lines of edible gifts found in the industry. Of the more than 400 gift items offered in the current catalog, though, well over half contain cheese of one type or another, most of them domestic but many carefully selected from among the best of the imports.

I found their Old World Pak (about $14.50) to be a delicious offering of the exotic and the familiar. In the box, one finds 3-ounce rectangles of aged cheddar, Edam, Colby, caraway, and brick; 1-ounce rounds of Hollander and Française; 5 ounces of aged Swiss; 3 ounces each of blue and smoked cheddar; 1-ounce wedges of Tuscany, Edel-Swiss, and kümin; 4-ounce cups of cheese spread and Port Salut; 2-ounce cartons of Fromage de Coeur and Korv-Ost; and, finally, two 3-ounce cuts of mellow American.

Cheese from The Wisconsin Cheeseman can be ordered in a number of interesting ways that would make fascinating, as well as tasty, gifts. For example, there is an electric hibachi (about

$29.50) that comes filled with cheddar, brick, kümin, Tuscany, and Amstel cheeses. Or you can choose four handsome teakwood wine goblets (around $18.95) that come packed with 3 ounces each of cheddar, brick, Zwiebel, Sorrento, Hollander, smoked cheddar, and cheese spread.

If you prefer bargains to beauty, a number of the more popular items are offered in bulk, without the gift packaging and at greatly reduced prices. Ordered in this way, cheddar, brick, Edam, Colby, Monterey Jack, and a number of other popular cheeses can be brought to your door at a cost of about $3.50 per pound—and if your local markets are like my own, you will agree that this is a remarkably low price to pay for quality cheese.

CHAPTER SIX

BAKED GOODS

It comes as a surprise to many to discover that fine baked goods can be delivered fresh to the door. Not only is it possible, it has become so common that I found it necessary to devote an entire chapter to firms that specialize in shipping unusual breads and baked goods to satisfied customers all over the United States.

These bakers and specialty shops send out Danish pumpernickel, Jewish rye, San Francisco sourdough, and breads made from cracked wheat, oats, and rye, and the loaves come in all shapes and sizes. There are firms that will send you famous regional specialties such as real water bagels from New York, pretzels made by the Pennsylvania Dutch, and Copenhagen-style pastries made in the "Little Denmark" region of Solvang, California.

Sweet baked goods are not overlooked. You can order a cheesecake from New York, a fruitcake from the Deep South, or a gingerbread house from half a dozen sources. You will also find that many firms listed here offer mixes for baking at home, including a few that offer mixes made from stone-ground whole grains and other ingredients that may be hard to obtain locally.

Although I have brought together in this chapter major sup-

pliers of baked goods and bread-related items, more limited
sources for such goods will also be found in other chapters, nota-
bly those for Natural Foods and Ethnic and Specialty Foods. Additional sources for sweet baked goods will also be found in the
chapter on Sweets and Treats.

□

ANNA'S DANISH COOKIES
3560 18 Street
San Francisco, CA 94110
Free price list. Accepts checks, money orders, Visa,
MasterCard, and BankAmericard.

A major part of Danish hospitality has always been a friendly
rivalry in serving *Danske Smaakager,* or small sweet cakes. Several generations ago, the most famous recipes were sought out
and manufactured by a family in Denmark. So successful were
they that "Danish cookies," as they are now commonly known,
attained worldwide fame.

Arriving in America in 1937, this same family established a
shop in San Francisco, and the same recipes are used to produce
cookies that are shipped throughout the world. They are made in
five different flavors—butter, vanilla, egg, oatmeal, and coconut—and come in cartons up to 5 pounds. They can be ordered plain, part chocolate, or all chocolate covered. A 1-pound
carton of plain cookies sells for around $5.60; a pound part choco-
late costs about $6.10; and 1 pound of all chocolate covered costs
approximately $6.40. A 5-pound carton of the plain cookies runs
$21.00 or so; part chocolate, a little over $23.00; and all chocolate, about $25.00. All prices include shipping and handling, and
lithographed tins are available at an additional cost of about $1.00
per pound. Discounts are offered on quantity orders.

□

G. H. BENT COMPANY
Corner of Pleasant Street and State Route 28
Milton, MA 02186
Free price list. Accepts checks and money orders
only; no CODs.

In 1801, a young man named Josiah Bent conceived the idea of starting a home business to bake and market a so-called water cracker, probably inspired by the presence of several clear-water springs, as well as a grist mill that produced quality wheat flour, in the vicinity of his home on the Neponset River.

The water cracker itself was not Bent's invention; it was the familiar ship's biscuit, or "hard tack," used by far-ranging sailing ships the world over. The crackers, nailed up in wooden kegs, could be broken out after years in storage, soaked in water, and still be edible. Today they are a New England tradition.

Though initially the crackers became popular due to a belief that they had therapeutic properties, aided digestion, and cured dyspepsia, their popularity increased as people learned what a welcome addition they were to soups, stews, and chowders, especially those made with seafood. Josiah Bent, who initially went from town to town selling the crackers out of his saddlebags, established what may be the oldest continuous manufacturing firm in the United States, and today his descendants manufacture his water crackers almost exactly as he made them nearly two centuries ago.

The crackers come in 14-ounce packages, two packages for around $4.60, with discounts given on larger orders: 12 packages, for example, for about $17.00. With any order you receive a small leaflet of authentic New England recipes that cannot be correctly made without the crackers. The preceding prices include postage.

□

BYRD COOKIE COMPANY
2233 Norwood Avenue
P.O. Box 13086
Savannah, GA 31406
(912) 355-1771
Free brochure. Accepts checks and money orders only.

The Byrd Cookie Company was founded in 1924 in the historic Old Fort section of Savannah, and its first hand-mixed, hand-cut cookies were packed in wooden boxes and delivered by Model T

Ford to local shops. Today their modern ovens produce up to 40,000 cookies per hour, and these cookies go out to about 2,000 gourmet and specialty shops around the country, as well as to thousands of consumers who order by mail.

The Confederate Cannon Ball, an onion and garlic flavored, bite-size cocktail bit covered with poppy and sesame seeds, is one of the newer and better-selling items produced by Byrd. Other baked snack items include Benne Bits, a cheese-flavored cracker; Railroad Trax, tiny nut-flavored crackers made with wheat germ; and Benne Straws, a spicy cheese, poppy seed, and sesame seed cracker—all at about $4.00 per 8-ounce box. The name "Benne," attached to many of the baked goods sold here, derives from the use of benne seeds, a spicy, honey-colored seed brought to Georgia and South Carolina by African blacks during the slave trade. They believed that the seeds brought health and good luck. A brief history of these seeds acompanies all Byrd products, which come in attractive lithographed tins.

Also still available at about $4.00 for an 8-ounce tin are the original Benne Wafers, a round, nutmeg-flavored sugar cookie that is famous throughout the South. A new price list was being put together when I contacted this company, so be sure to obtain that list before placing any order.

□

COLLIN STREET BAKERY
P.O. Box 79
Corsicana, TX 75110
(214) 872–3951
Free brochure. Accepts checks, money orders, Visa,
MasterCard, Diners Club, and American Express.
Full guarantee.

More than 85 years ago, this small-town bakery began turning out what many believe to be the best fruitcake in the world. Its first big order went to the troupers in John Ringling's circus (now Ringling Bros., Barnum & Bailey, and still regular customers of the bakery). As word spread, their list of regular customers grew to include such notables as Enrico Caruso, Will Rogers, John J. McGraw and "Gentleman Jim" Corbett. Last year, their only product, the Original Deluxe fruitcake was shipped to every state in the Union and 192 foreign countries. It has won awards throughout the world, including the prestigious Monde Selection gold medal for excellence, presented in 1978 in Geneva, Switzerland.

Fruit used in the cake comes from France, Italy, Hawaii, and the Pacific Northwest and is blended into a rich batter made crunchy with native pecans. Every step is done according to the original, secret recipe of August Weidmann, the baker who founded the company, and all cakes are hand-decorated. The result is a cake that is one of the best values in the food-by-mail industry. The 2-pound cake costs about $7.95; a 3-pound model sells for under $12.00; and the 5-pound cake goes for about $18.50 with discounts available on volume orders. All cakes come in a beautiful reusable tin that also holds a brief history of the company but absolutely no advertising. The bakery also promises that the name of the recipient will never be added to any mailing list as the result of the order—an offer some folks may appreciate almost as much as the cake.

□

THE FAMOUS AMOS CHOCOLATE CHIP COOKIE
7181 Sunset Boulevard
Hollywood, CA 90046
Free price list and brochure. Accepts checks and money orders only; no CODs.

Wally Amos has spent the last few years doing for the chocolate chip cookie what P. T. Barnum did for midgets and elephants—promoting it as if the circus were coming to town. But what else would you expect from the only cookie once managed by the William Morris Agency, where Amos once worked and where he became, he says, as the first black employed there, "the Jackie Robinson of the theatrical agency business." It was there, he admits, that he learned the techniques he uses in promoting his cookie, bestowing upon it dozens of awards that only Wally Amos can bestow, such as the "Golden Brown Chippie Award."

"I'm the theatrical agent for the cookie" is how he puts it.

According to its official biography, the cookie "was born at a very young age, on a pre-Teflon cookie sheet in Los Angeles, California, during the great crumb famine of 1970." With such hoopla, including published "interviews" with the cookie, Amos has made his creation a favorite of the Hollywood crowd.

The Amos cookie is more than just a PR job, though. It's a top-notch chocolate chip cookie, loaded with chips and pecans. Co-stars in the cast include chocolate chip with peanut butter and butterscotch chip with pecans. Minimum order is two tins— about $8.50 for a 1½-pound tin. Prices include mailing.

□

Harry and David's Bear Creek Bakery
Bear Creek Orchards
Medford, OR 97501
Free catalog on request. Accepts checks, money orders only; no CODs. Guarantees delivery in perfect condition only if delivery can be made when first attempted.

Harry and David have been shopping quality fruit and gourmet items for more than 40 years, and their Fruit-of-the-Month Club is one of the most successful club plans in existence. Over the years, they have accumulated a collection of what they believe to be the finest recipes for baked goods available to anyone, and recently they began putting these recipes to use in their new Bear Creek Bakery. If their catalog is an indication of things to come, it appears that the duo has another success story under way.

Start with three varieties of cheesecake—traditional, French chocolate, and strawberry filled. Weighing 2 pounds apiece and sold only in pairs, you can order two of any type for about $25.00. Follow this up with walnut plum, carrot pineapple, apple date, and several other specialty cakes (average price about $15.95 for a trio of 15-ounce cakes), and the catalog grows more interesting.

Most interesting of all, at least to me, is their *medjumurska gibanica*, a unique East European pastry made from paper-thin, hand-formed dough filled with layers of poppy seeds, sweetened ricotta cheese, raisins, walnuts, and apple strudel. According to the company, more than half an hour is spent shaping and filling each pastry, which makes the asking price of around $28.00 for a 2½-pound pastry seem entirely reasonable.

Bear Creek Bakery also offers baklava—another delicacy made with paper-thin dough, honey, and nuts that requires enormous amounts of time and labor to prepare—at a cost of about $25.00 for 3 pounds; and *croustilles,* the traditional French pastry first baked for Louis XIV, at about $17.95 for a package of about 85 pastries (2 pounds). Raspberry and blackberry tortes are offered at around $23.00 for two tortes weighing 2 pounds each.

You'll find all the more traditional baked goods here, too, such as chocolate chip cookies, pecan pie, and chocolate cake. To make it easier to send these as gifts, Harry and David have created the Bear Creek Bakery Club, offering a variety of plans that range in price from $54.95 for a 3-month gift plan to $249.95 for a plan that will keep the baked goods coming for a full year. My hunch is that it will become even more popular than their world-famous Fruit-of-the-Month Club.

□

MANGANARO FOODS
488 Ninth Avenue
New York, NY 10018
(212) 563–5331
Free catalog. Accepts checks, money orders, CODs.
Credit applications available.

For more than 90 years, Manganaro's has been one of the biggest importers of Italian specialty foods, as well as gourmet items from Canada, South America, and Eastern Europe. Probably their most famous item is their 6-foot-long hero sandwich, which unfortunately can be delivered only in New York City. Their new baked goods and pastry department, however, offers an excellent selection of breads, cakes, and cookies suitable for mailing.

There is anise toast at about $3.00 per pound, and Italian breadsticks at $1.05 or so for a 4-ounce package. Water biscuits and cocktail biscuits are sold at about $1.50 per pound, and both English cheese biscuits and boxes of assorted cocktail biscuits sell at about $3.95 per pound. Egg biscuits go out at about $4.00 per pound, and there are slices of honey- and almond-flavored *pappatelle*, butter cookies, chocolate hazelnut cookies, rum cake, cheesecake, and cassata cake—all at about the same price.

Amaretti, the dry, crisp Italian macaroons, come in tins or boxes at about $8.25 per pound. *Panettone*, the high, fluffy, semisweet Italian holiday cake, lemon-flavored and stuffed with citron and raisins, is about $5.50 per pound. It has very good keeping qualities and may be ordered well in advance of the holidays. *Panforte*, a slim, round, flat cake thickened with candied orange, citron, almonds and other goodies, sells at about $5.95 per pound. Manganaro's also sells a variety of Italian chocolates, nougats, and candied fruits, and makes up confectionery baskets packed with selections of pastry and candies ranging in price from $65.00 to $85.00. Charge accounts, something of a rarity in this business, are invited.

□

MATTHEWS 1812 HOUSE
Box 15
Whitcomb Hill Road
Cornwall Bridge, CT 06754
(203) 672-6449
Free brochure and price list. Accepts checks, money orders, Visa, and MasterCard. Full guarantee.

A love of natural foods and a desire to be self-employed inspired Deanna Matthews to launch a mail-order cake business five years ago from her restored colonial farmhouse. Preservative-free fruitcakes, made by a recipe used by Mrs. Matthews' grandmother, are the specialty here, and they are made with "just enough batter to hold the fruit and nuts together." Mrs. Matthews uses no candied fruit, rinds, peels, or preservatives. Even so, the cakes will last for months if refrigerated, and the claim is that their flavor improves with age.

Two versions are offered: the Fruit and Nut cake, which features a honey and brown sugar batter and is studded with pecans, dates, raisins, and apricots, and the Brandied Apricot cake, which features a lighter batter and is doused with a fine brandy. Price is around $12.00 for a 1½-pound cake of either kind, or approximately $21.00 for a 3-pound cake. All cakes are

sent out in attractive, buff-colored gift boxes. Shipping charges
are extra.

□

MISS KING'S KITCHENS
14114 North Dallas Parkway
Suite 320
Dallas, TX 75240
(800) 527–0739
Free brochure and price list. Accepts checks, money
orders, Visa, and MasterCard.

During the 1930s, Eunice King, a retired missionary and cooking
teacher, opened a cozy little tea-room called the Pecan House in
the town of Sherman, Texas. There she served her own special
pecan cakes to her guests in the Southern tradition of hospitality
and charm. She also developed a unique method of vacuum packing that would keep her cakes fresh, moist, and delicious without
any chemical preservatives or additives, in any kind of climate,
for months or even years.

During World War II, families and friends often wanted to
ship their loved ones a little bit of home in the form of baked
goods, but in those years it was almost impossible to ship fresh
foods long distances by mail. Because they would retain their
freshness, Miss King's tea cakes soon became a favorite of our
servicemen overseas, including General Eisenhower himself.

Today, though Miss King has long since retired, the bakery
she founded continues as a major force in the mail-order industry, sending its cakes to all parts of the world. To the original
pecan tea cakes have been added about half a dozen varieties of
cheesecake (including flavors such as lemon cream, chocolate
mocha, and Danish cream), apple spice cake, date and pistachio
cake, and more than a dozen varieties of fruitcake. Cakes range
in size from 3½ ounces to 2 pounds, with the most expensive
model being a 2-pound macadamia nut cake that sells for about
$21.00. The 3½-ounce cakes are put up in five-packs, all priced at
$10.50 or less. Chocolate chip cookies are offered at around $7.50
for a 1-pound tin, and all prices include shipping.

□

MORAVIAN SUGAR CRISP CO., INC.
Route 2
Friedberg Road
Clemmons, NC 27012
(919) 764–1402
*Free brochure. Accepts checks and money orders
only.*

"Truly a cookie with a personality," is how one customer described Moravian Sugar Crisp cookies, which are made according to an old family recipe that has been handed down for generations. Each sugar cookie is rolled and cut by hand, a costly method that assures the finest flavor. The cookies come in a number of shapes and are put up in 7-ounce, 1-pound, and 2-pound tins. Price is approximately $9.00 per pound.

Available for around the same price are paper-thin, spicy ginger crisp cookies, chocolate crisp cookies, and butterscotch- and lemon-flavored cookies. All prices include shipping.

□

PEPPERIDGE FARM
P.O. Box 119
Route 145
Clinton, CT 06413
(800) 243–9314; Connecticut residents call collect 669–9245.
*Free catalog. Accepts checks, money orders, Visa,
MasterCard, and American Express. $10.00
minimum on telephone orders.*

Pepperidge Farm is perhaps best known for the line of specialty soups that it distributes nationwide to fine food and gourmet shops—and, indeed, most of these are listed in the catalog and can be ordered by mail. But this company also specializes in fine pastry and baked confections, many of them baked by the firm itself and a few imported from around the world.

Their butter pretzels (about $9.95 for a 3-pound tin) are baked in the heart of the Pennsylvania Dutch country and come in either sticks or nuggets. Lightly salted and very buttery, they are as good as any I have tasted on visits to Lancaster County, where the pretzel was invented. Equally good as a snack are their cheese sticks (about $11.95 per pound), which are made with aged Vermont cheddar, Parmesan, and creamery butter, and are especially good when warmed in the oven a few minutes before serving. A slightly sweeter snack is their cinnamon stick, light pastry made with butter and cream cheese, that sells for around $11.95 for 14 ounces. Sweeter still is their cinnamon-apple Danish pastry that sells at about $9.95 for an 11-ounce reusable tin.

A dozen varieties of cookies, imported from Belgium and put up in 1-pound tins, are offered at $9.95 or so, and a 1-pound box of Pepperidge Farm's own Christmas cookies (gingerbread, molasses crisps, pirouettes, short bread, and sugar) goes for about $7.95. Other cookie assortments range in price as high as $16.50 per pound.

A number of breakfast mixes can be ordered here, but only as part of assortments. For example, one assortment includes 12 ounces of smoked bacon, 16 ounces of pancake mix, 16 ounces of whole-wheat pancake mix, 8 ounces of Vermont maple syrup, 1 pound of buttermilk pancake mix, 1 pound of hot cocoa mix, and 15 ounces of wild blueberries at a cost of under $25.00. Prices on other assortments vary, the most expensive being $43.95.

Whereas most fruitcakes are made with bourbon, rum, or brandy, the 22-ounce cake sold here (about $11.95) is laced with Grand Marnier, making it a true holiday delight. The 1½-pound Black Forest stollen, however, features the taste of Cognac; it sells for around $11.95. At the end of a traditional holiday dinner, you could also choose the most traditional of desserts—plum pudding with brandied hard sauce. The 1-pound pudding, thick with raisins, currants, and orange peel, along with enough hard sauce to cover it well, sells for about $8.50. With few exceptions, everything sent out by Pepperidge Farm is beautifully gift-packaged, which can save you a lot of time and trouble during the busy holiday season.

□

ARNOLD REUBEN, JR.'S CHEESE CAKES
15 Hill Park Avenue
Great Neck, NY 11022
(516) 466–3685
*Free price list. Accepts checks, money orders, Visa,
MasterCard, and American Express. Full guarantee.*

In 1929, famous restaurateur Arnold Reuben was served what
was then called "cheese pie" in a private home. It was a delightful, different dish, but one he knew he could improve on. With
his hostess's recipe and a pie she made with ingredients he provided, he set out to develop the perfect cheese dessert. Unlike
all others up until this time, this dessert was made with half cottage and half cream cheese, instead of all cottage. Reuben finally
eliminated the cottage cheese altogether. After more experi-
ments, he came up with a mixture that would, he felt, make the
perfect cake—if only he could find exactly the right, rich cream
cheese. But his regular cheese supplier laughed off his specifications as impossible. Then another manufacturer asked Reuben to
produce some cheesecakes for display at a World's Food Exposition. Reuben agreed, but only on the condition that cream
cheese of a certain butter fat content be made especially for the
baking. He baked, tasted, frowned, and then ordered cheese
with even more butter fat. Three times the butter fat content was
raised, and finally Reuben was satisfied. So were the judges at
the Exposition, who promptly awarded the cake a gold medal as
"the finest cheesecake in the world!"

Today, the son of that famous restaurateur continues to set
the same high standards in producing the famous cheesecakes he
ships out to all parts of the world. He has no other product, and
he needs none. This is cheesecake at its best, still the most
widely acclaimed product of its kind in the world. It is far superior to any of the imitations sold in markets and, perhaps because
of the quality of the cheese that goes into it, superior to that
found in almost any bakery or anything you might be able to
produce at home, at least in my opinion.

Reuben ships the cakes out in two sizes: a 6- to 8-portion cake
for about $11.95, and a 16- to 20-portion cake for around $22.95,
all postpaid. If you really get hooked on his cheesecakes, as well

you may, standing orders are accepted for monthly, semi-monthly, or holiday deliveries.

□

SAN FRANCISCO BAY GOURMET
311 California Street
Suite 700
San Francisco, CA 94104
Catalog 25 cents. Accepts checks, money orders,
MasterCard, and Visa. Full guarantee.

Five years ago, the founders of this company began with the premise that people all across the country would welcome a chance to order through the mails the most famous food product made in San Francisco, sourdough bread. That theory brought them immediate success, and they began adding more and more local food products that are hard to find elsewhere to their catalog, until today it is a real treasure trove of the finest California has to offer. But the original sourdough bread, made by a carefully guarded recipe and from a starter that is kept in a secret location, remains their pride and joy, their biggest selling item.

The hearty flavor and texture of this bread can really add life to an ordinary meal, and I found my samples especially good with spaghetti or seafood. Spread with garlic paste and lightly toasted, the sliced loaf makes the best garlic bread I have ever tasted. Two 1½-pound loaves cost about $9.50. Brown-and-serve sourdough French rolls are also available at a cost of about $8.75 for four packages of eight rolls; or you can order, for around $8.75, a sampler that holds two 1-pound loaves and two packages of rolls. And, while the company claims that you cannot duplicate their bread unless you have a million-dollar bakery, they do offer a kit for making sourdough pancakes and biscuits "like the Gold Rush miners made in their camps in 1849" for about $4.95.

To the original sourdough bread, the company has added a small number of other specialty breads. Pita bread, the flat loaf from the Middle East that is usually split and stuffed with a hearty filling for lunch or brunch, costs about $1.60 for eight 4-inch rounds, and with each order you get a list of suggested stuffings. A sweeter bread, *panettone,* is filled with raisins, diced candied fruit, and pine nuts from the Sierra Nevada. Two 1-pound loaves sell for around $8.95. Hawaiian bread, made from a recipe brought to the islands by early Portuguese settlers, I found to be especially good for making French toast, or just spread with jam as a simple dessert. Two one-pound loaves cost around $7.75.

A small number of West Coast cheeses are offered here. A cheddar made in Oregon's Tillamook Valley and Sonoma Jack, which is said to duplicate the cheese made by the padres of colonial California, are both offered in 3- and 11-pound wheels. A 3-pound wheel of either costs about $15.50, and an 11-pound wheel costs approximately $42.50.

If you become addicted to their bread or other products, the company will take monthly, semimonthly, or weekly orders in advance, but only if they can be charged to a credit card. Residents of California only can also order fine wines for delivery within that state.

☐

Toufayan Bakery
9255 Kennedy Boulevard West
North Bergen, NJ 07047
Free price list. Accepts checks and money orders only.

The pita bread baked by this company is put together according to a recipe the Toufayan family brought to this country from the Middle East. Pita, the hollow, flat, round loaf traditional to that region, comes made either with enriched white flour or stoneground whole-wheat flour. Vinegar is added as a natural preservative; no fats or chemicals are added. The round loaves weigh 2 ounces each, are put in cellophane packs of six, 12 packs to the box, and sell for around $5.40 a box plus shipping charges.

Pitettes are a thinner, lighter version of pita bread, weighing only 1 ounce each. In addition to the white flour and whole-wheat varieties, they can be ordered in onion flavor or with cinnamon and raisins added. Packed 96 to the box, these cost about $6.00 plus shipping charges.

Pita, in case you are not familiar with it, is known in Syria, where it originated, as "pocket lunch." This is because the bread, which looks like a small pillow when taken from the oven, opens to form a pocket that holds sandwich filling better than any ordinary bread or bun, making it particularly suited to fillings that are troublesome, such as barbecue. With each order Toufayan's sends a list of serving suggestions that range from the traditional to the unique.

□

WALNUT ACRES
Penns Creek, PA 17862
(717) 837–0601
Free catalog on request. Accepts checks, money
orders, Visa, and MasterCard. A handling charge of
$1.00 is added to all orders. All baked goods are
shipped at your own risk.

Walnut Acres, already mentioned as a leading source of health foods, is also a prime source for all types of bread, cookies, cakes, and other baked goods, as well as mixes for doing your own baking at home. All orders for baked goods are handled separately and sent out immediately after the baking is done, and only natural ingredients are used, of course.

Selling at about $1.00 for a 1¼-pound loaf are such breads as whole wheat, crushed wheat, rye, whole wheat with raisins, and Cornell loaf, which is made with whole-wheat flour, soy flour, wheat germ, molasses, corn germ oil, skim milk, and fresh well water. Specialty breads such as soya-carob and twelve-grain bread cost just pennies more per loaf.

Whole-wheat pita bread—the Syrian bread that opens to form a pocket for sandwich fillings, is also available; eight 1-ounce rounds cost 79 cents or so.

Cookies, all selling at about $1.59 per 12-ounce package, include black walnut, carob chip, date-nut, ginger, maple pecan, molasses, oatmeal, and peanut butter. As holiday dessert, there is a 2-pound fruitcake for about $6.00 and an 11-ounce plum pudding for about $1.20, with larger sizes of both available.

In addition to any kind of flour or meal you might need for your baking, Walnut Acres offer plenty of prepared bread and cake mixes, all available in 1-, 3-, 5-, and 25-pound bags. Prices given here are for 1-pound packages, but the per pound price drops as the size of the order increases. Bread mixes include whole wheat (about 80 cents) and soy-carob (about $1.20). Muffin mixes include bran (about 70 cents) and corn (about 60 cents). Quick bread mixes include apricot-nut (about $1.30), date-nut (around $1.00), granola maple (about $1.00), orange-nut (about $1.29), and wheat-free raisin cinnamon (about $1.15). Pancake mixes, also put up in 1-pound bags, include buckwheat (85 cents or so), rice (about 95 cents), triticale, which blends rice flour, soy flour, yeast, and buttermilk (about 75 cents), and 12-grain, which contains whole wheat, rye, corn, oats, barley, buckwheat, rice, soya and millet flours, as well as flax, sesame, and sunflower seeds (about 70 cents). A dry sourdough starter is also available at about $1.50 for a 2-ounce package, and it is said to make a bread or pancake with "a fine, rich nutlike flavor, moist and with good keeping quality."

□

CHAPTER SEVEN

VEGETABLES, FRUITS, AND NUTS

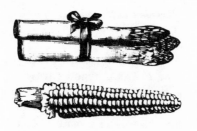

F ruit ripened on the tree, unsulphured dried fruits, nuts and seeds, and a wide range of organically grown vegetables—sources for all these will be found on the following pages. Suppliers range in size from small family operations to giant growers and importers who not only service the individual by mail but also, in many instances, supply the wholesale and retail trade. They provide exotic varieties of fruits and nuts from faraway places as well as local varieties of vegetables picked in their prime on small farms all across the country.

Apples, oranges, and dates are each available in a number of varieties, including many that may be locally hard to find, and the same companies frequently offer a large choice of confections made from these favorites. Pecans abound, as do the chewy concoctions made from them. Dried fruits range from the common choices such as apples and prunes to the less common like papayas, bananas, and guava. Vegetables are shipped out not only fresh but pickled, canned, or otherwise preserved.

Many sources will ship in bulk—often at a healthy saving to you—and nearly all offer small-size containers and gift assortments. Above all, you will find that most are friendly and easy to deal with, often sending out personal tips and recipes for using the good things they grow. I hope your experience in dealing with them is as enjoyable as my own. More sources for vegetables, fruit, and nuts may be found by consulting the chapter on Natural Foods.

□

BARFIELD'S
Polk City, FL 33868
Free catalog. Accepts checks and money orders only; no CODs. Full guarantee.

For more than forty years, the Barfields have specialized in the growing and selling of tree-ripened citrus fruit. If it's freshness you seek, this is the grower to contact. All their fruit, without exception, is left on the tree until your order is received, then picked and sent on its way in a matter of hours.

Grapefruits include the seedless Marsh, the seedless pink, and the giant, flavorful Duncan. Their juice oranges include the seeding, the pineapple, and the Valencia, all with seeds. For eating out of hand, they have the navel orange. Temples, tangelos, and tangerines are also available. Everything here is sold by the half-bushel (about $16.50), the three-quarter bushel (around $20.00), and the full bushel (about $23.75), and the Barfields will mix up a bushel just about any way you like.

An unusual offer is their Best-of-the-Month Club plan, which keeps the oranges, tangelos, and grapefruit coming from November till June, when the season ends. A bushel each month for the full eight months costs around $167.00; three-quarters of a bushel per month costs about $146.00; and half a bushel per month costs around $120.00. All prices include shipping charges, and everything is shipped by truck.

□

CALIFORNIA ALMOND GROWERS EXCHANGE
P.O. Box 1768
Sacramento, CA 95808
(800) 824–5891; within California, call (800) 952–5682.
Free catalog. Accepts checks, money orders, Visa, and MasterCard. Full guarantee.

The almond is California's largest tree crop, and the state itself is the world's leading producer of this delicious nut. The California Almond Growers Exchange, a grower-owned marketing association, operates the world's largest almond processing plant, and nuts from here go out to consumers all over the world. Their Blue Diamond brand almonds can be found in retail outlets all across the United States.

In addition to cocktail nibbles such as barbecued, hickory-smoked, onion-garlic, or cheese-flavored almonds (about $11.75 for one 6-ounce tin of each put up together in a gift box), and confections such as almonds that are honey-cinnamon or mint flavored (under $10.00 for a 20-ounce tin), the Exchange has several offerings that will please cooks. One of these is ground blanched almonds (about $12.50 for a 2½-pound tin) and another is a 4-pound tin of almond paste ($11.75). Almond oil for cooking is also available (about $5.95 for two 1-pint bottles), and there is a mix for whipping up your own almond macaroons at home (around $5.60 for a 24-ounce box). And, of course, there are plain almonds, in the shell or out, packaged in a number of sizes and ways—for example, a 3-pound burlap bagful of in-shell almonds for about $7.95, or a 4-pound tin of shelled or unshelled, unsalted nuts for around $16.50.

Almost everything that is shipped is attractively gift-boxed, and your personal greeting card can be added to any order at a cost of 75 cents. Discounts are given on orders of more than $400.00.

□

COVALDA DATE COMPANY
P.O. Box 908
Coachella, CA 92236
(714) 398–3441
Free price list. Accepts checks and money orders only; no CODs.

The Coachella Valley, at the foot of towering mountains, was once the bottom of an inland sea. Arriving there with his bride in 1920, Lee Anderson saw that the ultrarich soil was nearly ideal for the orchard that was his dream. Still, he also knew that all soil can stand some help, and he has spent the last sixty years building up his land with manure, cover crops, and compost. No chemicals have touched it during those years. Inactive now, the farm run by his children and grandchildren, Lee Anderson warns buyers that "there are a lot more organic foods sold than grown," but assures you that all his goods will always remain pure.

More than 800,000 pounds of dates are grown on his 100 acres of land each year, foremost among them the Deglet Noor variety, which accounts for about 90 percent of American date production. The Deglet Noor is a medium-brown-colored fruit that ranges in texture from moist to extremely soft, with a distinctive nutlike flavor. These sell at about $2.35 per pound, or around $3.10 per pound if pitted. Other varieties include Barhi, Halawi, Khadrawi, Medjool, Zahidi, and Thoori, and these range in price from $1.50 to $4.25 per pound, with substantial discounts offered on large orders.

Needless to say, with so many dates on hand, the Andersons use some to produce a number of date products. These include carob-pecan, date-almond, and coconut datelets, which are bite-sized confections, all at less than $2.50 per pound; date chips at $1.95 or so per pound; and there is even date butter, made with pure honey, at around $3.50 per pound. Dates stuffed with pineapple, walnut meats, or carob all sell at about $5.00 per pound.

Pecans ($1.65 per pound and up, depending on size) are also grown by the Andersons, and a number of other nut varieties— Brazil nuts, cashews, filberts, and pistachios among them—are bought from other growers and sold at prices ranging from $1.65 to $9.25 per pound. Dried fruits, purchased in the same manner, include apricots (around $6.15 per pound), black Monukka raisins (about $2.00 per pound), peaches (about $3.25 per pound), papaya (around $2.95 per pound), and currants (approximately $2.00 per pound). Shipping charges are extra on all orders of less than 100 pounds, with orders larger than that shipped by truck, freight collect.

□

DEER VALLEY FARM
R.D. 1
Guilford, NY 13780
(607) 764–8556
Free catalog. Accepts checks and money orders only;
no CODs.

Already mentioned as a major source of health foods, this large New York farm also ships out a number of fresh and dried fruits. As you would expect from this company, everything is organically grown.

November through May only is the time for ordering fresh fruit here, including four favorite apple varieties (McIntosh, Spy, Cortland, and Red Delicious) that sell at about $17.00 for a 50-pound box or 59 cents per pound on smaller orders. Oranges and grapefruit sell at about $19.00 per 50-pound box or 69 cents per pound on broken boxes, while tree-ripened lemons sell at around 95 cents per pound.

Among the unsulphured dried fruit offerings are apricots (about $2.99 per pound), Turkish figs (about $2.79 per pound), pears (about $2.89 per pound) and mixed dried fruit at approximately $3.20 per pound. Nearly any type of nut can be ordered here, including such favorites as peanuts, either raw or roasted, in the shell or out, at about $1.99 per pound; black walnut pieces at about $4.25 per pound; pecans, in the shell, at $2.70 or so per pound; and macadamias at about $10.50 per pound. Deer Valley asks me to remind you that all these prices may fluctuate widely from season to season and even from one month to the next.

☐

FIESTA NUT CORPORATION
P.O. Box 366
75 Harbor Road
Port Washington, NY 11050
(800) 645–3296
Free catalog. Accepts checks, money orders, Visa,
and MasterCard. $25.00 minimum on credit card
orders.

Raw and roasted nuts—salted or unsalted—dried fruit, candy, snacks and dessert toppings are featured items at Fiesta, and their prices are among the lowest I found. What's more, discounts are offered on very large orders ($250.00 or more).

Among the selections you can make for under $12.00 are 2 pounds of smoked or Jordan almonds, dried apple rings, stuffed dates, or Calimyrna figs; 3 pounds of raw shelled filberts, raw or roasted cashews, banana chips, or toasted sweetened coconut chips; 4 pounds of jumbo prunes or dried pineapple rings; and 5 pounds of sunflower seeds. In the same price range you'll find various-sized packages of carob-coated raisins, maltballs, peanuts, and bridge mix, yogurt-coated nuts and candies, and dried fruits such as pears, peaches, dates, and apricots.

Pistachios are a specialty here, and they are dry-roasted and lightly salted daily on the premises. One way to order them is in a colorful 2-pound burlap bag, the price around $14.00. Extra-large pistachios are available at a slightly higher price, and of course there are any number of nut assortments including one (priced at around $17.00) that contains one 11-ounce tin each of jumbo peanuts, cashews, pistachios, and mixed nuts. Other assortments cost as little as $6.50 and as much as $30.00. There is a charge of $1.00 on all orders shipped west of the Mississippi.

□

FIGI'S, INC.
Marshfield, WI 54449
(715) 387–1771
Free catalog. Accepts checks, money orders, Visa,
MasterCard, and American Express; no CODs. Full
guarantee.

Perhaps because cheese and fresh fruit go so well together, this giant company—where cheese has been a specialty for years—now offers an excellent selection of fruit, fresh as well as dried.

From October through December only, Florida oranges and grapefruit (varieties not given) can be ordered at around $20.00 for a 20-pound box, individually or mixed. Ruby Red grapefruit from Texas is available from November through April, the price about $14.95 for a decorative box of nine large grapefruit. October through January only, the firm offers its Fruit Buffet box (around $12.50), a gift carton that holds six juicy Anjou pears, four crisp Red Delicious apples, 5 ounces of assorted mixed nuts in the shell, 5 ounces of strawberry candy, and 4 ounces each of Colby and cheddar cheese; or, during that same period, you can choose the Apples 'n' Cheese assortment (about $14.95), a bell-shaped box holding an 8-ounce bell-shaped cheddar and eight large Red Delicious apples.

Dried fruits here are offered in a number of assortments, always put up in attractive rattan baskets or shipped on fancy reusable trays. As an example, for around $15.95, one basket holds a full 3 pounds of mixed dates, figs, apricots, pears, prunes, pineapple, cherries, and English walnuts. Or, for about $12.95, there is a 14-by-7½-inch wood tray loaded with 2 pounds of these same fruits. Unlike the fresh product, dried fruit assortments are available throughout the year.

Nuts, too, are available anytime you choose to order, including, for around $10.95, a 4-pound burlap bag of mixed almonds, filberts, English walnuts, Brazil nuts, and pecans; or, for about $18.95, 2½ pounds of pistachios, also in a burlap bag. Other nut selections are put up in attractive wooden barrels and buckets, with nutcracker and picks included, at about $15.95 for a 2-pound assortment. All Christmas orders must be in company hands by December 2 to assure preholiday delivery.

□

FRESNO TRADING COMPANY
5529 East Lamona
P.O. Box 7600
Fresno, CA 93747
(800) 228–5000
Free catalog. Accepts checks, money orders, Visa,
MasterCard, and American Express. Full guarantee.

California pistachios, grown on rich holdings in the San Joaquin Valley, are the leading item here, and you'll find them offered in a number of ways. There are natural unsalted pistachios, lightly salted dry roasted pistachios, roasted unsalted pistachios, whole pistachio kernels (raw or roasted, salted or unsalted), and pistachio pieces. The nuts, in any form, may be ordered by the single pound or in burlap bags holding up to 5 pounds of pistachios. Prices average around $8.50 per pound, though the whole kernels are a great deal costlier. The pistachios may also be ordered in a number of beautiful, refillable glassware containers including a replica milk bottle (circa 1890) that holds over 7 pounds of salted pistachios and costs nearly $80.00; a Wheaton canning jar that comes with 2¼ pounds of pistachios and costs around $25.00; and a 20-by-10-inch glass pig that holds 2½ pounds of nuts and costs around $45.00.

Pistachio candy is a newly introduced product of this company, and the catalog descriptions really make the mouth water. In addition to pistachio brittle, there are confections such as truffles, nougat Delilahs, pistaches, Moroccos, and Valentinos, all loaded with pistachios. Offered in a number of assortments, the candies sell at an average cost of about $8.00 per pound.

Almonds are another featured item here, though they have not yet been given equal billing with the pistachios. The almonds can be ordered roasted and salted; blanched, roasted, and salted; natural; or hickory smoked. Cost is around $12.00 for a 2½-pound burlap bag of any type, and all shipping charges are extra.

□

HADLEY ORCHARDS
P.O. Box 495
Cabazon, CA 92230
(714) 849–4668
Free catalog. Accepts checks, money orders, Visa,
and MasterCard. Minimum order: $10.00. Full
guarantee.

Nearly a century ago, Paul and Peggy Hadley began the development of their orchard in an oasis in the desert just west of Palm Springs, their idea being that the land would never be touched by chemicals and the fruit would be sold at prices everyone could afford. It was an idea ahead of its time, but the result was growth that, over the century, has made Hadley Orchards one of the world's largest retailers of fruit and nuts. And though the Hadleys are no longer associated with the business, the original idea prevails and their land remains untouched by chemicals.

The inventory of Hadley-grown products is impressive and

includes a huge selection of dates, nuts, dried fruits, homemade preserves, and honey taken from the hives of bees used to pollinate the orchard. Nearly 300 items can be ordered through the mail.

Among the sun-dried fruits are Thompson seedless raisins (about $1.95 per pound), banana chips (about $1.75 per pound), nectarines ($2.95 or so per pound), Calimyrna figs (around $3.35 per pound), and dates that range in price from $2.55 per pound to as much as $8.95 per pound for the waxy Medjool Noor variety.

Fifteen varieties of nuts are available. They come raw, natural, roasted, blanched, in the shell and out, and some are barbecue, cheese, onion, or ham flavored. They range in price from around $1.95 per pound for raw Spanish peanuts to about $8.55 per pound for roasted whole cashews, and there are several mixed boxes available.

The fruit trays and baskets sold here are some of the most tasty and beautiful found anywhere, ranging in price from $7.45 for a handwoven tray holding 2 pounds of dried apricots, figs, prunes, dates, and glazed cherries to $29.95 for a redwood tray loaded with 7 pounds of apricots, prunes, dates, pineapples, and figs stuffed with walnuts and cherries, plus a sprinkling of mixed nuts and date confections. The latter assortment was so beautiful I was reluctant to break into it, so tasty I know I will be ordering it again.

□

HARRY AND DAVID'S BEAR CREEK ORCHARDS
Medford, OR 97501
*Free catalog on request. Accepts checks and money
orders only; no CODs. All goods guaranteed if
delivery can be made when first attempted.*

Long before I began work on this book, I was a satisfied customer of Harry and David, having ordered their luscious fruit not only for my own use but also for those at the very top of my personal gift list. Due to the heavy amount of advertising they do, the name of this leading company will be familiar to most readers, so my only comment here will be that this is one company that always, in my experience, delivers the high quality it promises in its commercial advertisements.

Since 1933, the hottest item in their catalog has been their Royal Riviera pears, which Harry and David grow in their orchards in Oregon's Rogue River Valley. A hybrid of a variety originally grown in the area around Angers, France, these lushly delicious pears are available from November through January, a 6¾-pound box selling for about $14.95. During that same period, customers can also order, for around $19.95, five-pound boxes of their giant Red Delicious apples and receive in each box a ¾-pound brick of aged cheddar. Or choose a 4-pound box of thin-skinned Royal Mandarin oranges, grown especially for Harry and David, for about $12.95. Harry and David will also ship one box of each fruit (total net weight: 13 pounds) to one address for about $24.00.

Individual nut varieties are not sold here, but nuts are included in many of the gift assortments sent out by the firm, and the Fireside Favorite is a munchable mixture you might want to try sometime between October and May, the only time it is offered. At a cost of about $14.95 you get a handsome handwoven rattan basket with leather pockets for nutcracker and picks (all included) holding about 2 pounds of mixed English walnuts, California almonds, Georgia pecans, Brazil nuts, and Oregon filberts.

Harry and David pioneered the idea of the monthly shipment of food under a club plan, and their Fruit-of-the-Month Club is one of the most attractive and successful in the industry. Plans range in price from about $36.95 for the 3-month plan (pears at Christmas, apples in January, oranges in February) to around $150.00 for the 12-month plan that keeps such delicacies as pears, oranges, apples, grapes, pineapple, kiwi fruit, peaches, nectarines, grapefruit, and assorted fruit preserves coming throughout the year. Other plans include extra-elegant packaging at slightly higher prices, and when you buy a membership as a gift, each shipment carries your personal greeting.

□

HARWOOD HILL ORCHARD AND GIFT SHOP
Route 7A
Bennington, VT 05201
(802) 442-9524
Free brochure and price list. Accepts checks and
money orders only; no CODs.

This family-owned orchard produces 40 varieties of apples, all of which can be ordered in boxes of 15 (about $6.50), 30 (about $12.00), 45 (about $17.50), or 60 (around $23.00). Most popular are McIntosh, Cortland, Red Delicious, Northern Spy, and boxes of mixed varieties. Apples are also part of the many gift assortments offered here such as the Vermont Sampler (around $7.25), which contains 11 fancy apples, 8 ounces of Vermont cheddar cheese, and a pint of grade A maple syrup. Maple syrup (about $6.25 a pint, about $9.75 a quart, and around $27.00 a gallon) and honey ($2.25 or so per pound) can also be ordered separately from the Harwoods.

While apples are the only fresh fruit shipped out by the Harwoods, they do offer apple, blueberry, raspberry, and strawberry syrups (all at about $4.50 per pint), as well as a number of fruit butters, jellies, jams, and preserves. Jams include blueberry, blackberry, peach, strawberry, red raspberry, and strawberry-rhubarb. The butters are apricot, apple, and peach. Jellies include apple, blackberry, crab apple, grape, mint, quince, raspberry, strawberry, red currant, and that old-time goodie, wild elderberry. The jams, jellies, and butters are in 10-ounce jars, about $2.25 per jar, three jars for a little over $6.00. Shipping charges are extra on all orders here, and fresh apples, or gift boxes of which they are a part, are available only September through January.

□

HICKIN'S MOUNTAIN MOWINGS FARM AND GREENHOUSES
R.F.D. 1
Black Mountain Road
Brattleboro, VT 05301
(802) 254-2146
Free price list on request. Accepts checks and money
orders only; no CODs.

"That quality beyond taste . . . draws customers who hunger for things that taste as good as they used to," *Gourmet* magazine once said of the Hickin farm, tucked back off the beaten path in the Dummerston hills of Vermont. *Vermont Life* went a little further, saying, "The Hickin's products are beautiful. Often they are unusual as well, beguiling the gourmet who may have looked a dozen places before finally discovering just what he wanted at Mountain Mowings."

In an average season, Frank Hickin grows more than 100 varieties of fruit and vegetables. It is necessary to visit the farm in order to obtain most of the fresh produce, though bulk orders are sometimes shipped out on special arrangement following a telephone call to confirm prices. Without any special arrangement whatsoever, however, you can order, in season, apple varieties such as Cortland, Spy, Red Delicious, McIntosh, and Macoun, all at about $15.50 per bushel, with smaller boxes available. Also available without special arrangement are shallots at around $3.95 per pound, and Bear Paw popcorn, a highly regarded variety Frank Hickin helped save from extinction, at a cost of around $1.50 for three large ears.

Like many Vermont farmers, Frank Hickin has his own sugarhouse and produces his own maple syrup, which he sells, pure, in lithographed cans at about $4.50 a half pint, $9.95 a quart, or around $32.00 a gallon. Some of the excess syrup he combines with his vegetables and spices to make eight different types of the sweetest, crispest pickles I have ever tasted. Varieties are icicle cauliflower, cucumber chips, lemon cucumber, cucumber strips, mustard chips, sweet peppers, relish, and "crookzini," which combines three kinds of squash. Various size jars range in price from about $1.25 for the 2-ounce model up to $6.95 or so for the 32-ounce jug. Available at about the same price are a dozen kinds of dill pickles, including beans, tiny baby carrots, cauliflower, tomatoes, zucchini, and my personal favorite from among those I tried, kohlrabi. Relishes, also at the same price, include corn, pepper, pickled eggplant, red cabbage and old-fashioned bread and butter.

Fresh fruit syrups may be ordered sweetened or unsweetened, and prices range from around $2.50 for a 4-ounce bottle to about $12.95 for a 32-ounce jar. Thick and delicious, the flavors include wild blackberry, peach, wild black cherry, plum, blueberry, and half a dozen more. Pickled fruits, largely unknown outside Vermont but a tradition there, include elderberry, blueberry, blackberry, and red raspberry, all at around $4.25 per 6-ounce jar, with smaller jars available.

Hickin's offers nearly any kind of fruit jam, jelly, butter, spread, or preserve the mind could conceive, at prices ranging from about $1.25 for a 2-ounce sampler up to around $37.75 for gallon jugs. Familiar favorites include apple, plum, and pear butters; blueberry, peach, and strawberry jams; grape, apple, and elderberry jellies. Less familiar are parsley, watercress, dill, and tarragon jellies; yellow tomato preserves; and dill-tarragon butter, all of which should make very interesting condiments.

Offered as gourmet specialties are such rarities as dilled fiddleheads, snow peas, asparagus tips, Brussels sprouts, baby peas, and mixed vegetables, plus stuffed miniature peppers and boiled cider jelly, all at prices ranging from about $1.35 for a 2-ounce jar up to around $11.50 for a full 32 ounces. Hickin's combines many of these goodies into gift boxes that cost as little as $9.95 and as much as $37.95, and will also put together gift hampers to your own specifications.

□

THE HOUSE OF ALMONDS
5300 District Boulevard
Bakersfield, CA 93309
(800) 235–4070; within California, call (800) 582–3923.
*Free catalog. Accepts checks, money orders, Visa,
and MasterCard. Full guarantee.*

Early in the development of the California almond industry, Frank Slate and his son, L. L. Slate, started what was to become the nation's largest independent almond-processing firm. As a convenience for growers who brought almonds to them for processing, they opened a small retail almond shop in one corner of their plant, where they sold six flavors of almonds and almond brittle. In answer to customer requests, they began shipping almond gifts, and this was the real beginning of The House of Almonds, a company that now ships over 100 almond, food, and associated gift items to all 50 states and a number of foreign lands.

The House of Almonds seems to have done everything to an almond that can be done to it. The six basic flavors—roasted and salted; blanched, roasted, and salted; cheese; hickory-smoked; Ranchero (which is taco-flavored); and barbecued—are still available, along with candied almonds, almond-stuffed dates, almond brittle, caramelized almonds, and almonds flavored with garlic, onion, orange, banana, or coconut. The basic flavors are put up in just about any size package you could imagine, including 4-pound cans that sell for about $15.95 plus shipping. The six original flavors can also be ordered in a 1½-pound tin for about $8.95. Those with a sweet tooth will find goodies such as almond bark (approximately $13.95 plus shipping for a 1½-pound tin) and chocolate-covered almonds (about $9.95 per pound), and, when you're not in the mood for almonds, you can switch over to roasted, salted pistachios, 5 pounds in a burlap bag for around $29.95 plus shipping.

□

KAKAWATEEZ LIMITED
130 Olive Street
Findlay, OH 45840
(419) 422–5732
Free brochure. Accepts checks, money orders, and
CODs.

While living in Mexico, where they operated a poultry farm, Don Shieber and his wife tasted some nuts that had been processed by a Japanese-born citizen of Mexico. So enthusiastic were they about the unique flavor created by this process that they took out a loan and bought the rights to produce and distribute Totem-Kakawateez nuts anywhere in the world outside Mexico. (*Kakawateez* is the Mexican-Indian name for nuts.) First processing only peanuts, they later added to their line cashews from India and Africa and almonds from California (both at about $2.99 for an 8-ounce jar), macadamias from Hawaii (around $5.25 for 8 ounces), filberts from Turkey (about $2.75 for a 9-ounce jar), Brazil nuts (around $2.55 for 9 ounces), and pistachio nuts from Afghanistan (around $6.95 for 7 ounces). Peanuts, still their fastest seller, go out at about $2.35 for 7 ounces. All the nuts are coated and dry roasted in some secret fashion that gives them about the best flavor I have ever tasted in a nut from any source, and if you'd like to sample a few of each variety (except the peanuts, which are not included in the mixture), the company offers a 7-ounce mixed jar for $2.99. A minimum order, however, is 4 jars in any combination desired, and all shipping charges are extra.

□

KNOTT'S BERRY FARM
8039 Beach Boulevard
Buena Park, CA 90620
(714) 827-1776
Free catalog. Accepts checks, money orders, Visa,
BankAmericard, MasterCard, and American Express.

Knott's Berry Farm, with its vast theme amusement park that is second only to the two Disney parks in attendance and which, having recently celebrated its sixtieth anniversary, is the oldest theme amusement park in America, is a place known to millions of Americans. For those who have not been fortunate enough to visit the park, this is how it began.

When young Walter Knott, who had been instrumental in developing the boysenberry—a crossbreed of the blackberry, loganberry, and red raspberry—settled with his wife, Cordelia, on a 10-acre farm near Buena Park in 1920, he was pursuing a life-long dream of establishing a berry farm. Customers flocked to his tiny roadside stand to buy the juicy berries he grew, then tight money during the Great Depression forced the couple to add other foods to their line. From these modest beginnings sprang a booming restaurant business, and the Ghost Town and other attractions were added only as diversions for the long lines of hungry customers waiting for their chance at the fine dinners sold by the Knotts. Millions of meals were concluded with slabs of juicy boysenberry pie, and millions of diners, over the years, went home with jars of the jellies, jams, and preserves produced under the supervision of the Knotts. Odds are good that you have tasted these.

With the exception of the pie, nearly all of the Knott family's famous products are now available by mail. Their famous boysenberry makes dozens of appearances in the beautifully illustrated catalog, almost always in combination with other fruit products. Gift boxes abound here, and all are beautiful to behold. One example is a decorative box holding nine 8-ounce jars of assorted jellies, jams and preserves—boysenberry, apricot-pineapple, Bing cherry, plum, Kadota fig, peach, strawberry, grape, and orange—at a cost of about $13.95. Another is a rattan basket loaded with one 8-ounce jar each of boysenberry, apricot-pineapple, strawberry, and plum preserves, plus one 8-ounce jar of orange marmalade, the price around $12.30.

Then there are such goodies as boysenberry squares, jelly loaded with chopped California walnuts and covered with creamy chocolate, selling at around $7.75 for a 1-pound box; and party pastries, French vanilla cookies layered with delicate pastry cream and filled with your choice of apricot or boysenberry preserves, then dipped in chocolate or sweet pastel coating, at about $8.30 per pound.

Fresh fruit is not shipped by the Knotts, but they offer plenty in the dried form, for example an old-fashioned wood field crate holding 3 pounds of figs, apricots, dates, pears, prunes, and pears for just over $20.00. A rattan tray holding 3 pounds of date delicacies—some natural, some rolled in coconut and topped with almonds, some stuffed with walnuts, and all garnished with glacéed cherries or bits of pear—makes an attractive gift at under $12.00. Trays loaded with other dried fruits can be ordered at similar prices.

Visitors to this famous theme park know how delightful the fruit products of the Knotts can be, and their wares are no less delightful when received through the mail.

□

KOINONIA PARTNERS, INC.
Route 2
Americus, GA 31709
Free catalog. Accepts checks and money orders only;
no CODs.

Koinonia (a Greek word meaning "fellowship") was founded by a theologian in 1942 as an experiment in Christian communal living. The communal farm met with growing hostility in the mid-fifties because of its stand against racial prejudice, and a local economic boycott caused the collapse of the original chicken and egg business that had supported the commune and its residents. That forced Koinonia into the mail-order business, starting with pecans and peanuts, but now including fruitcakes, nut candies, pottery, and handicrafts. Profits help finance homes that are sold without interest to low-income families.

Pecans in the shell are offered in 4½-pound boxes (around $10.00) and 8½-pound boxes (about $18.50); or shelled for about $5.50 per pound. Hickory-smoked pecans cost around $5.95 per pound, and spiced pecans—sparkled with butter, sugar, and cinnamon—cost about $5.00 per pound. Shelled raw Georgia peanuts cost around $14.00 for a 10-pound box, while the roasted and salted peanuts sell at around $2.20 per pound. Spiced peanuts sell at about the same price as the salted ones. Peanut brittle (around $3.20 per pound), butterscotch (about $2.70 per pound), and carob-peanut crunch (about $2.90 per pound) are among the candies you will find here, and there is a boxed 2-pound 10-ounce fruitcake, baked on the farm, for around $8.50. Prices always include delivery, and substantial discounts are given on volume orders for fund-raising projects.

□

LEE'S FRUIT COMPANY
P.O. Box 450
Leesburg, FL 32748
(904) 753-2064.
*Free brochure. Accepts checks and money orders
only; no CODs.*

In 1945, after more than two decades spent managing a large Pennsylvania farm owned by others, Lee McComb was finally able to realize the lifelong dream of owning his own land. On that land he began to put to work some of his own ideas about how that land should be treated.

This involved not only fertilizing the land with natural compost and avoiding the use of any chemicals, but also the enrichment of the soil through the addition of sea solids, peat, and a type of clay that includes at least forty minerals. The method produces oranges that, according to laboratory tests ordered by the farmer, have 36 percent thinner skins, about 16 percent more juice, 78 percent less acid, 30 percent more vitamin C, and as much as 234 percent more mineral value than other oranges used in the study.

Lee's offers juice oranges, grapefruit, or mixed boxes of the two at about $20.00 of a bushel, $16.50 for three-quarters of a bushel, or about $13.95 a half bushel. Grapefruit include both pink Marsh and Duncan varieties. Navel oranges, Lee and Temple oranges, and Orlando tangelos are slightly higher: about $21.00 a bushel, $17.50 for three-quarters of a bushel, and around $14.95 for half a bushel. November through May is the season for most citrus fruits, but the Lee and Temple oranges are out of season by February, as are the tangelos, and the navel oranges can be ordered no later than the middle of January. All fruit is tree ripened, packed by hand, and shipped as soon as your order can be filled. Orange blossom honey, produced by bees used to pollinate the groves, is available at about $1.75 per pound, but only as part of a citrus order. Free delivery is made east of the Mississippi, but there is a $4.00 charge for shipments made to the west.

□

Manganaro Foods
488 Ninth Avenue
New York, NY 10018
(212) 563–5331
Free catalog. Accepts checks, money orders, CODs.
Credit applications available.

Manganaro Foods, the fine old Italian specialty shop that has been a New York landmark since 1893, ships out no fresh fruit or vegetables; however, their imported tinned vegetables and preserved fruits are so deliciously interesting that I would be remiss if I failed to mention them here.

From Belgium comes Vegetable Jardiniere, a "vegetable garden in a jar," the 10-ounce jar selling for about $2.75. It holds layers of baby carrots, shelled flageolets, peas, cut green beans, pickled turnip slices, and asparagus, each vegetable forming a beautiful design in its own layer. About a dozen other vegetable assortments, from half that many European countries, are offered at similar prices. Too, there are tins and jars filled with individual vegetables, gourmet items all: *clos du verdet* (fine green beans) from France at about $2.95 for a 14-ounce tin; miniature carrots from Greece at around $3.35 for a 12-ounce jar; 14-ounce tins of lentils, salsify, or endives from Belgium for about $2.50; Spanish or Italian olives, green, ripe, or dried, all at about $2.25 for 9 ounces—the list is an extensive one.

Brandied fruits, all in 16-ounce jars, all imported from Italy, and all selling at about $4.75, include pitted wild cherries, papaya, and even baby rosebuds. Mixed fruit in brandy is about a dollar higher. Among the many fruit preserves offered here, *mostarda* (around $3.25 for a 9-ounce jar) is one you might want to try. *Mostarda* is a sweet, spicy fruit relish consisting of candied fruits put up in a clear mustard sauce, and is utterly delicious alongside beef, lamb, or wild game dishes, especially venison.

□

MISSION ORCHARDS OF DAY AND YOUNG
2296 Senter Road
San Jose, CA 95150
(408) 297–5056
Free catalog. Accepts checks, money orders, Visa,
MasterCard, and American Express.

Fresh or dried, it would be difficult to find more appealing fruit than that shipped out by Mission Orchards. Sun-dried fruits include apricots, peaches, pears, and prunes, all put up in 2-pound bags at a cost of about $10.95 per bag. Comice pears are the leading fresh fruit, selling at around $9.95 for a 4½-pound box or approximately $14.95 for 7 pounds, and available November through January. Apples are sold November 15 through January 15, and varieties include Red or Golden Delicious, and the Granny Smith, all at about $13.95 for a 6-pound box. December through April, Ruby Red grapefruit is available, a box of six selling for about $10.95. During the same season, at a cost of $14.95

or so, you can order a 7-pound box of thin-skinned navel oranges. Mandarins, in boxes of 20 to 24 for about $16.95, are available in December only. Seedless Ruby Red Grapes, a rarity in by-mail shipment, can be ordered October 1 through January 7, in 3-pound crates for about $14.95; and luscious kiwi fruit, about $12.95 for a 2-pound box, is available November 10 through January 15.

In addition to numerous gift assortments, such as a white wicker basket (around $22.95) overflowing with six Comice pears, five Red Delicious apples, seven foil-wrapped dates, three walnuts, 2 ounces of candy kisses and a 1½-ounce jar of orange marmalade, Mission Orchards offers dozens of fruit-based candies. There are chocolate-covered prunes, for example, in 12-ounce boxes for around $11.95, or chocolate-covered, walnut-filled apricots in 14-ounce boxes for about $12.45. Macadamia cake, loaded with pineapple and nuts, costs about $11.75 for a 1¼-pound loaf, and a traditional 1½-pound fruitcake goes out for about $12.75.

A number of monthly ordering plans are available, the most costly being the 12-month plan (about $170.00). This brings pears in December, apples in January, grapefruit in February, tangelos in March, avocados in April, oranges in May, Bing cherries in June, plums in July, nectarines in August, grapes in September, kiwi fruit in October, and concludes with pears in November. Other plans cost as little as $48.50.

□

PINNACLE ORCHARDS
Medford, OR 97501
(503) 772–6271
*Free catalog. Accepts checks, money orders, Visa,
MasterCard, and American Express. Full guarantee.*

Developed in southern France in 1849, the Comice pear was for many years so rare that it was permitted only to the French nobility. In the late 1800s, however, a few trees were introduced to Oregon's Rogue River Valley, and today the Comice is by far the most popular fruit grown in that region.

Pinnacle Orchards has been growing and shipping these luscious pears for 44 years, and they have them in just about every size and type of container available, among them a peck basket (32 to 40 pears) for about $21.50, delivered, or a half-peck (16 to 20 pears) for about $16.95. The pears are available November through December.

The apple season is slightly longer, running November through January, when 6-pound boxes of either Red or Golden Delicious apples can be ordered for around $13.95. December through March, Texas Ruby Red grapefruit can be ordered at a cost of about $16.95 per 9-pound box, and the orchards offer almonds (around $12.50 for a 4-pound bag), hazelnuts (about $13.50 for a 4-pound bag), and pure raw honey throughout the year.

The monthly gift plan here differs from most others in that you are permitted to choose your monthly order from among several that are offered and can sign up for as many months as you wish. The choices include cakes and candies, jellies and jams, as well as the various fruits, and the monthly cost can be as little as $12.50 or as much as $19.50. Your personal greeting is included with each shipment, of course.

□

PIONEER SEMINOLE GROVES
P.O. Box 2209
Cocoa, FL 32922
(305) 452–3833
Free catalog. Accepts checks, money orders, CODs, credit applications, Visa, BankAmericard, and MasterCard. Free delivery east of the Mississippi; 10 percent delivery charge west of the Mississippi.

Over 56 years ago, Pioneer Seminole Groves began shipping their Indian River citrus fruit around the country at the special request of customers who had visited their groves. Today their fruit goes regularly to such distant points as Scotland, Luxemburg, Belgium, and Japan, and their groves are among the largest in central Florida.

Seedless navel oranges, ripened in the sun and available Thanksgiving through January 15, are their most popular fruit, offered at about $26.95 per bushel, $22.95 per three-quarter bushel, $17.95 a half bushel, or $13.95 a quarter bushel. Ruby Red, Duncan, and pink or white Marsh grapefruit, in season November through May, sell at the same price and the grower will mix a bushel of navels and grapefruit to meet your specifications.

Other varieties for eating out of hand include honey tangerines (March to mid-April; about $27.95 per bushel); Valencia oranges (March to mid-July; about $26.95 per bushel); and tangelos (January only; around $17.95 a half bushel).

Guava, lemon, orange, mint, mango, and papaya are a few of the tropical jellies, jams, and marmalades found in the catalog, all priced at about $7.95 for three ½-pound jars. Also offered is the world-famous Claxton Fruitcake, which you may have seen and tasted at the 1965–66 New York World's Fair, the 2-pound cake selling for around $8.95.

For convenience, you can place a standing order here, arranging for the monthly shipment of any quantity of the fruit of your choice, depending upon seasonal availability. Custom-made gift assortments are also available.

□

PRIESTER'S PECANS
Fort Deposit, AL 36032
(800) 323–1718
Free catalog. Accepts checks, money orders; no CODs.

For more than 45 years, Priester's has been billing itself as "the home of the Southern Kernel," and it appears that they have done just about everything with the pecan that can be done with it. Pecan halves, either natural or roasted and salted, are available in containers of all sizes, average price about $8.00 per pound, depending on the grade you order. Papershell pecans, in the shell, cost about $15.50 for 5 pounds. Then comes a parade of pecan cakes, cookies, and confections.

There is pecan bark (about $14.75 for a 24-ounce tin), toasted pecan brittle (about $9.95 for a 1-pound tin), cherry log candy, the traditional pecan log with a cherry center (around $12.95 for a 20-ounce tin), pecan divinity (about $9.25 per 1-pound tin), and pecan pralines in three flavors—vanilla, coconut, or rum (about $12.95 for a 20-ounce tin). Their 2-pound pecan fruitcake is said to be made from a recipe handed down from pre-Civil War days and contains far more fruit and nuts than those I have seen elsewhere; the price, about $10.25.

Citrus fruit is also shipped in season. November through March, Ruby Red grapefruit from Texas is available for about $16.95 per box of 18. November through January, at a cost of around $24.95 per bushel, or about $15.95 per half bushel, you can choose either Hamlin variety juice oranges or seedless navels for eating out of hand.

When ordering pecans or pecan products, although they are available throughout the year, I suggest that you remember that November is the month when these are harvested and that is when they should be purchased for the ultimate in freshness.

□

SUNNYLAND FARMS, INC.
Route 1
Albany, GA 31702
(912) 883-3085
Free brochure. Accepts checks, money orders, Visa,
and MasterCard. Full guarantee.

Sunnyland Farms offers a tremendous array of nuts and nut products, as well as a more limited selection of fresh and dried fruit. Jane and Harry Willson, who have been growing and shipping their products for more than 33 years, were in the process of restructuring their prices when we contacted them, however, so they could only tell us that their prices "will remain competitive with others in the market."

Natural nuts in their catalog include two varieties of pecans in the shell: Stuarts, which are the larger type most commonly seen in Georgia, and Schleys, smaller and with thinner shells. Shelled halves and pieces are offered, too; and there are other nut varieties such as California English walnuts, black walnuts from the Ozarks, cashews, almonds, hazelnuts, and Brazil nuts. Some of these come roasted and salted, and many are used in confections such as pecan logs, chocolate-covered nuts, nut brittles, barks, and pralines. Most can be ordered individually or as part of the many combination gift packages described in the catalog.

Apricots, dates, and figs, stuffed or unstuffed as you wish, are the only dried fruits offered here. These are grown for the Willsons in California, and can be ordered in bulk or in gift boxes. With any order, the Willsons send an interesting little booklet loaded with recipes and suggestions for serving the good things they sell.

☐

SUNRAY ORCHARDS
Route 1
Box 299
Myrtle Creek, OR 97457
(503) 839–4116
Free brochure. Accepts checks and money orders
only; no CODs.

Established in 1923, and in the hands of its present owners since 1948, Sunray Orchards is one of the nation's largest independent growers of prunes, raising four varieties and shipping them to all parts of the country. They have the slightly tart Italian prunes, the sweet Brooks and Moyer prunes, and the extra-sweet date prunes. Most shipments are in 25-pound bulk cases. Date prunes are the least costly, at about $17.50 per case. Brooks and Italian varieties sell at about $24.50 per case, and the Moyers sell at around $27.50 per case. If that sounds like too many prunes for your family, they offer a sampler (about $8.00) that holds three 1-pound bags of the Moyers and three 1-pound bags of the Italian. UPS charges are extra. With any order, you receive a pamphlet that contains many interesting recipes for using these processed plums.

☐

THE SWISS COLONY
Monroe, WI 53566
(608) 328–8400
*Free catalog. Accepts checks, money orders, Visa,
MasterCard, Diners Club, Carte Blanche, and
American Express. Charge accounts available. Full
guarantee.*

It may seem odd to order citrus fruit from Wisconsin, but a glance at the Swiss Colony catalog will convince you that this is one of the better sources. After years of demand by their customers, Swiss Colony acquired a small fruit company so they could provide top-quality fruit and nuts to accompany the fine cheese that is the backbone of their business.

November through May is the citrus season. During that period, Swiss Colony offers 15-pound boxes of Honeyball oranges for about $14.95, 10-pound boxes of seedless navel oranges for around $13.50, 9-pound boxes of Texas Ruby Red grapefruit for $11.95 or so, and (November 15 through January 15 only) 8-pound boxes of mandarin oranges for about $13.95. Also available (November 1 through January 15) are giant Comice pears, a 6-pound box for around $9.95. All fruit is available in larger boxes, and there are numerous mixed assortments, for example, the Tropical Treasure, which sells for about $29.95 and includes pineapple, pears, grapefruit, apples, oranges, avocados, lemons, limes, and walnuts (net weight 15 pounds). A monthly ordering plan is also available, with prices ranging from about $46.50 for a 4-month plan to approximately $150.00 for the 12-month plan.

In addition to many nut assortments, the catalog offers 3½-pound bags of papershell pecans (about $13.95), pistachios (around $27.95), and extra-fancy mixed nuts (about $10.85). A 14-ounce tin of spiced almonds is offered at about $8.50, and a 1½-pound tin of macadamias goes for just under $20.00. Everything is gift packaged, of course.

□

WALNUT ACRES
Penns Creek, PA 17862
(717) 837–0601
Free catalog on request. Accepts checks, money
orders, Visa, and MasterCard. A handling charge of
$1.00 is added to all orders.

If I keep returning again and again to this organic farm in the hills of Pennsylvania, it is only because I have found them to be not only an excellent source for the health foods that are their specialty, but for so many other kinds of food that are hard, if not impossible, to have sent by mail.

Fresh vegetables, especially, are difficult to obtain from mail-order sources. Walnut Acres, however, makes several kinds available, though none are shipped in very cold, freezing weather. All are shipped in 3-pound, 15-pound, or 45-pound boxes. Carrots cost about $1.59 for 3 pounds, $6.65 for 15 pounds, or $16.50 for 45 pounds. Beets are about $1.25 for 3 pounds, $4.80 for 15 pounds, or $11.50 for 45 pounds. Potatoes sell at about 85¢ for 3 pounds, $4.00 for 15 pounds, or $8.95 for 45 pounds, to give three examples. Garlic, onions, and bell peppers are other vegetables that can be shipped fresh.

Canned vegetables, all grown on Walnut Acres, processed there and put up in #303 tins with a net weight of 16 ounces, may be ordered singly or by the case. Good savings are realized on case orders. For example, one can of diced carrots will cost 72 cents, but 24 cans sell for only $13.95, or a savings of about 14 cents a can. Among the canned vegetables offered (with the single can price given) are beans and squash in tomato sauce (75 cents); diced beets (75 cents); sweet yellow corn (68 cents); peas (66 cents); pumpkin (86 cents); sauerkraut (83 cents); tomatoes (73 cents); zucchini (72 cents); and garbanzos ($1.00), with many more available. Prices fluctuate, so check before ordering.

Beans, peas, and lentils of every sort, all of which have good keeping qualities, are also listed here, the prices ranging from as little as 56 cents per pound for yellow soybeans to as much as $1.74 per pound for mung beans. In between, there are baby limas, azukis, garbanzos, peanut beans, and split yellow or green peas.

Dried fruits include apples (about $2.49 per pound), banana

flakes (about $2.80 per pound), apricots (about $4.10 per pound), pears (about $3.20 per pound), and pineapple (about $3.50 per pound). Among the canned fruits offered are blueberries (about $1.15 for a 1-pound can), unpeeled apricot halves (about $1.10 for a 1-pound can), peaches (about 90 cents for a 1-pound can), and Bartlett pears.

In addition to dry roasted almonds and dry roasted cashews (both about $4.00 per pound), the catalog lists about a dozen more nut varieties, including pine nuts (about $3.50 per pound), raw Spanish peanuts (about $1.40 per pound), and mixed raw shelled nuts (about $2.40 per pound). There are also about a dozen types of peanut butters, including such variations as banana peanut spread, date peanut spread, and coconut peanut butter—all priced at just over $2.00 for a 1-pound jar. For more exotic appetites, there are *tahini*, a spread made from roasted sesame seeds (around $2.25 per pound), almond butter (about $4.50 per pound), and raw peanut butter (about $3.00 per pound), which is made from blanched peanuts and is said to be far stronger in flavor than butter made from the roasted nuts. All these butters and spreads are made fresh daily and, like everything from Walnut Acres, without chemical additives or preservatives.

□

CHAPTER EIGHT

SWEETS AND TREATS

The vast majority of companies in the mail-order industry offer something for the sweet tooth. Usually these goods will be in some way related to the specialty of the firm. A company selling Southern-style smoked hams, for example, is likely to offer regional delights such as pecan pie, Georgia fruitcake, or New Orleans-type pralines. Most fruit companies sell jams, jellies, preserves, and marmalades. Cookies, tortes, and sweet pastries are on the list of most companies selling baked goods. Thus you should not overlook the catalogs of companies listed in other chapters when something sweet is your desire.

With the companies listed in this chapter, however, sweetness is more than a sideline. Here you will find companies selling elegant chocolates, saltwater taffy, fudge, candy kisses, caramels, gingerbread houses, mints of every kind, and sweets for every occasion. Many of the jams and jellies offered are homemade and come in exotic as well as traditional flavors. Most are far superior to the sugared-up, almost fruitless concoctions sold in supermarkets. Pure maple syrup, that uniquely American product so easily purchased at little roadside stands in New England but becoming nearly impossible to locate in local markets, is readily available from several sources listed here, and, along with the syrup, many offer maple-sugar candies, creams, and the old-fashioned maple sugar itself. Honey, straight from the apiary to you, can be ordered in many colors and flavors, and in many forms. There is liquid honey, out of the comb and free of crystals; honey in the comb, exactly as the bees made it; candied, creamed, or churned honey; and of course all the goodies that can be made with this natural sweetener. This is not to mention all the goodies you'll be able to make yourself using the recipe booklets sent out by most companies specializing in these natural sweets and treats.

□

ANDRE'S
5018 Main Street
Kansas City, MO 64112
(816) 561–3440
*Free brochure and price list. Accepts checks, money
orders, Visa, and MasterCard.*

Chocolate *truffes* (truffles), which many consider the queen of chocolates, are the specialtry at Andre's. The rich filling called ganache is made of whipping cream and bittersweet or milk chocolate; and in some varieties, the ganache is flavored by the addition of other natural ingredients. Among the varieties sold here are coffee, rum, marzipan, hazelnut, pecan, bourbon, orange-butter, strawberry, and pineapple. All are attractively gift packaged, and all are priced at approximatley $15.00 per pound, including a number of assortments. Other interesting sweets available from this source include candied apricots and candied ginger, both dipped in bittersweet chocolate, and mint thins, which are bittersweet chocolate around a fondant center and which come in flavors such as lemon, orange, and raspberry. The apricots and ginger are priced at around $12.50 per pound, while a pound of mints costs around $11.00. All prices include shipping.

□

ASTOR CHOCOLATE CORPORATION
48-25 Metropolitan Avenue
Glendale, NY 11385
(212) 386-7400
Free catalog. Accepts checks and money orders.

Some of the most unusual (and sinfully delicious) gift items I have
seen are produced by Astor Chocolate. Among them are a solid
chocolate chess set, with the pawns, rooks, knights, bishops,
kings, queens, and even the chessboard scupltured in fine white
and dark chocolate; greeting cards for all occasions (Happy Birthday, Happy Anniversary, Get Well, I Love You, etc.) carved
from blocks of pure milk chocolate; and chocolate Love Letters,
which are 6-inch, 6-ounce initials in pure solid milk chocolate.
Prices had not yet been set on the chess set and greeting cards
when we inquired (both are new products), but the chocolate
initials, in individual gift boxes, were priced at around $4.95
apiece.

How about having your portrait done in chocolate? Astor will
print your favorite photo in real chocolate on a 3-inch milk chocolate–flavored lollipop. It would be hard to beat these as presents
to pass out at birthday parties, weddings, receptions, bar
mitzvahs, or other celebrations, and the price is reasonable
enough: 50 lollipops for about $50.00. You may also have up to
four words of copy printed aroud each picture at no additional
cost.

Less unusual but no less tasty are the bittersweet chocolate
dessert shells made by Astor. These are designed to be edible
dessert casings and may be filled with such things as fruits, ice
cream, or mousse. Minimum order is 3 boxes at around $15.95.
Along with them you might order their mocha cups, tiny chocolate cups that you fill with cream, whipped cream, cognac or liqueur and float in cups of hot coffee, letting the chocolate
dissolve to make a sinfully delicious combination. Three boxes of
mocha cups sell for around $9.50, the same price Astor charges
for three boxes of its gold foil–wrapped after-dinner mints.

□

BAILEY'S
26 Temple Place
Boston, MA 02111
Free brochure. Accepts checks and money orders; charge accounts invited. Full guarantee.

Established in 1873, Bailey's has, throughout its more than a century of existence, enjoyed as enviable and growing reputation for luscious ice cream and handmade confections. Needless to say, you can't get the ice cream by mail. You can, however, order chocolates—dark, light, or bittersweet—at about $6.50 per pound, with your choice of any mix of fillings you might imagine. Among the more than 30 cream centers are banana, checkerberry, cherry, coffee, pineapple, pistachio, raspberry, and vanilla. Four fudge centers are available. Hard centers include peanut butter chip and molasses chip. Among the two dozen or so chewy centers offered are chocolate nut caramel, mint marshmallow, and pistachio nougatine. Nut centers include peanut, filbert, and almond. Apricot and orange peel are among the fruit centers. A good way to acquaint yourself with what is available is Bailey's 1-pound 6-ounce sampler, which sells for about $8.25 and includes 53 varieties with a chart to help you keep track of those you like best. Once you know your preference, Bailey's will custom-pack boxes to suit your taste, make a record of your order, and, if you like, take a standing order for boxes to be shipped at specified intervals.

The choice here is not limited to chocolates. Offerings include about a dozen hard candies such as horehound, peanut brittle, butterscotch squares, and rock candy (all at about $3.50 per pound); jelly candies such as jelly parfaits, fruit moss, and fruit slices (all at about $3.85 per pound); and a dozen types of fudge (about $3.75 per pound). Any candy you choose can be ordered in a colorful Swiss candy box at no additional charge, or in an imported lithographed tin for about $3.00 extra.

□

BISSINGER'S, INC.
205 West Fourth Street
Cincinnati, OH 45202
(513) 241–8182
Free catalog. Accepts checks, money orders, Visa,
and MasterCard. Charge accounts invited.

In *The Chocolate Bible* (G. P. Putnam's Sons) author Adrianne Marcus says:

> Bissinger's is to chocolate candy what Emperor Louis Napoleon III was to Karl Frederick Bissinger: royalty. It was that emperor's loss when Bissinger took his leave of France, way back in 1863, and brought to the United States the recipes he had perfected as confectionist and candy maker to the emperor. There's no way anyone will mistake these chocolates for anything but noble. They're done correctly, with impeccable taste, and that includes the box.

In another book by the same author and publisher, *Quest for the Best*, Bissinger's was singled out as the finest chocolatier in America.

Though they have been in business well over a century, Bissinger's remains a small firm, and all its candy is made by hand in small batches, using many of the original formulas brought to this country by Karl Frederick Bissinger. The candy is not inexpensive, but that, according to the firm, is because they refuse to use anything but premium ingredients despite spiraling costs.

In a sampler called Our Famous Assortment, Bissinger's offers a bit of just about everything they make—nut centers, cream centers, fruit cordials, crisps, and nougats. At about $8.95 per pound, and available in a number of weights, it is their most popular offering. If you prefer an assortment with a greater concentration of nut centers and other more expensive fillings, try the Empire Selection at about $10.95 per pound.

Certain varieties from Bissinger's have become famous throughout the country and, because of their fame, are offered individually. Chocolate nut balls, created for Louis Napoleon, are prime among these. Freshly ground almost paste is packed in between plump pecans and walnuts, then hand dipped in fondant and chocolate. These are huge candies, each a dessert in itself. They sell at around $10.95 for a box of 16, with a net weight just under 2 pounds. Chocolate Bissys, another original formula, make a delightful after-dinner refresher. These are made by working milk chocolate to a creamy consistency, coating it with a special dark vanilla chocolate, adding a hint of coffee or mint flavor (your choice), and cutting to size. Ten-ounce boxes are offered at about $5.50. Sinfully rich opera creams, their vanilla cream centers coated with dark vanilla chocolate, are another favorite made by an original recipe. Also in 10-ounce boxes, these sell for just under $5.00.

Bissinger's features unique packing for all its products. Standard assortments are put up in rich-looking taupe boxes with blue lettering and tie-cord, and bear the seal: Confiseur Imperial by appointment to Emperor Louis Napoleon. If that's not impressive enough, then browse through the catalog and you'll find a 1½-pound assortment in a suede paper box embossed with silver lettering; 2 pounds of chocolates in a tin with a beautiful floral design; 4 pounds of chocolates in an elegant tin with a hinged lid and a scene embossed in silvery metal; and 5 pounds of chocolate in a tin with a black enameled background with birds on a branch reminiscent of a Chinese painting. But it is what's inside the box that counts, and I join with others in telling you that nobody puts better chocolate in a box than the folks at Bissinger's.

□

Callaway Gardens Country Store
Pine Mountain, GA 31822
Free catalog. Accepts checks, money orders, Visa, MasterCard, and American Express. Guarantees delivery in perfect condition.

The muscadine grape is a vine native to the Southeastern United States, bearing clusters of large, dull purple fruit that early settlers found being put to heavy use by the American Indians. Though many horticultural varieties have been developed from it and the closely related scuppernong grape, which bears amber-green fruit, and though all the varieties are uniquely sweet and may be used to produce jellies, syrups, sauces and preserves that are delicious to taste, these sweets remain strangers to most people in the United States. Callaway Gardens hopes to change all that.

Muscadine sauce, jelly, and preserves are the featured sweets in their beautifully illustrated catalog, which also includes a number of recipes—such as muscadine bread—for using these unusual delicacies. All are put up in 12-ounce jars, and for around $10.50 there is a sampler box that holds one jar of each.

With the exception of 2 pounds of jelly beans in an old-fashioned canning jar for about $15.50, all the sweets sold here are distinctively Southern in flavor. In addition to the muscadine products, there are wild huckleberry and blueberry preserves, crabapple and blackberry jellies, and raspberry, boysenberry, or peach preserves, all made by original recipes and all selling at about $5.00 per 20-ounce jar.

Gallberry honey is offered only as part of a package that incudes 32 ounces of honey in the comb, 16 ounces of honey removed from the comb, and 2 pounds of old-fashioned breakfast grits. The package sells for around $14.50.

□

CATHERINE'S CHOCOLATE SHOPS
Stockbridge Road
R.D. 2
Box 32
Great Barrington, MA 01230
Free catalog. Accepts checks, money orders, Visa,
and MasterCard.

Catherine Kereszetes represents the third generation of a candy-making family that entered the business in Savannah, Georgia, then later moved north to open a series of shops in Manhattan, the Bronx, White Plains, and New Jersey. Despite the growth of the company, everything is still hand-dipped, in very small batches to ensure freshness, by skilled confectioners. House specialties are stemmed cherry cordials, buttercrunch, caramel nut delights, chocolate nut bark, and pecan rolls, all put up in various assortments that sell at around $7.50 per pound.

Most popular of Catherine's offerings is the Berkshire Assortment, selling at about $6.50 per pound. It consists of nut, fruit, hard, chewy, and soft centers, hand dipped in your choice of milk, white, or bittersweet chocolate, or a combination of the three. At about $7.50 per pound there is the Yankee Fruit and Nut Assortment, or the Colonial Cream Assortment, which concentrates on centers such as butter cream, maple walnut, coffee, orange cream, raspberry, and coconut, with a few thin mints thrown in for good measure. Both are available in your choice of chocolate coating.

Creamy fudge in such forms as vanilla nut, penuche, plain chocolate, chocolate nut, peanut butter, and maple walnut is about $4.95 per pound, and fresh-from-the-kettle peanut brittle sells at around $4.50 per pound. For the small fry, there are chocolate lollipops at about $3.95 per pound, and, when the urge for something sweet but out of the ordinary strikes, you can always turn to the chocolate-covered pretzels Catherine's sells at around $6.95 per pound. There is an extra charge of $1.00 on all orders for special insulated packaging to protect your candy against temperature, but the company will add an embossed card bearing your personal greeting, when requested, at no additional cost.

□

CLARK HILL SUGARY
Canaan, NH 03741
(603) 523-7752
Free brochure. Accepts checks, money orders, Visa, and MasterCard.

"I am led to expect that a material part of the general happiness which heaven seems to have prepared for mankind will be derived from the manufacture and general use of maple sugar," wrote a citizen named Benjamin Rush in a letter to Thomas Jefferson, a few years after the American Revolution.

That "general happiness" can still be found at this tiny sugary located deep in the woods near the small town of Canaan, where a local family does all the work of tapping the trees, boiling down the sap, jugging the syrup, making the candy, and shipping their heavenly products to customers all over the world. This is maple syrup as I remember it from my childhood in New England—so pure and sweet that a taste at breakfast is in your thoughts all day—and it comes in attractive jugs that make unusual kitchen decorations. It sells at about $17.00 the half gallon, $10.00 per quart, or $6.00 per pint, with a shipping charge of $2.00 per jug.

When available, the sugary also mails its jarred maple butter and pure, old-fashioned maple-sugar candy in 1- and 2-pound tins. As with the maple syrup, there is a $2.00 postage charge on each order. A 20 percent discount is given on all orders of more than 100 units.

□

EARLY'S HONEY STAND
Rural Route 2
Spring Hill, TN 37174
(615) 486–2230
Free catalog. Accepts checks, money orders,
MasterCard, and Visa; no CODs.

Today Early's Honey Stand is nationally famous for the high quality of its smoked meats and other Southern-style food. But about sixty years ago, when it all began with a little roadside stand in the Tennessee Hills, honey made by their own bees was the only product offered by the Earlys.

The bees are still busy in the Tennessee countryside, and the honey still flows. Most of the honey the bees make from the pollen of the local Dutch white clover, and this the Earlys offer at about $6.35 per quart, or around $3.70 for a 12-ounce bear-shaped squeeze-bottle. Also available is the new Honeypak (about $10.95)—four 1-pound jars of honey in a gift box. There is one jar of liquid clover honey, one jar of clover honey with the honeycomb still in, one jar of wildflower honey—actually a blend of several different varieties, and one jar of the rare and delicious sourwood honey. Included at no extra cost is a booklet with 68 recipes for using honey in cooking.

Among the other sweets sold by Early's are such old-fashioned delicacies as pear, strawberry-rhubarb, and rhubarb-raspberry preserves. For about $8.85 you can order a box holding one 11-ounce jar of each preserve plus a 9-ounce jar of old-fashioned green tomato relish. Other unusual goodies include corncob jelly and sweet watermelon-rind pickles, five 7½-ounce jars for about $11.15. Also available is sparkling apple cider. Put up in 25-ounce champagne-style bottles and gift boxed, two bottles are offered for just under $10.00.

Few old-time sorghum makers are around today, but Early's has contacts with one, and they say he cooks the sorghum in an open pan, just as in the old days. In any case, the molasses comes out a beautiful amber color, just the right thickness. It sells at about $7.95 per quart. Or you can order a pair of ceramic "moonshine" jugs—both filled with 12 ounces of sorghum, both filled with honey, or one of each—for around $9.25. Because of the shipping methods used by Early's and the way they calculate shipping and handling charges, prices will vary slightly according to where you live.

□

FERRARA FOOD & CONFECTIONS, INC.
195-201 Grand Street
New York, NY 10013
(212) 226-6150
Free brochure and price list on request. Accepts checks and money orders only. There is a $10.00 delivery charge on orders of less than $150.00.

Ferrara Foods, as the oldest Italian confectionery company in the United States, offers a tremendous array of sweet specialties from around the world. The average buyer encounters certain problems here, however, mainly because of their high minimum order requirement and the fact that so many items are sold only by the case. If you are involved in fund raising, have a very long gift list, or have a group of friends willing to split an order with you, then such problems become no problem at all and the Ferrara catalog is one you will want in your possession. Remember that I am giving single-unit prices here and that, in nearly all instances, you must buy a case of 12 or 24 units if your order is to be accepted.

A number of sweet syrups (almond, mint, raspberry, and grenadine among them) are offered at 92 cents per 4-ounce bottle. Cherries in brandy, imported from Italy and made with the world-famous cherries that grow in the countryside around Bologna, sell at 85 cents per 12½-ounce jar. For an additional charge, your private label can be put on either of these items.

Imported chocolate includes gold foil–wrapped chocolate snails from Switzerland and French cooking chocolate (both at $4.50 per pound), as well as four types of Swiss chocolate bars (au lait, semisweet, fruit and nut mix, and hazelnut), the 3-ounce bars priced at 76 cents each. Wrapped mints, available in a number of flavors, are priced at $1.35 per pound. Fourteen-ounce nougat bars, available in vanilla, orange, lemon, or assorted flavors, are priced at $2.68 per bar. Petit babas, delightful little cakes gently bathed in rum that are especially good with custard or ice cream, are put up in 14-ounce jars and tins that sell at $1.60 apiece. These have extremely good keeping quality, so that need not be a worry when ordering the quantity required by Ferrara.

□

FIGI'S, INC.
Marshfield, WI 54404
(715) 387–1771
Free catalog. Accepts checks, money orders,
MasterCard, Visa, and American Express; no CODs.
Full guarantee.

Once again I must mention Figi's, a company that seems to offer something for every taste and every budget, as well as for most holidays and all seasons. When you contact Figi's, you receive not just one but a number of catalogs, each devoted to a specific holiday and gifts especially suited for that occasion.

Hundreds of sweet gifts are pictured in the Valentine's Day edition, among them chocolate Love Letters, the word LOVE spelled out in solid milk chocolate 2½ inches high, weighing about 5 ounces and beautifully boxed. The Love Letters sell for around $5.95. In addition to the ordinary heart-shaped boxes of chocolates, Figi's offers a heart-shaped confection cake, 1 pound of cherry-chocolate batter loaded with candied fruit and crunchy nuts, then topped with candied cherry halves, at a cost of just under $8.00.

For Mother's Day, a few selections from their special catalog include Sweet Thoughts, a beautifully boxed assortment that includes 8 ounces of crispy honey-nut popcorn, 6 ounces of creamy Danish mints, 7 ounces of assorted chocolate mints, 2 ounces petits fours, 2 ounces macaroons, and 10 ounces hand-decorated party cookies. The price is about $16.95. Hearts 'n Roses, selling for about $8.95, is a simple yet elegant box of long-stemmed poly-silk roses and 7 ounces of gold foil–wrapped milk chocolate hearts. Corsage and Candy, for about $13.95, is a beautiful 1-pound box of milk chocolate Bavarian mints topped with a poly-silk corsage that, according to the catalog, can be worn again and again.

Interesting gifts fill the Easter catalog. My eye was quickly caught by a frilled Easter bonnet filled with 7 ounces of Danish mints, and by the Candy Carousel, a 15-ounce lithographed tin of pastel Jordan almonds, chocolate-covered toffee brittle, and crunchy almond butter toffee squares. Also very tempting is the Easter Collection, an 11-inch white wicker basket overflowing with various mints, milk chocolate eggs, and Jordan almonds. Net weight of the candy is 1 pound; the price is under $12.00.

Sweets fill pages in the special Christmas edition of the catalog. You can order 2 full pounds of Jelly Bellies, the gourmet jelly beans made famous by their appearance on the desk of President Reagan, in an 8-inch fluted glass jar with a lid resembling the Capitol dome. The fifteen flavors include such jelly bean rarities as coffee, tangerine, and coconut, and the jar sells for just under $17.00. Available not only at Christmas but throughout the year is Honey Bunch, four 4-ounce jars filled with basswood, buckwheat, clover, and wildflower honeys, at a cost of about $12.00. To excite the young at Christmastime, though, the ideal offering is a honey-sweet gingerbread house with a hinged roof that lifts to reveal 1½-pounds of old-fashioned hard Christmas candy; the price, around $11.00. Young and old alike will be delighted by the 11-ounce foil-wrapped pure chocolate kisses that sell for about $5.95 apiece, or by the bright red wooden crates loaded with 16 ounces of small milk chocolate hearts wrapped in red, silver, and gold foil. Each crate sells for around $7.95. Fudge lovers will appreciate a decorative box that sells for around $8.50 and holds 6 ounces each of chocolate walnut, chocolate black walnut, vanilla nut, and maple nut fudge. For those who prefer the crunchier sweets, Figi's offers a 1-pound tin of butter almond toffee squares, each square laced with almonds and dipped in milk chocolate, then topped with crushed, toasted almonds. The tin sells for just under $10.00.

Special holidays aside, Figi's offers, throughout the year, literally hundreds of sweets and treats so enticing that their catalog belongs in the collection of anyone who orders food through the mail.

□

GREEN MOUNTAIN SUGAR HOUSE
R.F.D. 1
Ludlow, VT 05149
(802) 228-7151
Free brochure. Accepts checks, money orders, Visa, and MasterCard.

The family that operates Green Mountain Sugar House began making maple syrup and candy nearly fifty years ago. Today, with two sugarhouses—one on the main road and one hidden deep in the woods—the company is one of the largest producers in southern Vermont. Strawberries from surrounding fields and cold, fresh cider from an old-fashioned press are sold to visitors during the summer and autumn. The sugarhouse produces candy on a weekly basis to ensure freshness, and the country gift shop on the premises sells not only maple products but such regional favorites as cheese, cob-smoked bacon and ham, rum-flavored mincemeat, cider jelly, and Indian pudding. Nearly all of these are shipped by mail, singly or in various combination packages, but maple products account for most of the business done by this firm.

There are three grades of Vermont table syrup, plus one grade generally used only for cooking. All are made to weigh 11 pounds to the gallon. Those with the lightest color and the most delicate flavor are the most expensive. Vermont Fancy, most expensive of all, ranges in price from about $7.05 per pint to around $28.60 per gallon. Vermont Grade B, least costly of the table syrups, sells at around $6.75 per pint or $27.00 per gallon. Grade C, suitable for cooking and not offered in pints, sells at about $8.00 per quart or $21.00 per gallon. Shipping costs for syrup are extra but they are included in the price of all other items.

Fresh maple candy, molded into the traditional maple-leaf shapes, sell at about $7.00 for a 10-ounce box. Maple fudge, made with pure maple syrup, cream, and nuts, sells at around $6.70 per pound. Solid blocks of old-fashioned hard-grained maple sugar, delicious when cut and eaten as candy, sells at about $9.60 per pound. Maple cream, which is pure maple syrup cooked down to a thicker consistency, then beaten to make a granular cream that will spread easily on toast or graham crackers, costs around $7.85 for a 1-pound jar. Creamed honey, another delightful spread, sells at about $4.35 per pound. For those not familiar with the pure maple products but wanting to give them a try, there is a combination package that includes 1 pint of Grade A maple syrup, a 1-pound jar of maple cream, and 6 pieces of maple candy for around $15.25.

□

HARBOR SWEETS
P.O. Box 150
Marblehead, MA 01945
(617) 745-7648
Free brochure. Accepts checks and money orders only.

Some years ago, Ben Strohecker, who had worked as an executive for a candy manufacturer, began to make candy in the kitchen of his home with the help of his wife and teenage children. It was purely a hobby until he donated a batch to his church for sale at a fund-raising fair. His candy was a tremendous success, friends and neighbors began asking to buy more as gifts, and Ben Strohecker was almost literally forced into the candy business. But he loves it, as you will love his candy. Sales have reached $750,000 per year, his candies have been made on special order for New York's Lincoln Center, the Metropolitan Museum, the Boston Symphony, and companies throughout the United States. Publications such as *Gourmet* and the *Boston Globe* have rated him one of the finest chocolatiers in America.

Strohecker claims a burning ambition to make "the very best chocolates in the world, regardless of cost," a pursuit that, he admits, has put Harbor Sweets in the "very expensive" category, meaning his candy is priced by the piece rather than by weight.

The Sweet Sloop, his most famous confection, came about through improvising. "I had been planning to make a pennant in a triangular shape, because everyone else seemed to be making them square and I have an aversion to doing what everyone else does. I had been making an almond butter crunch, cutting it into triangles, covering it with dark chocolate, and then dusting the outside with chopped nuts," he explains. "But I ran out of dark chocolate one day and dipped the top in white chocolate because it was all I had on hand. All of a sudden, it looked very different. My son said, 'It's a sailboat!' and my wife suggested we call it 'Sweet Sloop.'" Thus legends are born. The outlines of a sloop is clear in these candies; the mainsail and the jib are the white chocolate; the crushed pecans at the base are the spindrift; the dark chocolate is the sea. The delicious almond butter crunch inside, I suppose, you could call the cargo. Sweet Sloops cost around $11.50 for the basic box of 28 pieces (about 12 ounces), and are available in larger boxes, a number of decorative containers, or in combination with other candies made by Harbor Sweets.

Sand Dollars rank second in popularity among these. These are pecan halves sunk in a spoonful of soft, creamy caramel, then dipped in dark chocolate to emerge as round as the small sea creature after which it was named. It is then stamped with the striations that mark the real one and, like everything else here, wrapped in gold foil. Sand Dollars cost about $11.50 for a box of 17; around $21.00 for a box of 34.

Next in line come Marblehead Mints, "a rounded sea and sky of bittersweet chocolate delicately flavored with peppermint starlights and embossed with a sailboat." Marblehead Mints are priced at approximately $11.50 for a box of 30 silver dollar–sized pieces; around $21.00 for a box of 60.

When Strohecker polled his customers, asking, "If you could eat but one more chocolate, what would it be?" the leading response, he says, was "toasted almond bark." So he created his own nautical version, Barque Sarah, dark chocolate so full of toasted almonds it's almost guaranteed to break into bite-sized pieces. Each slab, of course, bears the imprint of a seagoing barque. An 11-ounce slab, wrapped in gold foil and placed in a bright red box with a mahogany satin ribbon, sells for around $11.50.

Personal service is a specialty of Harbor Sweets, and, in addition to the many gift assortments they have already made up, they will make up orders to your specifications if you call them. They will even arrange, at your request, for a local florist to supply and deliver fresh flowers along with your gift of candy, a unique idea my husband might consider.

□

HARRY AND DAVID'S BEAR CREEK CONFECTIONERY
Bear Creek Orchards
Medford, OR 97501
Free catalog on request. Accepts checks and money orders only; no CODs.

Bear Creek Confectionery, the newest addition to the little empire Harry and David seem to be building out in the Pacific Northwest, sends out a temptingly illustrated catalog no lover of good food should overlook when seeking a source for the finest in sweets. The goodies pictured here are so rich looking one is tempted to ask them for a loan.

Assorted chocolates, made from scratch on the premises, are put together from an impressive list of ingredients: French vanilla dark chocolate, creamy milk chocolate, cashews, macadamias, walnuts, filberts, Khadrawi dates, whole cherries, apricot morsels, rum, mint, and custom-made peanut butter. These go into confections that are all made by original recipes, and approximately $28.00 brings a 2½-pound box with 12 varieties.

Hand-decorated petits fours, especially useful as a fancy dessert that can be served on the spur of the moment, sell at about $12.95 per pound, and there is Fruitcake Confection, which won a gold medal for Harry and David in international competition at the Monde Selection trials in Geneva and which is more akin to candy than to cake, at around $14.95 for 2 pounds of sweetness.

Harry and David offer their own version of that elegant

French dessert, Mousse au Chocolat, actually a 1-pound block of fine milk chocolate that sells for about $12.95. An extravagant chocolate torte, each layer separated with chocolate buttercream and the 9-inch-high torte thickly coated with chocolate fudge and milk chocolate sprinkles, sells for around $26.95. It weighs nearly 4 pounds and serves 20, so the price is not really excessive.

When considering sweet things from the kitchen of Harry and David, don't overlook the award-winning fruit preserves they have been selling for years. Made in small batches from fruit native to the Pacific Northwest, the five varieties are strawberry, red raspberry, peach, wild blackberry, and wild plum. A ¾-pound tin of each variety costs about $14.95. Postage is always prepaid on orders from Harry and David.

□

HAWAIIAN HOLIDAY COMPANY
P.O. Box 707
Honokaa, HI 96727
(800) 367–5150; within Hawaii, call 775–7221
Free catalog. Accepts checks, money orders, Visa,
and MasterCard. Full guarantee.

At Hawaiian Holiday, the macadamia nut is king. Five years ago, when this nut-processing plant was taken over by Paul De-Domenico—who had been an executive with a chocolate company back on the mainland—and his wife, Anita, the company was one of the smallest in the business, and its list of products was limited to the macadamia in all its usual forms. Then Paul DeDomenico put his candy-making and marketing experience to work, and today Hawaiian Holiday is one of the largest companies of its kind in the industry, selling more than 160 nut and candy products to over 400,000 customers throughout the world. The macadamias can still be had roasted, dry roasted, salted or unsalted, flavored or unflavored. They are put up in cases of six 5-ounce tins, and sell at about $18.60 per case. A number of assortments are available at slightly higher prices. From that point on in the catalog you will begin to see some sweetly amazing things done with the macadamia—described by this company as "the perfect nut."

A few of the items, such as macadamia nut brittle and macadamia nut–coconut brittle (about $8.95 for one 8-ounce tin of each) are among the expected. Then you begin to encounter items such as jams that combine macadamia nuts with guava, pineapple, papaya, strawberry, or ginger and orange (five 10-ounce jars, one of each flavor, for approximately $17.95); macadamia nut blossom honey and macadamia nut honey spread (two 12-ounce jars of each for around $16.95); and Diamond Heads, which are perfect whole macadamias dipped in rich creamy chocolate (about $16.95 for three 5-ounce boxes).

These are followed by nut clusters, Rocky Road (nuts and marshmallows in milk chocolate), Islanders (a milk chocolate and nut crunch), Tikis (nuts and raisins in milk chocolate), Nut Chews (nut-filled caramels in milk chocolate), and Coconut Islanders (coconut added to the Islanders described above)—all at around $6.95 for two 6-ounce boxes.

Also available from Hawaiian Holiday is Kona coffee, one of the rarest of all coffees and thought to be the finest of all by many coffee connoisseurs. Grown only on the Big Island of Hawaii, the coffee is nearly impossible to obtain elsewhere. Hawaiian Holiday has it in three forms: roasted whole beans, pure Kona coffee, and a blend. For around $17.95, you receive one 7-ounce tin of each type, with other assortments available. A macadamia nut cookbook is sent free with any order of $100.00 or more.

☐

HERSHEY'S CHOCOLATE WORLD
Mail Order Department
Park Boulevard
Hershey, PA 17033
(717) 534–4900
Free catalog. Accepts checks, money orders, Visa,
and MasterCard. Full guarantee.

Milton Hershey was the epitome of the American dream. Although his early years were marked by several business reversals, by the time he was 40 he had achieved success as the owner of a caramel factory in Lancaster, Pennsylvania. He had already been studying the chocolate market, and his research convinced him that the nation was ready for a tasty, inexpensive chocolate bar with nutritional value. In 1900, at the age of 43, he sold his caramel business for a million dollars. Returning to his birthplace near Derry Church, Pennsylvania, he set out to test his theory by starting a chocolate factory near the dairy rich farms of south central Pennsylvania. The location was chosen so he could rely on the availability of the fresh milk so essential to his basic product—milk chocolate. The company achieved immediate success. Production began in 1906, and sales had reached $5 million by 1911. Today the plant has more than 3 million square feet of floor space, uses the daily milk production of more than 50,000 cows, turns out over 125,000 cases of chocolate products daily, and Hershey's confectionery products are sold to some 65,000 wholesalers and retailers in 20,000 towns and cities.

Nearly all the familiar Hershey's products are shipped by mail, including what may be the ultimate chocolate bar. A full foot and a half long, it weighs in at 10 pounds and sells for around $40.00. For lesser appetites, there is a bar the same length but weighing just 5 pounds, which is available for about $27.50. A giant foil-wrapped kiss (weight not given) is offered for about $3.00, and standard-sized kisses are offered in a number of different packages, most priced at about $4.50 per pound.

The Golden Almond bar, which consists of roughly equal parts of nuts and chocolate, is one of the newer members of the family. Five bars (net weight 1 pound) sell for about $4.85, and a number of gift boxes are available. All the candies of the Reese's Company, including their famous Peanut Butter Cups, are also found in this catalog, since this company was acquired by Hershey's a number of years ago.

□

HUTMACHER CHOCOLATES
40-32 162 Street
Flushing, NY 11358
(212) 445–9011
Free brochure and price list. Accepts checks, money orders, Visa, and MasterCard.

Hutmacher offers only imported Swiss chocolates, "delicately blended by master *confiseurs* using only fresh sweet cream, farm fresh butter, and pure natural ingredients without preservatives or artificial colors." All chocolates are flown from Zurich to New York via Swissair, arriving the same day, and all orders are filled from the newly arrived shipments, never from inventory.

All this is expensive, of course. The smallest box of chocolates offered (219 grams, or 7½ ounces) costs nearly $12.00 plus shippng, while the largest box (1,800 grams, or 64 ounces) costs well over $100.00. Filled truffles include varieties such as vanilla, mocha, champagne, caramel, nougat, white chocolate, and solid dark chocolate centers. A number of nut centers are also available, and all chocolates are shipped in deluxe fabric-covered boxes.

□

DAN JOHNSON'S SUGAR HOUSE
Route 1
Box 265
Jaffrey, NH 03452
(603) 532-7379
Free price list. Accepts checks and money orders only.

Dan Johnson, who operates an old-time maple syrup business in the foothills of Mount Monadnock, swears that his maple syrup is thicker and tastier than the competition's. It is packed in attractive jugs from a half pint (around $5.50, or 6 for about $22.75) to a half gallon (about $17.00, or 6 for around $87.50). By advance notice, you can reserve syrup from the first run—usually the best—each season. Johnson says syrup from the first run is lighter in color, higher in sugar content and maple flavor, and strongly urges his customers to place reserve orders.

Johnson also runs a school for those hardy souls who might be thinking of entering the maple syrup business. The two-day course costs around $245.00 per person and is available throughout the year, since Johnson has located a year-round source for sap. It covers all phases of sugaring, from learning to identify and tap the trees to marketing the syrup, and each student goes home with a gallon of maple syrup he or she has made. For more information about transportation, accommodations, and the school itself, call Johnson's.

□

LAMME'S CANDIES
P.O. Box 1885
Austin, TX 78767
Free brochure. Accepts checks and money orders
only. All prices include delivery anywhere in the
continental United States.

In 1885, when cattle were still crossing the Old Chisolm Trail through Austin and pecan trees lined the banks of the Colorado River where it wound through the city, D. T. Lamme opened a small candy shop near the Texas capitol. During the next few years, he began buying up the locally grown pecans and using them in a variety of recipes, and soon he had developed the confection he eventually named the Texas Chewie Pecan Praline, a sweet he made only in small batches for friends and special customers. Soon visitors to Austin began asking that they be added to his list, and by 1920 Mr. Lamme had been drawn into the mail-order business. Today the colorful little brochure put out by his company and his candy reaches thousands of customers throughout America and the world.

Texas Chewie Pecan Pralines are just what the name suggests, an irresistible blend of rich caramel and Texas pecans so chewably moist that to bite into one is to enter into a delicious taste experience you will not soon forget. The toasted pecans temper the sweetness of the caramel, making the taste less cloying than most pralines, and it is little wonder that, after all these years, the Texas Chewies remain the most popular candy sold by Lamme's. The cost is around $7.75 per pound.

Texas Longhorns, another popular offering, are Texas pecans clusted in caramel and covered with milk chocolate. They sell at about $6.85 per pound. Slightly higher in price (at $7.25 or so per pound), Lamme's Almond Crunch is a crisp English toffee with an almond butter flavor and a coating of milk chocolate, topped with toasted almonds.

In addition to these house specialties, Lamme's offers a number of other candies, including mint kisses (around $7.60 per 2-pound box), pecan divinity (about $7.30 per pound), almond toffee (about $5.00 per pound), and a number of chocolate assortments, average cost about $7.00 per pound.

□

LIBERTY ORCHARDS COMPANY, INC.
Cashmere, WA 98815
(509) 782–2191
*Free brochure. Accepts checks, money orders, Visa,
and Mastercard.*

Back in 1920, two Armenians, Armen Tertsagian and Mark Bal-
aban, began using fruit juices and walnuts from America's Pacific
Northwest to produce a confection similar to the *rabat lacom,* or
"Turkish delight," they had known back in their native land.
Their cooking process used fruit juices, corn syrup, confectioners'
sugar, and a secret blend of flavors. After the candy was boiled,
the walnut pieces would be added, and the candy chilled, cut,
and dusted with cornstarch and powdered sugar. They sold this
delicious candy at roadside fruit stands throughout the state of
Washington. For many years, only an apple-flavored candy, sold
as Aplets, was made, then came the apricot-flavored Cotlets, and
finally Grapelets. No other products are made by the company,
but this trio has been so successful that white-clad workers now
manufacture more than 9,000 pounds of candy daily, and 15,000
visitors tour the plant each year to see this unusual candy being
made.

Long familiar to retail buyers in the Pacific Northwest but
largely unknown outside that region, Aplets, Cotlets, and Grapelets are ultrasweet, jellylike confections with just a bit of walnut
crunchiness in each nugget. The natural fruit flavor comes
through loud and clear in each variety, and those I received
gained quick favor with the youngsters around my house. A 5-
ounce box of any flavor costs around $3.80, and there is a 13-
ounce box, half Aplets and half Cotlets, available for about $7.25,
or a 13-ounce box of Grapelets for around the same price. Candy-
bar sized (¾ ounce) pieces are a new addition to the line, with 24
of any flavor offered for just over $10.00. Though all these come
in attractive satin-finish boxes suitable for gifts, a number of special holiday gift boxes (Christmas, Valentine's Day, etc.) are offered, none costing more than about $10.00. Prices include
delivery.

□

Li-Lac Chocolates, Inc.
120 Christopher Street
New York, NY 10014
(212) 242–7374
*Free brochure and price list. Accepts checks, money
orders, Visa, MasterCard, American Express, and
Diners Club.*

Li-Lac Chocolates has been a Greenwich Village landmark since
1923, when the original owner and creator of the master formulas, George Demitro, opened his shop at its present location.
Today, the third owner, Edward Bond, continues the tradition by
creating Li-Lac Chocolates from the same closely guarded formulas that pleased customers when the store first opened. All
chocolates are handmade and hand-dipped fresh daily in small
batches, using only the finest ingredients.

One of the special features of this store is the wide selection
of bars and rolls, including nut truffle rolls, plain and nut caramel
rolls, mocha rolls, napoleon rolls, rum and chocolate mousse
rolls, raspberry jelly and fudge bars, and the French roll dipped
in chocolate and sprinkled with jimmies (most are 95 cents each).

Offerings include the French Assortment, an appealing collection of dark chocolates filled with mocha, praline, rum, *truffe,*
creams, and marzipan; the Continental Assortment, a selection of
pecans, walnuts, pistachios, Brazil nuts, filberts, almonds, and
cashews dipped in dark or milk chocolate; and the Fruit & Nut
Assortment, featuring dark and milk chocolate over raisins, figs,
dates, walnuts, pistachios, almonds, apricots, cherries, pineapple, and more. These three popular assortments are all priced at
about $16.00 per pound.

Far less expensive, but no less popular are candies such as
fudge, peanut brittle, almond bark, and cashew, pecan, or walnut
chews, these offered at prices ranging from $6.00 to $12.00 per
pound. Shipping charges are extra here.

□

MARY OF PUDDIN HILL
P.O. Box 241
Greenville, TX 75401
(214) 455-2651
Free catalog. Accepts checks, money orders, Visa,
MasterCard, and American Express. Full guarantee.

Back in 1947, Mary Lauderdale and her husband, Sam, were having a hard time making ends meet on the $90 a month they received under the G.I. Bill. So Mary, who had just received her degree in home economics, took a few cases of fruit donated by her parents and entered the fruitcake business. That first year she baked and sold 500 pounds of fruitcake, but the cake was enthusiastically received by the public, the business grew rapidly, and this year Mary of Puddin Hill will ship more than 175,000 pounds of fruitcake to customers all over the world.

The fruitcake, which holds far more nuts than most and ranks as one of the best I tasted, is still the Lauderdales' most popular item and is available in a number of sizes: a large round ring (4½ pounds, about $24.00), a loaf cake (2¾ pounds, around $16.50), and a small loaf cake (1¾ pounds, about $11.95), all prices including delivery. By using her original recipe but substituting English walnuts for the pecans, Mary came up with a deliciously different version of the traditional cake that she sells at slightly lower prices. Then there are Little Puds—bite-sized pieces of the pecan fruitcake that Mary boxes up with spiced, sugar-coated pecan halves. For about $16.00, you receive 16 of the Little Puds and 11 ounces of the glistening, sugar-coated pecan halves.

Fruitcake may well have started it all, but today Mary of Puddin Hill is much more than a fruitcake bakery; it is a full-line confectionery that offers some of the most interesting, most delightful candies you will find in any catalog.

As expected, this being a Texas firm, there are pralines, creamy, chewy and crammed with pecans. They can be ordered in a 2-pound box for about $14.50, or in a 1-pound miniature, reusable bushel basket for around $10.95.

Less expected are Fan-taste-ics, which, according to the Lauderdales, were created when their daughter, Pud, had a hard time choosing between a piece of fruitcake and a piece of chocolate. The answer? You guessed it: bite-sized pieces of chocolate-covered fruitcake. They come in dark or light chocolate, 25 pieces of each (net weight 21 ounces) for just under $15.00.

Then there are Scutterbotches, golden morsels of pure, old-fashioned butterscotch laced with liberal helpings of peanuts and raisins, selling at about $10.95 per pound. Thingamajigs, another original, are made with a base of rich caramel and fresh pecans, then coated with fine white chocolate. They sell at about $11.25 per pound.

In addition to old-fashioned hard candies (4 pounds in a decorative tin pail, around $18.50), chocolate truffles (1 pound in a reusable wicker basket, around $24.95), coffee crunch (a 14-ounce box for about $10.50), almond toffee (about $12.50 for a 1-pound 2-ounce box), and pecan fudge balls (about $11.95 for a 1½-pound box), Mary of Puddin Hill offers what may qualify as the most unusual confection offered by any company in the mail-order industry: Cotton Bolls. These are clusters of creamy white chocolate generously mixed with roasted cotton seeds, a remarkably tasty idea. The Cotton Bolls arrive wrapped in a burlap sack so the package resembles a cotton bale, and the 1-pound box sells for around $11.95. Hush my mouth!

□

PEPPERIDGE FARM
P.O. Box 119
Clinton, CT 06143
(800) 243–9314; within Connecticut, call collect 669–9245.
Free catalog. Accepts checks, money orders, Visa,
MasterCard, and American Express. $10.00
minimum on phone orders.

Among the many reasons for obtaining the Pepperidge Farm catalog is the fact that they are one of the few by-mail sources for world-famous Godiva chocolates, a brand held in the highest regard by chocolate lovers the world over. And not only does Pepperidge Farm distribute the sweet artwork produced by Godiva, it also buys bulk chocolate from this famous confectioner and uses that in many of its own delicious concoctions. For example, there are chocolate petits fours, thin layers of cake and raspberry buttercream filling coated with Godiva chocolate. Ten ounces in a red-and-white gift box costs about $9.50. The same combination of raspberry buttercream filling and Godiva chocolate goes into their Torte à la Godiva. It weighs over 1 pound, serves 10 to 14, and sells for about $12.95.

For those who have never enjoyed the Godiva experience, there is a 1-pound sampler tin for around $20.00. It contains an assortment of milk and dark chocolates, each piece a work of art. Pieces are shaped like feathers, hearts, walnuts, crowns, and scallop shells, and they hold all the favorite fillings—creams, fruits, pralines, mocha, even Cognac. These are chocolates to be savored slowly, on special occasions, with coffee or a cordial.

If you are already a devotee of Godiva chocolates, as millions are, you can order from Pepperidge Farm entire boxes of just your favorite pieces, all in fancy, beribboned ballotins that hold hours of eating ecstasy. Specialties such as chocolate-covered cherries with kirsch, chocolate mousse in milk chocolate, butterscotch caramel in milk chocolate, raspberry buttercream in milk or dark chocolate, and fruit and nut centers are available. Average cost is $14.00 for a box of about 11 ounces.

Sculpted chocolate is Godiva's forte and they offer chocolate artwork to match every interest and occasion. There are chocolate golf balls, the center of each dimpled ball filled with pralines and buttercrunch (three balls, 4½ ounces, about $9.00); tennis tins filled with butter creams flavored with Grand Marnier (around $15.00 per tin, weight not given); and even chocolate shotgun shells, boxed exactly like the real ones, each chocolate shell loaded with praline filling, gold foil at the end making them look like they could be used for hunting (11½-ounce box of 25 shells, about $25.00). My personal favorite is the open oyster, a milk chocolate piece in the shape of an open bivalve, with a center of praline and dark chocolate. The oysters cost about $14.00 for a 10½-ounce box.

For after-dinner elegance, there are Godiva liqueur cups, each with an outer cup of gold foil, making it possible for you to serve your favorite liqueur in some of the world's finest chocolate, a box of 24 cups selling for around $12.00. And for another exciting dimension in dessert creativity, there are Godiva toppings, available in six intriguing flavors: chocolate with crème de menthe, with Cognac, with crème de cocoa, butterscotch with rum, strawberry with bourbon, or raspberry with cognac. All sell at about $5.50 per 10½-ounce jar, and all sound like excellent choices when it comes time to top off your most elaborate dinner party.

□

PLUMBRIDGE
30 East 67 Street
New York, NY 10021
(212) 371-0608
Free brochure. Accepts checks, money orders, Visa, MasterCard, Diners Club, and American Express.

Where did Jacqueline Bouvier shop for candy when she was in Manhattan? She headed—as Mrs. Onassis still does—for Plumbridge, a shop many regard as the Cartier of confectioners, a shop that, since opening its doors to the carriage trade in 1883, has been catering to old-line New York families like the Roosevelts, the Belmonts, the Rockefellers, and the Fricks. These days its clientele includes such celebrities as Paul Anka (who simply gives the store a budget and has them send out hundreds of gifts), Frank Sinatra, Liza Minnelli, and Claudette Colbert. One anonymous movie star is said to have spent $14,000 there during a single day of Christmas shopping.

That Plumbridge candies are expensive even the owner, Douglas Petrillo, does not deny. But that frequently is because of the ingenious packaging—which ranges from a tiny $2.50 heart-shaped chrome box for cinnamon candy to a nineteenth-century Chinese porcelain bowl filled with jelly beans at $1,250—and because of the special care that goes into making up each order.

"Before we make up gift orders," Petrillo explains, "we like to know everything about the recipients, what they like, whether they own a horse or a yacht. We are so finicky we even have major debates about what kinds of ribbons to put on the packages."

You may not own a horse or a yacht, you are probably not a Kennedy or a Rockefeller, and you may not even be able to visit the old New York brownstone that houses Plumbridge. but their fairly new mail-order service does make it possible for you to enjoy the many luxurious confections they offer. Chocolates are not shipped during the hottest months of summer, but even then Plumbridge will make up assortments guaranteed to win the heart and soul of any fancier of fine sweets.

Several New York writers have suggested that the Plumbridge experience would be incomplete without a taste of their spiced pecans (about $15.00 per pound), which are coated with brown sugar and cinnamon, and roasted fresh each day. These are their hottest item, followed closely by the chocolate-coated French mocha nuts (about $13.00 per pound) and their dragée chocolates, dripping layers of semisweet chocolate with fillings such as coffee, orange peel, raisins, and nearly everything that has ever been glazed with chocolate (about $14.00 per pound).

Caramels, whipped creme mints, Russian mints, chocolate-covered coffee beans, orange peel bits in dark chocolate, and chocolate truffles—all sell for about $13.00 a pound. Tiny pectin jelly beans, and assorted fruit and spice jelly candies are $5.00 to $6.00 per pound, and there is a special 1-pound gift selection of the most popular chocolates for about $15.00.

Queen Bees are an unusual candy you might enjoy. Each Queen Bee is a candy shell with a liquid center of pure clover honey. You can order these in a number of delightful packages, including a hive-shaped tin swarming with ¾ of a pound of Queen Bees for around $12.50, or in a handmade picnic basket that holds a canning jar filled with 16 ounces of pure clover honey, a 6-ounce bag of Queen Bees, and a 6-ounce bag of peanut-butter filled candies, for about $20.00. Alone, the Queen Bees are about $5.00 per pound.

Special packages featured in the brochure range from burlap bags that cost nothing extra to wooden cabinets for which you may be charged as much as $90.00. Plumbridge will fill these almost any way you like, and you are invited to call in your special orders, or stop by for free samples whenever you are in New York City.

□

THE POPCORN FACTORY
966 North Shore Drive
Lake Bluff, IL 60044
(800) 621–5559
Free catalog. Accepts checks, money orders, Visa,
MasterCard, and American Express. Credit
application sent on request.

Laura Cretors, owner of The Popcorn Factory, says it was her
five-year-old daughter, Annie Cretors, who inspired the trade-
marked symbol, "Annie's Best," for their popcorn products. But
she also points out that popcorn has long been associated with
the Cretors name; it was little Annie's great-great-grandfather,
Charles Cretors, who patented the first popcorn-popping ma-
chine and founded C. Cretors & Company, which has been producing them in Chicago for over 95 years.

Founded just five years ago, The Popcorn Factory has met
with amazing success. Perhaps in response to the question asked
on the front of their catalog, "How can you forget someone who
sends you 6½ gallons of popcorn?" the public has swamped the
little factory with orders, especially at Christmastime. Its sales
have more than doubled during each year of its existence.

About that 6½ gallons of popcorn, the featured offering of The
Popcorn Factory:

> We begin with our own specially grown hybrid popping
> corn. Then each kernel is popped to perfection in pure
> coconut oil. But even though each puffy piece is already
> superior to the popcorn most people are familiar with, we
> make it even better. We coat it with pure creamy butter
> flavor, aged Cheddar cheese, or homemade caramel.
> Then, while it's still warm, we pop it into airtight cans, so
> when people open our popcorn, it will be just as fresh and
> satisfying as when we popped it.

The 6½-gallon can may be ordered with all buttered popcorn for
about $18.95, with half buttered and half cheese-flavored for
around $21.00, with one-third buttered, one-third cheese, and
one-third caramel (the most popular assortment) for about
$25.00, or half buttered and half caramel for about $30.00. For

lesser appetites, there is a 2-gallon can, all buttered for about
$12.50, or divided into thirds of buttered, cheese-flavored, and
caramel-coated for under $18.00. All cans are beautifully litho-
graphed, with a number of themes available.

If you prefer to do your own popping, or prefer to give un-
popped popcorn as an unusual gift, there is a kit available for
about $14.95. It includes enough hybrid popcorn, pure coconut
oil, and special seasoned salt to produce, according to the company, 6½ gallons of popcorn. And if you are a real popcorn en-
thusiast, The Popcorn Factory may have just the item you have
been searching for. It is a professional popcorn popper quite similar in appearance to the pushcart types first turned out by the
Cretors family nearly a century ago. It has a stainless-steel cabi-
net, Plexiglas doors, plugs into any household outlet, and will
pop 160 one-ounce servings per hour. The price? Just $1,395.00,
delivered.

The Popcorn Factory has recently added chocolates to its line.
Christmas Meltaways, as they call them, are, according to the
catalog, "made of pure whipping cream, real butter, and hand-
dipped in the very finest chocolate. Then . . . each piece is carefully decorated by hand." As the catalog adds, "They're almost
too beautiful to eat." A box of 18 pieces sells for about $9.95. Also
available during the Christmas season is a 6½-pound chocolate
Santa Claus. Standing 14 inches high and made from an antique
mold discovered by the Cretors in Germany, the candy Santa
consists of a special white chocolate, plus milk and dark semisweet chocolate, and is handmade only after your order is received. The price is around $60.00, and you must allow at least 4
weeks for delivery.

They have been doing some unusual things at The Popcorn
Factory, to say the least, but most unusual of all is the last item
added to their catalog, a 1-pound chocolate pizza. It's made from
rich milk chocolate, krispies, and nuts, laced through and
through with white chocolate and cherries, and sells for about
$15.00. Believe it or not, the chocolate replica looks very much
like a Chicago-style deep-dish pizza, and they even deliver it in a
cardboard, take-home pizza box.

□

SAN FRANCISCO BAY GOURMET
311 California Street
Suite 700
San Francisco, CA 94104
(415) 965-1261
Free catalog. Accepts checks, money orders, Visa,
and MasterCard. Full guarantee.

For those who live within the state of California, San Francisco Bay Gourmet offers one of the most unique services in the mail-order industry: the delivery of fine wines by mail. In addition to most major brands, the company offers two major specialties. First, they offer private labeling of high-quality varietals at what the catalog describes as "surprisingly low costs." Second, they have quality wines with labels personalized for individuals or organizations. They ask that you write or phone for details on current prices and availabilities, because "this will be a constantly changing situation."

Those living outside California are not able to order wine by mail, but SFBG does offer an excellent substitute gift for wine connoisseurs living outside the Golden State. As you probably know, especially if you have a liking for "the fruit of the grape," wine lovers are used to selecting their potables according to the varietal grapes from which they are made, as well as by vintage. Well, San Francisco Bay Gourmet is the only company I encountered that makes it possible for you to select jam on the same basis. They offer three kinds of grape jam—made in the Napa Valley, home of California's most famous red wines—made from the same grapes used in making America's finest wines. Flavors are Pinot Noir, Cabernet Sauvignon, and Zinfandel. Each jar is labeled with its vintage year, and you receive one 10-ounce jar of each variety, packed together in a colorful corrugated box, for about $10.00 plus shipping.

If varietal grape jam is not unusual enough for the taste of those on your gift list, you might consider shipping them a jar of killer bee honey. No, the infamous killer bees haven't invaded the West Coast; San Francisco Bay Gourmet has the honey imported from Brazil. Packed in a striking gift box complete with a leaflet telling the story of the killer bee, the 6 ounces of dark, rich honey sells for about $5.50 plus shipping.

Visitors to Ghirardelli Square seldom forget the long lines waiting to get into the Ghirardelli soda fountain, a remnant of times now past. One of the great attractions there has always been the hot cocoa made from Ghirardelli's special blend of chocolate. This ground chocolate, which is useful in a number of ways, can now be ordered through SFBG at a cost of about $3.95, plus shipping, for a 1-pound tin.

In addition to other unusual sweets, such as glacéed apricots, prunes, and pineapple chunks and dates dipped in chocolate (which can only be ordered as part of larger gift packs), SFBG also offers candy from another San Francisco institution, The Fudge Works. Four types of fudge are offered, in various combinations, at a cost of around $11.75 per 36-ounce box, shipping included. Flavors include chocolate walnut, vanilla walnut, penuche, and Kona coffee, and the claim is that all are made from pure cream and creamy butter.

Port of San Francisco chocolates—shipped September through May only—are a new addition to the catalog. Only three different 8-ounce gift boxes are presently offered, but all three are sure to tempt real lovers of chocolate. Grant Avenue Chocolate Gingers, "spicy morsels of crystallized ginger, coated with dark, bittersweet chocolate," according to the catalog, cost around $7.50 plus shipping. Nob Hill Cocoa Amandettes, roasted almonds covered with a grillage dipped in pure chocolate and dusted with selected imported cocoa "from a well-guarded secret recipe of one of San Francisco's turn-of-the-century salons" are about $8.00 plus shipping charges. Chocolate Cappucino Blend, ground chocolate that San Franciscans mix with milk, cream, and brandy to create a favorite cold-weather drink, using no coffee, is around $6.00 plus shipping. All three of these chocolate specialties can be ordered, packed together in a colorful gift carton, for about $19.95 plus shipping.

San Francisco Bay Gourmet, which entered the mail-order business just a few years ago with a single product, sourdough bread, has been adding new and interesting food items to its line with each issue of its catalog. Next year, I am told by the owners, will be no exception, so their catalog will be worth ordering if only to see what surprises it holds.

□

SEÑOR MURPHY, CANDYMAKER
P.O. Box 2505
Santa Fe, NM 87501
(505) 988-4311
Free price list. Accepts checks, money orders,
MasterCard, and BankAmericard.

Piñon nuts and piñon nut candies are just two of the unusual offerings of this small company. The imported nuts come shelled, roasted, and lightly salted, and sell for about $13.00 per pound. The piñon nut candies (priced at around $10.00 per pound) include brittle, caramels, nougats, toffee, tortuga rolls, and clusters. More familiar selections include English toffee, cashew crunch, pecan turtles, and bolitas, a fudge center dipped in dark chocolate and rolled in toasted almonds; average price for these is around $8.50 per pound. Also offered, at about the same price, are Bour-bons, a chocolate confection made with 100-proof Kentucky bourbon. For about a dollar more, the company also offers one old-fashioned canning jar each of green and red chile jelly, gift-packed with a pamphlet of suggestions for using them. Shipping charges are included in this company's prices.

□

THE SILVER PALATE
274 Columbus Avenue
New York, NY 10023
(212) 799-6340
Free brochure, newsletter, and price list. Accepts
checks and money orders, Visa, MasterCard, and
American Express.

Sweet sauces, brandied fruits, and preserves made from perfect whole fruit get featured billing in the small but attractive brochure put out by this firm.

Sweet sauces to drizzle over ice cream, sorbet, mousses, or waffles or for use as fondue with fresh fruit are put up in 16-ounce jars that sell for $9.00 to $10.00 apiece, depending on the flavor selected. Those flavors include fudge sauce, raspberry-fudge sauce, caramel pecan, pineapple-rum, and several more.

Chestnuts in Grand Marnier, fruit melange in cognac, brandied peaches, and brandied winter fruit are among the brandied fruit choices found here. All come in faceted crystallike decanters, with prices ranging from around $14.00 for a 14-ounce jar of mixed winter fruit to approximately $40.00 for a 40-ounce decanter of fruit melange in cognac.

Around two dozen varieties of fruit preserves are offered, all in 12-ounce jars. Average price is slightly less than $7.00 per jar. Among the many interesting varieties are apple-ginger, chestnut cream, wild strawberry, boysenberry-crabapple, and fig. More common but no less enticing are such flavors as black currant, peach, cherry, orange, and blueberry.

Less sweet, but no less interesting to the gourmet are a large number of chutneys, mustards, vinegars, and oils. The chutneys are in 13- and 14-ounce jars, priced at $9.00 to $10.00 per jar. Sweet, tart, and spicy, the chutneys include blueberry, tomato-apple, plum, spiced cranberry-apple, and half a dozen more. Gourmet mustards, in 8-ounce jars that sell for approximately $4.50 per jar, include such exotic blends as orange mustard, green peppercorn and garlic mustard, and tarragon and shallot mustard. Champagne, sherry, tarragon, wild thyme, blueberry, raspberry and red wine vinegars are a few of the choices you'll find for use in marinades and salads, and to go with them there are oils such as walnut, basil, and green peppercorn. The oils and vinegars are in 12-ounce bottles, priced between $5.50 and $9.50 per bottle, and shipping charges are extra on all items.

□

SPRING GLEN FARM KITCHEN
Box 518
Ephrata, PA 17522
(717) 733–2201
Free brochure. Accepts checks and money orders only; no CODs.

Located in Lancaster County, in the heart of the Pennsylvania Dutch country, Spring Glen Farm Kitchen is a family-operated business that turns out many of the regional specialties for which the Amish are noted. Among these are "barrel molasses," actually a blend of corn syrup and refiners syrup, said to be especially good on scrapple; apple butter made from fresh apples and without spices; and apple schnitzel. Another Amish specialty is chow-chow, a blend of eleven garden vegetables in a sweet and sour syrup, and yet another is sweet and sour salad dressing, especially good on tossed salads.

But Spring Glen Farm Kitchen has recently begun to devote more of its attention to the production of sugar-free jams, jellies, and spreads, less to the traditional Amish foods. These sugar-free spreads are sweetened with sorbitol and saccharin and are said to be suitable for a diabetic or sugar-restricted diet. Spreads are available in 8- or 15-ounce jars, and flavors include black raspberry, strawberry, pineapple, wild huckleberry, and apple butter. Jams and jellies are in 7-ounce jars, and flavors include red raspberry, black raspberry, strawberry, cherry, peach, wild huckleberry, apricot, and pineapple. To spread these on, if you like, the company also has 7-ounce sugar-free coffee cakes.

Spring Glen Farm Kitchen, when I contacted them, advised me that all prices were undergoing a reevaluation; therefore, I can only pass along their promise to provide prices upon request.

□

HENRY AND CORNELIA SWAYZE
Brookside Farm
Tunbridge, VT 05077
(802) 889–3737
Free price list. Accepts checks and money orders
only. Full guarantee.

The Swayzes explained in a letter to me that

> Syrup making is akin to wine making in that no two days' production tastes exactly the same. Also, the syrup from one grove of maple trees has a different flavor from that made from another grove of maple trees. Our maple syrup operation differs from others in that we store all of our production in small batches until after the boiling season is over and then select only complementary flavors to blend when we package our retail containers. Those batches which don't suit our taste are disposed of in bulk

to commercial packers, and only the finest is sold to you under our label. The syrup, too, is as organically pure as we know how to make it. We use no sprays in the groves, no pellets in the tapholes, no artificial defoamers in the evaporators, no preservatives in the syrup. It is pure maple syrup.

In spite of all this care and effort, the Swayzes still manage to sell their syrup at very reasonable prices: about $6.00 per pint, $8.50 per quart, and $25.00 per gallon, with discounts offered on large orders. Lower quality syrup for cooking sells at around $8.00 per half gallon or about $25.00 for a 5-gallon drum. Prices do not include shipping.

□

THE WISCONSIN CHEESEMAN
P.O. Box 1
Madison, WI 53782
Free catalog. Accepts checks, money orders, Visa, MasterCard, and American Express. Delivery in perfect condition guaranteed.

Among the candies featured in the catalog are dark chocolate rum balls (about $6.95 per pound); brandy-soaked, chocolate-covered cherries (about $7.95 per pound); fudge logs in flavors such as chocolate, maple, vanilla, and strawberry, all packed with cashews, walnuts, and Brazil nuts (four 5-ounce logs for about $7.95); candy-coated pistachios (around $8.95 per pound); and a 1-gallon bucket filled with a mix of candy kisses, strawberry chews, chocolate crunch, and saltwater taffy for about $8.95. In the International Candy Assortment (about $9.50), you are offered nine different candy treats—2½ pounds—from around the world. Included in the box are assorted éclairs, chocolate Neapolitans, coconut crunch, English toffee, strawberry tips, butterscotch, chocolate crunch and more—gathered from Scotland, Ireland, Colombia, England, France, Austria, Holland, Argentina, and Denmark. A smaller assortment (1¼ pounds) is available for about $5.75 and includes English toffee, chocolate crunch, strawberry tips, and assorted éclairs, all put together in a woven bamboo basket. Also imported are the miniature, foil-wrapped chocolate bottles that come filled with fruit-flavored, nonalcoholic liqueurs. You receive a box of 20 bottles for about $7.50 with a variety of flavors that include cherry, apricot, raspberry, strawberry, and black currant. In case you have never tried these, the fruit flavor inside blends with the chocolate to make one of the most luxurious after-dinner cordials you will ever serve.

Among the more than 400 gift packages illustrated in the catalog of The Wisconsin Cheeseman are a fair number of honeys, jams, jellies, chocolates, hard candies, and other confections, many of them imported. Everything here is beautifully packaged, and many of the items can be ordered in bulk, at greatly reduced prices.

Featured honey flavors include white clover, noted for its mild flavor, fragrant basswood, hearty buckwheat, and the very delicate wildflower, with a flavor that will vary according to the type flowers visited by the bees. One of the many ways in which these can be ordered is in a wooden pine crate that holds half a pound of each in authentic reproductions of 1876 Muth honey jars with cork stoppers. The price is just under $15.00.

The catalog features an abundance of unusual jams and jellies, often packaged in combination with the honey. The Jamboree assortment is a good example. Selling for about $9.95, it holds tiny 3-ounce jars of white clover and wildflower honeys; 2½-ounce jars of jams and jellies, such as wild chokeberry, wild blueberry, wild plum, and wild grape; and 2¾-ounce jars of jams and jellies including such unusual varieties as purple plum, black cherry, lemon butter, red currant jelly, and ginger marmalade. Those who prefer the more familiar, however, can always choose such items as the 5½-by-5-inch white plastic bucket, which comes filled with 2 pounds of strawberry preserves and sells for about $9.95, and is attractive enough to be used as a planter or for serving potato chips and popcorn.

For a more traditional dessert, there are tiny cordial cakes, each consisting of three cake layers with liqueur-flavored fillings and pastel or chocolate coatings topped with bits of candied fruit. The box of 24 cakes sells for around $6.50, and the filling flavors include crème de cacao, brandy, rum, raspberry, orange, and apricot, among others. These are, of course, in many ways similar to petits fours, the French dessert confections, which can be ordered here in boxes of 20 (about $5.00), 32 (about $7.50), or 40 (around $10.00).

Tortes are regarded by many as the ultimate dessert, and here you will find nearly all the favorite varieties. Weighing in at 1¼ pounds apiece, these include the famous Vienna torte, which will win the heart of any chocolate lover, for around $6.95; a chocolate fudge torte, which features a coating of chocolate and chopped nuts, for about $8.50; a torte flavored with rum and with a filling made of Dobosh creme, for about $7.95; and, finally, a chocolate torte, with alternating layers of crème de menthe filling, for $7.50 or so.

Nearly everything mentioned here can be ordered as part of one or more of the dozens of gift assortments you will find illustrated and described in the colorful catalog of The Wisconsin Cheeseman, and a few are available as part of the monthly gift plans that are also offered by the company.

. □

MILTON YORK
Box 416
Long Beach, WA 98631
(206) 642-2352
Free brochure and price list. Accepts checks, money
orders, Visa, MasterCard, Diners Club, and Carte
Blanche.

In 1882, a young candy maker from Portland, Oregon, set up a tent on the Long Beach Peninsula in the state of Washington, and over the upper front of the tent he hung a wooden sign saying, simply, CANDY. With recipes collected from his apprenticeship days in Portland and learned from immigrant candy makers, Milton York made his candy over open fires heated by native alderwood. During warm weather, he remained at the tent to sell the candy he produced, but during the winter he sold it door to door in Portland and other cities.

By 1894, the young man had built his first permanent business establishment. On the lower floor, he sold candy from display cases that are still used, while living with his family on the upper floor. At this same location, more than 50 years ago, he built the structure that presently houses Milton York Candies.

The master candy maker who owns Milton York Candies today uses the secret recipes originated back in 1882. All chocolates are hand-dipped; all ingredients are fresh, natural, and of the highest quality. In spite of all this, Milton York candies are remarkably low in price. The most expensive candies offered in the catalog are priced at just over $7.00 per pound, and many are priced well below that.

If you truly love chocolate, try the Milton York Special, three layers of light and dark chocolate fused together with a center layer filled with chopped almonds. If fruit fillings are your preference, you'll be interested in offerings such as honey-glazed apricots or pineapple dipped in your choice of chocolate, chocolate-covered ginger, orange sticks, prunes, and cranberry jells. Barks include butterscotch almond and milk chocolate cashew, and there are log rolls such as pecan, cashew, and Brazil nut. There is a shipping charge of $2.85 on any order up to 3 pounds, plus 30 cents for each additional pound.

CHAPTER NINE

COFFEE AND TEA, HERBS AND SPICES

Among the great pleasures in life are the rich aroma of freshly roasted coffee and the delicious fragrance of brewing tea. From burlap sacks, wooden barrels, and chests bearing the names of distant lands come the brewables offered by companies listed in this chapter. They make the exotic seaports of the world as close as your mailbox. Coffee varieties by the dozen are made available to you, and tea varieties number in the hundreds. Most are superior products, better than the supermarket varieties not only in the quality of the bean or leaf, but also in the care that goes into roasting or blending them. Freshness and proper grinding also add to the quality of the brew.

The great variety available makes it worthwhile for you to experiment until you find the drink exactly right for you and your family. Many of the companies make this easier by offering sampler packages. Along with numerous house blends, you will find many unblended teas and coffees with which to experiment, and a few of the firms will even blend coffees and teas to your own specifications, keeping the recipe on file for use each time you order; some provide a standing order service by which tea or coffee are sent out to you at regular intervals. Nearly all will

193

grind coffee to order, but may I suggest using the whole bean and a home grinder for a fresher, more flavorful brew? Many of the catalogs offer grinders, pots, and other equipment that will help you obtain the best beverage possible.

Teas come loose or bagged, and varieties include all the herbal blends that have been used for centuries and currently are enjoying renewed popularity. Like the coffees, the tea varieties are easily shipped, the shipping charges adding little to the total cost, so you pay about the same when buying by mail as you would when buying locally—but you obtain your tea or coffee from a specialist in that field. And while coffee and tea prices fluctuate so wildly that the prices given here should be considered a general guide and nothing more, you can be sure that the specialty companies described are in a position to sell you the finest teas and coffees at their fair market value, sometimes, surprisingly enough, at prices lower than can be found locally.

Herbs, spices, and extracts also come from faraway lands, as well as from tiny farms scattered across America, and the choices seem almost limitless in number. Where all but a few dozen common varieties may be difficult to find locally, any variety known can be ordered by mail. Because many of the sources grow (or have grown for them) their own herbs or import their spices directly, and because all of them specialize and deal in large volume, freshness (of utmost importance with herbs and spices) is guaranteed. I assure you that you will be reluctant to buy supermarket herbs and spices once you have known the quality and freshness of those sold by mail. And if quality and freshness are not enough to gain your patronage, these companies will surely win it with price—for, even when the negligible charges are added in, herbs and spices are generally cheaper by mail than in the local markets.

While all the companies described here specialize, or have a department that specializes, in coffee, tea, herbs, and spices, some also offer specialty and hard-to-find cooking ingredients, or, in a few cases, prepared foods. Likewise, some of the companies described in other chapters of the book include in their catalogs a limited variety of coffees, teas, and so on—but the following firms are the specialists, and it is to them you should turn when you seek the very finest in these categories.

□

APHRODISIA PRODUCTS, INC.,
45 Washington Street
Brooklyn, NY 11201
(212) 852-1278
*Catalog: $1.50. Accepts checks and money orders;
makes COD shipments. Charge accounts available
with one bank and three credit references.*

Though they specialize in botanicals and herbs for medicinal purposes and most herbs for cooking are sold only in quantities
(usually 1 pound or more is the minimum order) too large for use
by the average family, the catalog of Aphrodisia Products does
offer a number of herb teas, packaged herbs, and specialty products that can be purchased in smaller amounts, frequently at excellent savings to you.

The San Francisco brand of herb teas, sold in retail outlets nationwide, includes about two dozen blends of tea, all at $1.29 or so per
package (package weight not given in catalog). Varieties include Minty
Lemon, Quietly Peppermint, Mildly Chamomile, Refresh Mint (a
blend of alfalfa and mint), Orange Spice, and Oriental Blend, to name
just a few. The full line of the famous Celestial Seasonings teas is
offered, too, but only by the case, with most varieties selling at about
$15.00 per case of 24 boxes of tea bags.

Packaged herbs include such familiar varieties as catnip, cay-
enne pepper, peppermint leaves, and sassafras root bark, plus
lesser known types such as black cohosh root, passion flower,
senna leaves, and skullcap herb. Listed along with these, you will
find at least 65 more herb varieties, but if you are a novice in the
herbal field, be forewarned that the catalog offers almost no information about their uses, though the company does sell a number
of books and guides you can use to educate yourself.

Offered, too, are more than 100 varieties of herb tablets and
capsules, these at savings of about 50 percent off the price you
would pay locally. The list includes Korean white ginseng capsules, Tienchi ginseng capsules, burdock root capsules, comfrey
capsules, and all the special herbal mixtures used by millions
who practice herbal and preventive medicine. As I said earlier,
this is not a good source for cooking herbs, but it is a fair source
of herb teas and an excellent place to turn if you are looking for
the hard-to-find herbs that are used in countless other ways.

□

Armanino Farms of California
1945 Carroll Avenue
San Francisco, CA 94124
(415) 467–3500
Free brochure. Accepts checks and money orders; no
CODs. Full guarantee. There is a $1.00 handling
charge on orders of less than $10.00.

Established in 1951, Armanino Farms is probably best known for its San Francisco Seasoning, a product it sells through retail outlets nationwide and which is a blend of spices and herbs including freeze-dried shallots, chives, basil, leeks, garlic, and paprika. The seasoning, which is suggested for use on "all foods," but which I found especially good on crab and other seafood, is sold through the mail at around $2.00 for a 2-ounce jar or about $3.50 for a 4-ounce tin. I think it is a worthwhile addition to your spice shelf.

All herbs sold by Armanino undergo this freeze-drying process, and a letter from their corporate office explains why:

> Our herbs are freeze-dried, which is quite different from dehydrated. The freeze-drying process allows the product to have a more natural color, a fresher flavor, [it] reconstitutes instantly, and is very light in weight since 98% of the water is taken out during the process. Our products have even been to the moon as part of the astronauts' food program.

Other freeze-dried herbs offered by Armanino Farms include a 2-ounce tin of shallots, a ½-ounce tin of chives, a ¾-ounce tin of green bell peppers, a ¼-ounce tin of red bell peppers, a ⅞-ounce tin of Italian parsley, and a ¾-ounce tin of leeks, all priced at about $3.00 per tin. There is also a five-jar gift package (for around $10.00) that includes chives, shallots, Italian parsley, San Francisco Seasoning, and dill (the last is not sold separately).

Though I still find fresh herbs preferable for my own cooking, I do agree that the freeze-drying process turns out the nearest thing to fresh herbs that money can buy, and I hope that public acceptance will eventually cause Armanino and other firms to make a greater variety available.

□

BARCLAYS COFFEE, TEA & SPICE COMPANY, LTD.,
9020 Tampa Avenue
Northridge, CA 91234
(213) 885-7744
Free brochure and prist list. Accepts checks, money
orders, MasterCard, and BankAmericard.

In the seventeenth century, England had a famous trading company known as Barclay's, Ltd., a company that was known around the world for the care with which it selected and roasted its coffee beans, and for the bulk tea it imported in wooden chests from faraway places with strange-sounding names. Three centuries later, in 1973, a group of San Francisco businessmen set out to re-create the Barclays tradition and establish for themselves the same kind of worldwide reputation for the very best in coffee, tea, and spices. Just a decade later, they seem very close to achieving their goal.

Barclays retail store is a quaint shop filled with heady aromas where customers can help themselves to a free cup of coffee while they browse. Teas from Barclays are shipped out in sealed wooden chests, a technique that has ensured freshness since well before the Boston Tea Party. Coffees that are nearly impossible to obtain elsewhere are made to seem almost, but not quite, commonplace on their list. Their house blend coffee is already famous among connoisseurs around the world. That house blend, which was selling at a very reasonable $4.79 per pound when we checked, is their best-selling coffee, but their list of more than 20 coffees includes many others with which you may be familiar or which you may want to try.

The most expensive coffee on the list, and probably the most highly prized in the world, is Jamaican Blue Mountain, which sells for $9.95 or so per pound. Next highest in cost, when we checked, was Mocha, described as having a "rich, creamy taste," at $6.59 per pound. All other coffees, whole or ground to your specifications, were selling at prices ranging from $4.99 per pound to $5.69 per pound, and they included such imports as Brazil Santos ("mild . . . Brazil's finest"), Columbian Supremo ("full body . . . sweet aftertaste"), Costa Rican ("mild and smooth"), Ethiopian Harrar ("taste full roast without extra roasting"), Java ("very aromatic"), Kenyan ("medium . . . fantastic aftertaste"), Mexican ("mild, nutty aftertaste"), and Sumatran ("round, full taste").

Three dark roasts are listed, all at $4.99 per pound when I checked. These include Viennese ("lightest of the dark roasts"), Espresso ("most popular for espresso and cappuccino makers"), and French ("our strongest coffee, perfect for blending").

A dozen varieties of decaffeinated coffees, all whole bean, with 98 percent of the caffeine removed, are listed at prices ranging from as little as $5.89 per pound for your choice of Brazilian, Columbian, or Viennese to as much as $7.99 per pound for Javan, Kenyan, or Ethiopian. Four flavored coffees are on the list, all at less than $6.00 per pound. Flavors are almond, cinnamon, Bavarian chocolate, and Swiss almond chocolate. Only natural flavorings are used in these blends.

Tea is priced by the quarter pound. English varieties all sell for $2.00 to $2.50 per ¼ pound. Those offered are Darjeeling ("winey taste"), Irish Breakfast ("full body"), English Breakfast ("a good pick-me-up"), Earl Grey "(fantastic flavor and aroma"), lapsang Souchong ("smoky tasting"), and Ceylonese ("the most bracing tea"). In case you are wondering how much to order, ¼ pound of loose tea makes 62 to 65 cups, depending on how strong you like your tea.

The traditional Oriental teas range in price from around $2.25 per ¼ pound for gunpowder ("mild and subtle"), jasmine ("the pungent flavor of jasmine blossoms"), and Chinese oolong ("served in the better Chinese restaurants") to about $3.75 per ¼ pound for Dragon Well ("the fabled Lung Chin green tea") and $4.00 or so per ¼ pound for Mandarin Keemun ("very rare . . . finest black Congan"). A Russian tea is also available at around $2.25 per ¼ pound.

New on the Barclays list are three decaffeinated teas—English Breakfast, Earl Grey, and spiced orange—all selling at about $3.75 per ¼ pound. New, too, are about a dozen kinds of flavored teas, all priced at about $2.25 per ¼ pound. All these are flavored with natural fruit extracts and spices. Choices include almond, Berry Delight, black currant, Cashmir (cinnamon-flavored), jasmine spice, spice orange, vanilla, wild cherry, and strawberry, among others.

Barclays also offers a tea gift sampler (around $7.00) that includes packages of wild cherry, English Breakfast, black currant, Chinese oolong, Darjeeling, jasmine, and Earl Grey teas. There is also a Celestial Seasonings herb tea bag sampler (under $2.50) that holds four tea bags each of such Celestial Seasonings favorites as Red Zinger, Morning Thunder, Roastaroma, Chamomile, Mo's 24, and Mellow Mint.

The Barclays catalog also offers a full line of coffeemaking equipment, including grinders and espresso coffee makers, and discounts of 20 percent are given on all tea orders of 5 pounds or more. All coffee customers are given a free pound of their favorite blend with each twelfth pound they purchase, which helps compensate for the fact that all shipping charges are extra when you order from Barclays.

□

BETTER FOODS FOUNDATION, INC.
300 North Washington Street
Greencastle, PA 17225
Catalog $1.00. Accepts checks, money orders, and food stamps.

More than 150 fresh herbs and herb teas are stocked by Better Foods. They also make a very unusual offer: If the herb or tea you want is not on their list, just send them its name and a check for $1.50; they will send you the herb or refund your money. But their list is so complete, it is unlikely you will have to take them up on this offer.

In addition to chives, sage, thyme, and all the other herbs commonly used in cooking, their catalog lists such hard-to-find herbs as licorice root, papaya leaf, wild-cherry bark, and blackberry leaf.

Among the herb teas put in tea bags are alfalfa leaf, chamomile, comfrey leaf, rose hip, and ginseng. Better Foods also distributes Barth brand herb teas, which are sold in retail health food shops across the country. At an average price of $1.60 for a package of 32 tea bags, the Barth line includes blends such as Rose-Mint, Taste-O-Pep and Gossip. Several caffeine-free blends are also offered, all at 76 cents or so for a package of 16 bags.

No coffee is sold by Better Foods, but they do offer a number of all-natural coffee substitutes. At an average price of less than $2.50 per pound, these potables consist of ingredients such as chicory, carob, barley, wheat, soybeans, buckwheat, rye, molasses, or even okra seed, roasted singly or blended in a number of ways. Many have been used as coffee substitutes for years, and others are as new as Better Foods itself.

A number of all-natural seasonings and condiments are listed and described in the catalog. These special blends consist of ingredients such as sea-salt crystals, special yeasts, toasted onion and onion powder, orange powder, soy flour, celery leaf powder, dill, garlic, sea greens, natural Indian curry, organic herb and vegetable extracts, etc.—but never any white sugar or flour. They are combined into special blends for use with soups, noodles, fish, gravies and sauces, spaghetti, and more, and they are sold at an average price of about $2.39 per pound. Please note that Better Foods is one of the few companies in the industry that accepts USDA food stamps.

□

W. ATLEE BURPEE COMPANY
Warminster, PA 18974
Free catalog. Accepts checks, money orders, Visa, and MasterCard. Minimum order on credit cards: $20.00. Full guarantee.

If you have been cooking with commercially dried herbs primarily because of the difficulty of locating fresh herbs, then perhaps it's time you considered growing your own. A small space in a flower or vegetable garden, or even a window box or a few pots set in a sunny window, is all you need to grow a few herb favorites. You say you're not a gardener? For 25 cents Burpee's offers the leaflet "Herbs," which contains growing charts, other helpful information, and even recipes for using the herbs you grow. But, most important of all, they will ship to you, if ordered before May 3, healthy, sturdy young plants of the most popular herb varieties, well rooted in the proper growing medium and ready to set out in your garden, window boxes, or other containers. They'll grow fast, with almost no care, and in just days be ready for any recipe that needs a flavor brightener. Some are perennials and will last for years if given some winter protection. Plants are packaged in units of three of one kind. Three or six plants of any kind should provide enough of that herb for even the largest family.

The minimum order is two units (6 plants) for about $9.45. You can order three units (9 plants) for around $13.50, four units (12 plants) for about $17.25, or five units (15 plants) for around $20.85. Available in this way are such useful cooking herbs as sweet basil, chives, lavender, lemon balm, sweet marjoram, oregano, curly parsley, peppermint, sage, spearmint, and thyme. Also offered, at a cost of about $15.45, is an assortment of three plants each of chives, parsley, sage, and sweet basil. And for those who are really interested in herb variety, there is a 39-plant assortment that includes three plants of all the varieties mentioned above, plus three each of catnip and chamomile, all the basic herbs, at a cost of about $45.00. Herb seed of every variety is also available at a cost of 75 cents per packet.

□

CARAVANSARY
2263 Chestnut Street
San Francisco, CA 94123
(415) 921-3466
Free brochure and price list. Accepts checks, money orders, Visa, MasterCard, and American Express.

Caravansary offers gourmet coffees by the pound, by the half pound, or through a monthly ordering plan that allows you to have a designated amount of your favorite grind delivered to you on or around the first of each month and billed to your credit card. All coffees are dry-roasted daily in small batches and shipped to you within 24 hours of roasting.

Light-bodied coffees on the list include Hawaiian kona and Mexican altura. Medium-bodied coffees include Brazilian santos,

Guatemalan, Guatemalan Antigua, and Kenyan Arabica. Heavy-bodied coffees on the list come from Colombia, Costa Rica, Java, Yemen, and Sumatra. Dark roasts include French, Italian, and Viennese, and there are three decaffeinated grinds, including a decaffeinated chicory.

In addition to the house blend, there are mixtures such as Aram's blend ("an excellent full-bodied after-dinner coffee"), Mocha espresso ("medium-bodied, mellow"), and New Orleans blend ("a rich mixture of chicory and French roast"). Custom blending is also available.

Prices are very reasonable here. When I checked, the great majority of the coffees were selling at less than $5.00 per pound, with the most expensive beans listed going at about $7.50 per pound. Coffee prices do fluctuate wildly, though, so always check before ordering, and remember that shipping charges are extra.

□

CHINA BOWL TRADING COMPANY, INC.
80 Fifth Avenue
New York, NY 10011
(212) 255-2935
Free brochure and price list. Accepts checks, money orders; no CODs. Minimum order $7.50.

China Bowl Trading Company not only handles all the spices, herbs, and sometimes-hard-to-find ingredients essential to the preparation of authentic Chinese cuisine, it serves as national distributor for Grace Rare Teas, a line that includes some of the world's finest rare teas, some hand-fired for this company alone.

All Grace Rare Teas are packaged in elegant black 8-ounce canisters with tasteful labeling that has won awards in the food industry for "the most beautiful and creative packaging." Inside these canisters, you will find carefully blended loose teas that have won high praise from connoisseurs the world over.

The most expensive blend is Superb Darjeeling 6000, at about $8.80 per canister. Grown 6,000 feet above sea level in the Himalayas of northern India, where the low temperature promotes slower growth and gives the smaller leaves a greater flavor, this tea is hand picked only once a year, in early summer, so the supply is always limited. It is regarded as the jewel among teas, and would be an excellent gift for anyone who enjoys fine tea.

Next in line, at around $8.55 per 8-ounce canister, is Formosa Oolong Supreme, a hand-picked tea from northern Taiwan. It is described as a tea that "can be enjoyed in large quantities without jading the palate and so it is a particular favorite with Oriental cuisine. Professional tea tasters regard it as the Champagne of Teas because of its delicate taste and eloquent fragrance, [which] is likened to fresh peaches."

Winey Keemun English Breakfast Tea (about $8.00 per canister) is described as "a tea with unusual depth, body, color and a fine winey flavor"; lapsang souchong, Smoky No. 1 (about $6.50 per 8-ounce canister) is "one of the rarest of all teas, famous for its unique smoky flavor. Exotic woods are used in the old method of hand-firing summer leaves to impart an unusual and pleasant taste." Other teas include a house blend (about $8.15 per canister); The Original Earl Grey Mixture (about $6.85 per canister), said to be exactly as it was blended for Earl Grey, who was twice premier of Great Britain, by a Chinese mandarin; and Before the Rain Jasmine (about $6.55 per canister),

> . . . picked at the height of its flavor in the spring before the rain and prior to its period of fast growth. Then held with special care until the summer when the finest flowers are available for blending to impart their rare and delicious perfume. Truly a tea among teas.

If the cost of these teas seems high, be reminded that 8 ounces of loose tea should produce at least 100 cups of hot beverage, making fine tea one of the least expensive drinks money can buy.

In addition to the full line of sauces, flavorings, and prepared foods described in the chapter on Ethnic and Specialty Foods, China Bowl Trading Company imports and ships out a number of spices, herbs, and Oriental cooking ingredients that are sometimes difficult to find locally. These include Szechuan peppercorns, star anise, and small Hunan chilis (all at about $1.00 per ounce), fragrant green coriander, or Chinese parsley (around $1.20 for ⅙ ounce), Chinese mustard powder (around $1.00 for

2½ ounces), five-spice powder (2 ounces for about $1.65), and more. All prices include shipping charges if delivery can be made by UPS, but for Parcel Post delivery there is an additional charge of 20 percent of the total price of the order.

□

O. H. CLAPP & COMPANY, INC.
47 Riverside Avenue
Westport, CT 06880
(203) 226–3301
*Free price list. Accepts checks and money orders
only. Delivery in perfect condition guaranteed.*

This company is a major importer of teas, and it sells large quantities of the unblended product to the major packers in the United States and Canada. Clapp & Company also offers six "vintage" teas in small quantities to mail-order customers. In addition to Formosa oolong ("the briskness of black tea without sacrificing the tenderness of green tea") and Darjeeling ("the subtle flavor of black currant"), there are four teas from mainland China: keemun ("heady, full-bodied"), jasmine ("a golden green tea gently touched with the fragrance of jasmine blossoms"), oolong ("keen and tangy"), and Yunnan ("wickedly exciting"). Keemun, it is interesting to note, was the tea dumped into the harbor during the Boston Tea Party. The teas come packed in attractive miniature wooden tea chests with the name of the blend printed on the lid at a price of about $7.50 apiece. If 12 or more chests are ordered, they sell at around $5.00 apiece. A sampler of 2 ounces of each of the six varieties is also available, at a cost of around $5.00. Clapp also offers a tea taster's set that is imported from Sri Lanka (Ceylon) and consists of a pot with a serrated edge that allows the liquor to drain off while holding back the leaves, matching lid, and bowl, all in white porcelain. The set sells for approximately $11.50 (shipping charges are included, as they are in the tea prices given above).

□

THE GOOD TIME SPICE COMPANY
P.O. Box 189
Tiburon, CA 94920
(415) 232-2570
*Free price list. Accepts checks and money orders
only; no CODs.*

The hand-packed spices and blended culinary salts from this company arrive in old-fashioned glass-topped canning jars with a
rubber ring and wire closure, making them particularly attractive. The specialty salts include "survival salt," a mixture of raw
sea salt, kelp, sesame, garlic, and parsley; and "garden salt," a
blend of sea salt, sesame, kelp, dill, parsley, celery seed, and
ginseng, both priced at about $6.25 per 8-ounce jar. Five vari-
eties of herbal teas may be ordered in canning jars, tins, or
boxes, at around $6.75 for the jars, $4.00 for the tins, and $2.75
for the boxes. (Weights for each type of package vary slightly due
to differences in the ingredients.) The varieties include Comfort
Tea, a blend of alfalfa, spearmint, chamomile, and catnip; Spice
Tea, which combines raspberry leaves, dried orange peel, and
cloves; Peaceful Tea, a mix of peppermint and orange blossoms;
Good Time Tea, which combines cinnamon with rose hips and
the dried peel of oranges and lemons; and Pleasure Tea, a very,
very sweet tea that blends together licorice root bark, fennel
seed, ginseng leaves, and sarsaparilla. Two black teas mixed with
herbs are also available, in either 4-ounce canning jars or decorative tins, the jars selling for about $6.75, the tins for approx-
imately $4.00. Lemon Mint Tea, first of the two, combines black
tea with lemon peel and spearmint; and the other, Sunblossom
Tea, is a blend of black tea, rose hips, and hibiscus flowers,
which gives the final brew a glowing reddish color and a stronger
flavor.
    Also available in a 4-ounce storage jar is a special blend of
"mulling spices," a mixture of stick cinnamon, cracked nutmeg,
whole cloves, and dried orange peel designed to add zest to
warm wines, ciders, and meads as well as teas and coffees. The
jar of spices sells for about $8.50, with shipping charges addi-
tional, as they are on all the items described above.

□

THE KOBOS COMPANY
The Water Tower at Johns Landing
5331 Southwest Macadam
Portland, OR 97201
(503) 222–5226
Free brochure. Accepts checks, money orders, Visa,
and MasterCard. Minimum order $5.00; $10.00 on
credit card orders. Shipping charges are additional.

David Kobos and his wife, Susan, roast and blend their own coffees in a renovated furniture factory and sell it through four of
their own retail outlets in the Portland area, and, believe me,
they do an excellent job. I was lucky enough to sample several
varieties from their roaster, and all ranked right up there with
the best brews that ever filled a cup.

Kobos offers not only a very good selection of straight coffee
growths and blends, including several dark roasts, such as French
espresso, Vienna, Sumatra, and Turkish (all at around $4.95 per
pound), but also a large selection of teas and one of the most
extensive stocks of culinary herbs and spices to be found anywhere, as well as a large and varied line of cookware, accessories,
and gadgets.

Coffees sent out to mail-order customers are packed in poly-
lined bags, which are then heat sealed, extending the freshness
considerably. When ordering, you should indicate whether you
want whole bean or ground coffee and specify the grind—per-
colator, drip, automatic drip, extra fine, espresso, etc. If you are
unsure of which grind to use, simply tell this company the brand
name or type of your coffee maker and they will choose the
proper grind.

Regular roasts include Arabian mocha (around $7.95 per
pound), described as "heavy in body with complex flavor and
mysterious aroma—one of the world's great coffees"; Colombian
(about $4.75 per pound), a coffee "with medium body and a rich,
smooth flavor"; Guatemalan Antigua (about $4.50 per pound),
with "a distinct nutty flavor and exquisite aroma"; and Ethiopian
Harrar (about $5.50 per pound), "a rich coffee similar in taste to
Arabian mocha, though not as heavy." Peruvian coffee ($6.95 or
so per pound) is described as "a light pleasant coffee, sweet and
uncomplicated, and Java beans (about $4.95 per pound) produce

a brew with "a sturdy deep flavor, smooth, but sweet and highly aromatic." At around $5.25 per pound, there is Kenyan, "the heaviest in body and snappiest of all coffees." At $6.95 or so per pound, the company offers Kalossi Celebes, "the most romantic of the Indonesian coffees, and the most highly prized." Mocha Java, which costs $5.95 or so per pound, is a mixture of three types of Java coffee beans. Unblended coffees include Costa Rican (about $4.50 per pound) and New Guinean (around $5.25 per pound). The house blend, which the coffee drinkers around my house loved, is about $4.75 per pound, and those who like chicory can order it here at just $2.00 or so per pound.

If you are not really familiar with the great coffees of the world but wish to give them a try, I'd suggest that you order one of Kobos' coffee gift packs, as I did. For about $15.00, you receive 6½ ounces each of five different coffees: Colombian, Kenyan, Bistro (a blend of Colombian and mocha coffees with just a bit of French espresso added), Mocha Java, and the Kobos house blend. None is less than excellent.

Teas, blended or unblended, are sold in 8-ounce packages, nearly all at $4.00 per package. The blends include the famous Earl Grey mix, Irish and English breakfast teas, jasmine, mint blend, spice blend, and Russian "caravan" teas. Unblended varieties are Darjeeling and Darjeeling gold-tipped varieties, which are slightly higher in price, Ceylon, Formosa oolong, keemun congou, Lapsang souchong, gunpowder green, and Assam.

The Kobos Company is particularly and justifiably proud of its extensive stock of culinary herbs and spices. Just to list those on hand would require pages. They include all those commonly used in the American kitchen plus such gourmet items as Turkish bay leaves, Chinese cassia buds, whole Zanzibar cloves, whole Jamaican allspice, Italian juniper berries, Chinese mustard flour, Iranian cumin, real Hungarian paprika, and vanilla beans from Madagascar, the last not priced and available only by special order. Kobos offer this service with any spice you have difficulty locating elsewhere: If he doesn't have it, he searches until he finds it.

□

LE JARDIN DU GOURMET
West Danville, VT 05873
Free catalog. Accepts checks and money orders only;
no CODs.

Culinary herbs, including numerous varieties of shallots, leeks, and garlic imported from France, hold center stage at this small Vermont company. Shallots and garlic are sold in boxes of about a dozen bulbs each, which can be divided and replanted to produce at least 50 bulbs with almost no care. Young leeks, ready for use in gourmet cooking or ready to transplant, are shipped out in boxes of 50. Prices range from $2.75 per box to $4.00 per box, depending on the variety you choose.

Live herb plants of almost every variety are shipped out in 2-inch plastic containers, ready for planting in your garden, window boxes, or under artificial lights. Most will be producing useful herb material in a matter of weeks, and just a few plants should fill your needs. All varieties are priced at less than $1.00 per plant, and they include angelica, basil, bergamot, dill, horehound, rosemary, rue, French sorrel, and tarragon, to name just a few of the 50 or so varieties offered. If you are unfamiliar with the fairly simple techniques used in growing herbs, the company sells a number of books that will explain these, and a few of the more popular herb varieties are sold dried and ready for use, at prices competitive with local markets.

Also available are herbal teas imported from Germany. Eight varieties are offered, all in boxes of five flow-through tea bags, all priced at about 40 cents per box. Flavors are peppermint, chamomile, verbena, fruit, linden, malven blossom, peppermint-linden, fennel, and a spice mixture for adding to mulled wine and other hot wintertime drinks.

Although an imported espresso (around $4.60 for a 12-ounce tin) is the only coffee offered, the company does carry nine varieties of Twinings brand tea, imported from England. All are shipped in 8-ounce tins and are priced between $5.50 and $5.95 per tin. Those available are English, Irish, and Ceylonese breakfast teas, the famous Earl Grey blend, an Orange Pekoe Black, Darjeeling, Prince of Wales blend, Formosa oolong, Queen Mary blend, jasmine, and a Lapsang souchong. Once you are on the mailing list of Le Jardin du Gourmet, you can also expect to receive occasional notices of reduced prices on many items, including their herbs, teas, spices, and seasonings. Those offers alone make their catalog worth ordering.

□

MARIA'S
111 South Stratford Road
Winston-Salem, NC 27104
(919) 722–7271
Free catalog. Accepts checks, money orders, Visa, and MasterCard. There is a $3.00 handling charge on orders of less than $30.00.

With the exception of Hawaiian kona (which sells for approximately $7.50 per pound), all the coffees offered here sell at prices ranging from $4.85 to $5.95 per pound, and the choices are many. All beans are fresh roasted daily, to ensure freshness, and grinding is done to your specifications, though the company wisely suggests you order whole beans and grind them yourself.

Among the whole beans rarely seen elsewhere are Tanzanian, Mexican Altura, Sumatran Mandheling, and Jamaican Port Royal beans: blends include Scandinavian, French, mocha Java, and Colombian. Also offered are a number of flavored blends including Swiss chocolate almond, chocolate rum, and café amaretto. Also offered (for about $12.50) is a coffee sampler that holds a little over ⅓ pound each of the house blend, mocha Java, Colombian, and Mexican Altura coffees, gift-packaged.

The only teas offered are in a sampler that sells for around $8.00 and holds one package each (weight not given) of English breakfast, jasmine, Earl Gray, Orange spice, Queen Mary's blend, and Lapsang souchong teas.

Herbs, too, are available only in an assortment. For about $10.00, you receive packaged (weight not given) blends for chicken, beef, omelets, salads, fish, Greek and Italian dishes, vegetables, and, finally, a *bouquet garni*. Prices do not include shipping.

□

MCNULTY'S TEA & COFFEE COMPANY, INC.
109 Christopher Street
New York, NY 10014
(212) 242–5351
Free brochure and price list. Accepts checks, money
orders, Visa, MasterCard, and American Express.
Full guarantee.

McNulty's brochure lists an incredible variety of teas, both straight and blended. Many of these are rare and difficult to find elsewhere. Listed by country of origin, the teas range in price from $5.00 to $15.00 per pound, though smaller amounts may be ordered, of course. The unblended teas include three varieties of Darjeeling, two kinds of Assam, a long list of teas from China, and some interesting Japanese imports such as uji-gyokura, known as "pearl dew," and denmai-cha with toasted rice. The tea list goes on and to to include special blends and exotic items such as orange blossom mint, blueberry leaf, and anisette. The list includes the famous Twinings teas from England, the lesser known Jackson's English teas, all the Celestial Seasonings herbal teas, and its own line of blended teas. Many of these are available in tea bags as well as loose.

Coffee prices start at less than $5.00 per pound. The most expensive bean on the list is the famous Jamaican Blue Mountain, selling at around $15.00 per pound when I checked. Priced in between those extremes are dozens of special roasts, blends, and gourmet coffees from all parts of the world. Among the last you'll find Hawaiian kona, Yemen mocha Sanani, old crop Colombian, and Haitian. Flavored coffees include almond, chocolate, cinnamon, orange, maple-walnut, and more. A full line of coffee-making equipment rounds out the list. Prices do not include shipping.

□

MR. SPICEMAN, CHARLES LOEB
615 Palmer Road
Yonkers, NY 10701
(914) 961–7776
Free catalog. Accepts checks, money orders, Visa,
and MasterCard. Full guarantee. Minimum of $25.00
on credit card orders.

If you use a lot of herbs and spices—and perhaps even if you don't—Charles Loeb is the man to see. According to his own estimate, many of his herbs and spices are priced as much as 94 percent below current supermarket and grocery store prices. He contends that "when you buy by the pound, the savings on most items are 40 to 60 percent," and my own survey shows that he is correct.

In many instances, of course, a pound of a single spice or herb is far too much for the average family to use. However, Loeb offers nearly all the popular varieties in smaller, family-size jars and canisters, and even then his prices are incredibly low.

And his list is remarkably complete. If it can be defined as spice, herb, or seasoning, you will probably find it offered in his catalog; if not, Mr. Loeb will be happy to get it for you at the lowest possible price.

This company has recently begun to expand its horizons, adding teas, candies, and kitchen gadgets to its catalog. Though these new lines are presently somewhat limited, the prices are so low that they deserve your attention. The tea list, for example, is not as complete as one might hope, but it does include about 100 blends, straight, and herbal teas, at prices ranging from $4.50 to $7.50 per pound. Bargain hunters should keep an eye on this company.

□

PAPRIKAS WEISS IMPORTER
1546 Second Avenue
New York, NY 10028
(212) 288–6117
Annual subscription to catalog costs $1.00. Accepts
checks, money orders, Visa, and MasterCard;
telephone orders accepted, but no collect calls.

In Chapter 3, I briefly described the founding of Paprikas Weiss, a dynasty that was started by a Hungarian immigrant who went into the business of importing and selling paprika and other spices simply because in this country others were unable to supply spices that would meet the high culinary standards set by his own wife. In reading about Paprikas Weiss, it is possible you may have gotten the idea that the company's expansion has caused it to forsake its roots and place less emphasis on the selling of the quality herbs, spices, coffees, teas, and extracts that were the cause of its success. Forgive me if I have misled you. Nothing could be further from the truth.

After more than half a century of growth, imported paprika (the company sells more than 200,000 pounds a year) and other spices continue to account for much of Paprikas Weiss's business and much of its fame. The Hungarian paprika is sold in sweet, half-sweet, and fiery hot concentrations, and one gourmet-writer has said, "By comparison, all other paprikas taste like brick dust." To quote the Weisses, "It seduces the taste buds, nips at the nostrils, and enchants the eye." The price is around $4.98 per pound, $23.00 for 5 pounds, or $42.00 for 10 pounds.

About 150 more spices and herbs are available, all put up in handsome 4-inch-high apothecary jars. All sell at about $2.59 per jar, the amount inside each jar varying with the variety and relative cost. Also offered, at about $4.00 per ½ gram, is pure Spanish saffron, that most expensive of all herbs.

A number of coffees are offered, 17 to be exact. All are priced at around $6.98 per pound, $19.00 for 3 pounds, or $36.00 for 6 pounds. A few of the varieties are a Hungarian blend ("full-bodied, with a zing"), a Jamaica ("mellow"), Hawaiian Kona ("breezy"), and green coffee beans for those who want to roast their own.

The English Royal line of teas offered by Weiss comes in your choice of ¼-pound boxes, 8-ounce canisters, or 1-pound boxes. The price is about $1.50 for ¼ pound, $5.00 for the 1-pound box, or $5.98 for the 8-ounce decorative canister. Black India, Assam, Russian Samovar, an apple blend, an orange spice blend, and a Japanese green are among the types available. Certain products ordered from Weiss will be gift wrapped on request, and your satisfaction is fully guaranteed. A $3.90 charge is added to all orders to cover shipping and handling.

□

SCHAPIRA COFFEE COMPANY
117 West 10 Street
New York, NY 10011
(212) 675–3733
Free brochure. Accepts checks and money orders only; no CODs.

This old, family-owned and -operated company, located in New York's Greenwich Village, built a national reputation with its Flavor Cup Coffee. This house blend was for many years the only blend they sold. A blend of three Colombian beans and currently priced at around $4.15 per pound, Flavor Cup is available in three styles: brown roast, a darker French roast, and, darkest and strongest of the three, Italian espresso roast. The house brand still accounts for a great percentage of the business done by Schapira, but over the years it has been joined by nearly every type of coffee known to man. This is a coffee house that offers real variety.

Among the unblended coffees on the list you will find are such rarities as Maracaibo, the most highly regarded coffee of Venezuela, at about $4.20 per pound; Ethiopian Mocha, known for its light flavor and exquisite aroma, at about $4.50 per pound; and, rarer still, Djimmah, another Ethiopian bean known for its spicy flavor, at $4.40 or so per pound.

Other straight coffees include Java, Colombian ($4.35 per pound), Mexican, and Costa Rican, all priced at around $4.50 per pound.

Blended coffees include a New Orleans mixture that combines a French-roasted coffee with chicory (about $3.75 per pound), a Viennese that is a mixture of Maracaibo and French-roasted Mexican beans (about $4.25 per pound), and a Turkish blend (around $4.20 per pound) that is a finely ground mixture of Venezuelan and Mexican coffees, dark roasted. A decaffeinated espresso blend sells at about $5.25 per pound. For those who like a little extra flavor in their coffee, Schapira offers ¼-pound packages of such additives as chocolate, lemon, cinnamon, chocolate-rum, and chocolate-orange-cinnamon, all at about $2.00 per package. For those who'd like to experiment and find the coffee most suited to their individual taste, there is a coffee sampler (about $13.00) that brings five ½-pound packages of any five coffee varieties selected; and, for those who really want to splurge and order what most connoisseurs consider the ultimate coffee, there is Jamaican Blue Mountain, 100 percent pure—priced at $10.00 or so per ½-pound.

Just as the first Schapira coffee was called Flavor Cup, its original house blend of tea—first sold more than 60 years ago—bore, and still bears, the same name. A blending of rare Indian and Chinese leaves, this house brand sells at around $5.75 per pound. Like all other teas sold here, the Flavor Cup blend can be ordered in ¼-pound, ½-pound, or 1-pound packs.

All loose teas here are priced by the pound, those prices ranging from as low as $4.25 per pound to as much as $5.50 per pound. On the list are all the favorite Chinese and English blends, as well as Russian and Ceylonese. Also offered (at about $3.00 per pound) are a number of naturally flavored teas, including black currant, raspberry, apple, and almond.

Bagged teas sell at around $2.25 for a box of 50, and varieties include jasmine, Darjeeling, Earl Grey, Chinese green and oolong, Lapsang souchong, Ceylonese, Russian, and orange spice. To explore the virtues of several varieties, try the tea sampler that is offered for approximately $2.75. It brings you four bags (or enough loose tea for a potful) of each of any eight varieties you choose. Prices do not include shipping.

□

SHOFFEIT PRODUCTS CORPORATION
420 Hudson Street
Healdsburg, CA 95448
(707) 433–5555
Free brochure. Accepts checks and money orders
only. Full guarantee.

Wanderer, dreamer, inventor, well-dressed hobo, and unsuccessful trapeze artist, Bill Shoffeit edged his way into the food business as the result of a near fatal heart attack he suffered several years ago. The tasteless foods and bitter salt substitutes suggested by his doctor made him realize that millions of Americans must be yearning for salt-free seasoning blends with real flavor, and he set out to find them. Several years were to pass before his first blends were perfected and approved by the necessary bureaucrats, but he believes it was time well spent. I agree with him there, because the samples I received were the very best salt substitutes I have ever encountered and I have been using them regularly to add zest to my own cooking. For those on a low-sodium diet they are essential, but I believe they also belong in the pantry of everyone who likes good food.

Under his own label, Shoffeit markets about 40 different seasoning combinations, six of them suggested as salt substitutes, and about a dozen of them billed as "natural seasoners" containing no preservatives or MSG. All contain lemon, which acts as a natural flavor enhancer to many foods. The salt substitute varieties include a meat seasoner, lemon teriyaki blend, herb mix, lemon-onion, shake-on dry lemon juice, and a deluxe herbal blend. A gift pack containing a shaker of each sells for just under $12.00. The natural seasoners include lemon-onion, luau, lemon Louis, Italian, garlic, and flavor crystals, a shaker of each for around $10.00. There are seasonings for meat, fish, or salads, and others that can be added to sour cream to create flavored dips. They are offered in a number of assortments, including a two-tiered hardwood spice rack with 10 different seasoners for about $24.00. Other assortments cost as little as $5.00, with shipping charges included in all prices. You also receive a free gift pack of seasoners, worth $5.00, with any order of $25.00 or more.

□

SIMPSON & VAIL, INC.
53 Park Place
New York, NY 10007
Free brochure. Accepts checks and money orders,
Visa, and MasterCard.

Simpson & Vail, a purveyor of coffees and teas familiar to many New Yorkers, offers about a dozen different choices in the whole bean or ground to individual specifications. Foremost on the list are a Mocha-Java-Colombian blend, a Hawaiian kona blend (which is one of those held in highest regard), and a house blend. All are available in 8-ounce canisters for sampling. More than two dozen teas and tea blends, including a special iced-tea mix that is said not to cloud when cold, are also listed, as well as a dozen or so herbal teas. Bagged teas are also sold. Gift combinations include coffees and teas, along with decorative canisters and coffee mills.

Specific prices were unavailable at the time of this writing because the Simpson & Vail catalog was undergoing revision and prices were being adjusted to compensate for inflation. The firm promises, however, that those prices will "reflect our commitment to provide our customers with the finest quality at reasonable rates."

□

SPECIALTY SPICE SHOP
2757 152 Avenue Northeast
Redmond, WA 98052
(206) 883-1220
Free price list. Accepts checks, money orders, Visa,
and MasterCard.

Since 1911, The Specialty Spice Shop has been selling teas, coffees, and spices to shoppers in Seattle's Pike Place Market, and the company also wholesales these products throughout the country. Most of its products, however, are offered only in quantities far too large to be of interest to the average consumer.

The exception is its Market Spice Tea, a secret blend put together more than 20 years ago by Ruby Rutelonis, wife of the company's owner. This very dark tea produces a heady, fragrant cup that is brisk and spicy without loosing the goodness of the teas. It is one I will be ordering again. The loose tea sells at approximately $6.00 per pound, $3.30 per ½ pound, or $1.85 for ¼ pound. A decaffeinated version costs about $10.00 per pound, $5.65 for ½ pound, or $3.05 for ¼ pound. Tea bags are available only as part of a gift box that contains one box of loose Market Spice Tea, one box of Market Spice Tea bags, and one box of Market Spice all-purpose seasoning, the price around $10.00. Also available is a pine spice rack holding eight cork-stoppered glass jars filled with specialty seasonings such as vanilla powder, barbecue spice, and Italian seasonings, priced at about $20.00. There is a handling charge of $1.00 on orders of less than $10.00, and shipping charges are extra.

□

THE SPICE HOUSE
102 North 3 Street
Milwaukee, WI 53203
(414) 272-1888
Price list: 50 cents. Accepts checks, money orders; no
credit cards. Makes COD shipments. There is a
$2.00 handling charge on orders of less than $25.00.

At 50 cents, the 33-page "price list" sent out by The Spice House, owned by Bill and Ruth Penzey and located in Milwaukee's historic Old World shopping district, is a true bargain. Much more than a simple price list, it not only gives price information on their very complete line of fresh bulk spices, herbs, seeds, and seasonings, but is loaded with helpful, accurate information about each herb and spice and offers dozens of gourmet recipes.

Did I say their list is "very complete"? Take a look. Fresh herbs and spices are offered by the ounce, quarter pound, half pound, and pound, in most cases. Here you are likely to find every type seasoning already known to you, as well as many with which you may not be familiar. Rare seasonings include the pink peppercorns so frequently called for in the French nouvelle cuisine and costly Madagascar vanilla bean "chops" for making old-fashioned, pure extract at home. You'll find three kinds of bay leaves, four kinds of chili powder, five kinds of cinnamon, four curry powders, three varieties of Hungarian paprika, perhaps a dozen peppercorn varieties, and at least three kinds of sage. Just reading about the choices is a fascinating experience.

Those looking for salt substitutes are not forgotten here. Put up in ½-cup shaker jars that sell for approximately $3.00 each are individual flavors and blends that include powdered basil leaves, minced dill leaves, toasted onion powder, diced leeks, powdered lemon juice, minced celery flakes, powdered tarragon leaves, steak seasoning, Parisian *bonnes herbes,* Italian herb mix, and at least a dozen more choices. Those on a salt-free diet should also look at the blends offered under the Sunny label. Omitting all sugar and MSG as well as the salt, the company offers six different blends under this label. At prices ranging between $1.00 and $2.49 per ounce, choices include Sunny California, a blend of sweet red and green peppers, black pepper, garlic powder, and white onion powder; Sunny New Mexico, consisting of ground sweet chili pepper, tomato powder, sweet paprika, ground cumin seeds, garlic, oregano, coriander, allspice, and cloves; Sunny Spain, made up of black pepper, powdered lemon peel, citric acid, garlic and onion powder, and ground shallots; and Sunny Warsaw, a blend of European forest mushroom powder, black pepper, minced green bell peppers, and garlic powder.

A number of interesting seasonings to use in making your

own salad dressings are available here, as well as others for making dips and spreads. Salad dressing blends, all priced at well below $1.00 per ounce, include buttermilk, creamy French, Green Goddess, Italian, and Thousand Island. A number of soup bases are available, too, all put up in bulk paste form in 4-ounce jars that sell for prices ranging from $1.89 to $2.69 per jar. Flavors include beef, chicken, ham, onion, French onion, and turkey.

All the blends sold here are hand-mixed; when grinding is called for, spices are ground with stone mills, and the quality of the products I received and tested was so high that I find it difficult to say enough good things about this 25-year-old company. I can only sum up my feelings by saying I believe their catalog belongs in the hands of all who love fine food.

□

Sugar's Kitchen
P.O. Box 41886
Tucson, AZ 85717
(602) 299-6027
Free brochure and price list. Accepts checks and
money orders only.

When you long for the tart bite of mustard, nothing else will suffice. There are English, French, German, Russian, and American mustards, all of which differ considerably in texture, flavor, and utility. Some are simply flavor enhancers; others serve as emulsifiers and condiments. A mustard in the latter category that has been receiving a lot of favorable attention is a fairly new product called Arizona Champagne Mustard Sauce.

Craig Claiborne, writing for *The New York Times,* called it "One of the most interesting no-salt products to find its way into my own refrigerator . . . fairly spicy and somewhat sweet . . . among the best of the mustards." And Gene Benton, expressing his opinion in the pages of *Bon Appétit,* had this to say: "This is one of the best homemade specialty mustards I've tasted in years. If you enjoy a mild, sweetly piquant mustard, this is one you'll want to try."

Arizona Champagne Mustard Sauce is the creation of a young

woman named Sugar Birdsall. Thick and lightly colored, the sauce is a blend of English dry mustard, champagne wine vinegar, whole eggs, and just a hint of arrowroot. A box of three ½-pint jars sells for around $10.00 plus shipping charges.

Following the success of her first product, Ms. Birdsall has added three new items to her line. These include a hot version of the mustard, called Arizona Fire, a dip for raw vegetables, and a salt-free herbal dip. Like the original mustard, these new products are offered in boxes of three ½-pint jars, and all are priced at around $10.00 per box, plus shipping. Substantial savings are offered on large orders.

□

TONY'S COFFEES & TEAS
1101 Harris Avenue
Bellingham, WA 98225
(206) 733–6319
Free price list. Accepts checks, money orders, Visa, MasterCard, and CODs.

This company began as a small herb shop, later began selling a few teas, and finally acquired a roaster and began selling coffees of gourmet quality. All coffees are roasted daily, "the old-fashioned way—by sight." Visitors to Bellingham are invited to stop by for a free cup of coffee while looking over the cheeses, pastries, and other foodstuffs, which are sold on the premises but not by mail

A very complete line of coffees is available by mail, however. Coffees from Brazil, Costa Rica, and Guatemala are grouped together on the list as "light-bodied." Coffees from Columbia, Mexico, and Nicaragua are described as "medium-bodied." "Full-bodied" roasts include Kenyan, Javan, Sumatran, Mocha Yemen, Mocha Java, and Ethiopian Harrar. Dark roasts all sell for just over $5.00 per pound and include Viennese, Italian espresso, French roast, and continental blend. Hawaiian kona is found here, and there is a coffee with chicory added in the New Orleans fashion.

Teas may be ordered in ½- or 1-pound boxes. In addition to Indian teas, such as Assam and Darjeeling, and Chinese teas, such as green gunpowder lychee and jasmine, there are teas from Sri Lanka, Formosa, and Russia, and blends that range in price from about $2.40 for ½ pound of black currant to around $5.90 for ½ pound of Mandarin orange spice. Shipping charges are extra.

□

CHAPTER TEN

DEHYDRATED FOODS

This chapter is for those who love the outdoor life. Setting aside my search for fine, rare, and exotic delicacies, I have turned my attention here to companies who specialize in dehydrated foods—foods that are light in weight, tasty, yet nutritious enough to sustain you when you leave home for a one-day fishing trip, a weekend stay at the campgrounds, or a three-week hike along the Appalachian Trail.

Those who pursue such interests will have an idea of what is needed in the backpack. Food must be nonperishable, light in weight, and nutritious, providing the proper proteins, fats, and carbohydrates, but it should also meet certain standards of edibility. While it is true enough that most food tastes better in the crisp air of the mountains, the salty breezes of the shore, or alongside a favorite lake, it is equally true that a lousy meal is a lousy meal, no matter where it is eaten, and the serving of poor food is the surest way to ruin any excursion.

The removal of water is the principal means of reducing weight and preventing the spoilage of food. This is done either by simple dehydration or by the more complicated process of freeze-drying, which is one of the benefits of the space effort. No matter how the water is removed, you simply replace it in camp and the food is restored to a fair approximation of its former self. Firms listed in this chapter offer complete meals in dehydrated form, as well as separate items such as fruits, vegetables, snacks, and desserts. For additional flavor and nutrition in trailside soups and stews, there are beef-, ham-, and chicken-flavored vegetable protein additives made from freeze-dried soybean flour, and there are a number of foods in highly concentrated form.

Freeze-dried foods are not, of course, the only foods useful in such situations. In going through the catalogs described in other chapters of this book, you will come across dried fish, shrimp, meat, fruit, and vegetables, as well as high-energy candies and high-protein drink mixes, all of which would be welcome at camp. Beef jerky, salami, and certain other sausages are especially fitted to outdoor living. Take these along, by all means. But do try some of the dehydrated food described in the following chapter. If such foods are new to you, I think you will be pleasantly surprised by what these companies are doing.

☐

AMERICAN OUTDOOR PRODUCTS, INC.
Dri-Lite Foods Division
1540 Charles Drive
Redding, CA 96003
(916) 241–9280
Free brochure. Accepts checks and money orders only; no CODs.

Some 300 freeze-dried foods are listed in this brochure. A wide choice of staples such as breakfast mixes, main-course entrées (with or without meat), vegetables, and soups is accompanied by a selection of fruit varieties, spreads, high-energy snacks, and desserts. All are available in single servings, double servings, or four-person packets. Prices given here are for the four-person packages.

Breakfast items include scrambled eggs (around $2.00), buttermilk pancake mix (around $1.40), maple syrup mix (about 90 cents), French toast mix (about $1.60), and coffee cake mix (around $2.00). A precooked bacon bar to go with all this costs $2.90 or so.

A few of the other meat offerings are pork chops (about $5.00), precooked meatballs (around $3.15), and precooked diced chicken, beef, or ham (all for about $3.10 each). Entrées with meat include beef stroganoff (around $6.65), noodles with chicken (about $5.45), mashed potatoes and gravy with meatballs (about $5.00), and shrimp creole (approximately $8.65). Half a dozen vegetarian entrées are priced between $2.00 and $3.60.

Freeze-dried fruits include applesauce (around $1.80), pineapple tidbits (about $1.90), banana chips ($1.30 or so), and fruit cocktail (about $2.95). For dessert, the company has gingerbread mix (around $2.20), cheesecake mix (around $3.00), and chocolate or butterscotch pudding ($2.50). All shipping charges are extra.

□

CHUCK WAGON FOODS
780 North Clinton Avenue
Trenton, NJ 08638
(609) 392-0122
Free brochure. Accepts checks and money orders only. There is a $3.00 service charge on orders of less than $25.00.

Throughout World War II, Chuck Wagon Foods was a major supplier of such dried foods as biscuits, milk, eggs, and fruit and nut bars to the armed forces. When that conflict came to an end, the company assembled food packages for industry, and in 1957 it began producing dried and dehydrated foods for campers, backpackers, and other outdoor recreationalists.

Nearly 100 varieties of food include breakfast items, fruits, vegetables, soups and chowders, main dishes, desserts, baking mixes, and beverages. Everything is guaranteed to remain edible for at least two years. Food comes in packages that serve two, four, or six people. Prices given here are for the four-serving packages.

The Stack of Cakes breakfast package, priced at around $5.80, includes orange drink, pancakes, and maple syrup—all dehydrated, of course. Or, for about $6.00, your party of four can have cocoa, prebaked biscuits, scrambled eggs, and hash brown potatoes. Other breakfast packages, in the same price range, include fare such as bacon-flavored scrambled eggs, French toast, and Western omelets.

Among the lunch packs are the Liverwurst Deli, which sells for about $7.00 and includes liverwurst spread, biscuits, fruit drink, and granola bars; and the Tuna Fish package, which sells for about $9.00 and contains a ready-to-serve tuna spread, pre-baked biscuits, chocolate milk-shake mix, and fruit-flavored gelatin dessert. Other lunches include items such as chili-mac, peanut butter and jelly sandwiches, cheese and crackers, and dehydrated luncheon meats.

Packaged suppers include the Chicken A La, selling for about $8.50 and containing individual servings of bouillon, chicken à la king, rice, chunky applesauce and fruit drink; and the Alpine, priced at about $8.90 and containing beef-flavored rice, green beans, stewed fruit, and a fruit beverage. Nearly all the items in these breakfast, lunch, and supper packages can be ordered separately; or, for around $11.50, you can order The Sampler, which brings you a complete breakfast, lunch, and supper for two. According to the company, meals in this package were chosen "from a cross section of thousands of orders from satisfied customers." One advantage of ordering the complete meals is that you will know in advance exactly what food costs will be for the trip you have planned. However, there will certainly be times when, and reasons why, you will prefer to order individual dishes, especially if one or two fussy eaters are going along.

Just a few of the dishes that can be ordered include peach slices; oatmeal with sugar, cinnamon, and fruit; potato slices and puffed carrots; vegetable-beef soup; rice and beef with beef gravy; spaghetti with tomato sauce; egg noodles with turkey and turkey gravy; Chinese-style rice and beef; and macaroni in tomato sauce. All are reasonably priced. Prices include shipping, and substantial discounts are given on orders totaling $100.00 or more.

□

FOOD RESERVES, INC.
710 Southeast 17 Street Causeway
Fort Lauderdale, FL 33316
(305) 524–2929
Free catalog. Accepts checks, money orders, Visa, MasterCards; makes COD shipments.

Started about a decade ago, this company was founded because the owners believe that there will be an "ever growing need for the storage of food for various reasons: inflation, famine, the ravages of war or nature." Dehydrated foods listed in the catalog include fruits, vegetables, grains, beverages, plant and animal protein dishes, fats and oils, seasonings, sweeteners and desserts, snacks, and main course dishes for breakfast, lunch, and dinner. Not only can nearly every item in the catalog be ordered in large amounts that would help you survive any long-term crisis, but nearly everything can be ordered in smaller foil pouches that could be carried along on outdoor excursions. Most of these portions hold servings for two.

Breakfast courses include bacon and eggs, granola and blueberries with milk, buttermilk pancake mix, and precooked sausage. Luncheon entrées include, among others, chicken salad, tuna salad, cottage cheese, and applesauce. Dinner entrées include macaroni and cheese, spaghetti with meat and sauce, chilimac with beef, and noodles with chicken. You also have your choice of beef stew, chili with beans, shrimp creole, beef chop suey, chicken chop suey, or any of about a dozen more entrées. All items are priced at $1.60 or less per serving.

Dehydrated peas, green beans, corn, and carrots all cost about 50 cents per serving. Fruits such as pineapple, peaches, pears, and apples cost just under $1.00 per serving. For dessert, there is even ice cream—your choice of chocolate, vanilla, or strawberry—all priced at around $1.50 for a pouch of two servings.

If you agree that the world is headed for disaster, you might want to check out the various food reserve packages put together by this company. These are said to meet the nutritional guidelines set forth by Howard Ruff in his best-selling book, *How to Prosper During the Coming Bad Years* (Times Books, New York, 1980) and each package consists of canned, dehydrated foods intended to sustain a certain number of people for a designated period of time. The basic unit, said to hold enough food to sustain one adult for 12 months, weighs 320 pounds and costs about $645.00. A smaller unit, weighing 80 pounds and selling for just over $200.00, holds food to supply the needs of one adult for 90 days. A package that is supposedly capable of feeding a family of five for a full year is priced at around $3,175.00, and there is even a gourmet unit, for those, I assume, who intend to eat well even in the face of disaster, that weighs 210 pounds, holds enough food to feed an adult for 120 days, and sells for about $820.00. Food Reserves guarantees that its products will remain edible for at least two years, and all freight charges are included in its catalog prices.

□

MOUNTAIN HOUSE FREEZE DRIED FOODS, INC.
3025 Washington Boulevard
Ogden, UT 84401
(801) 621–7022 or (800) 453–9210
Free catalog. Accepts checks, money orders, Visa,
and MasterCard.

The Smithsonian Institution's Museum of Air and Space Science maintains a display of "freeze-dried space foods" that went to the moon with the Apollo missions in the 1960s. The company that helped pioneer these foods, Oregon Freeze Dry Foods, Inc., now produces Mountain House Foods for recreation, storage, industrial, and military needs. More than 80 food varieties are listed in its retail catalog. They offer greater variety, I believe, than any other company in the dehydrated food business.

Most Mountain House products are put up in resealable cans—either #2½ or #10, depending on what goes inside—and, according to the company, the food keeps very well even after the can has been opened and resealed with the plastic top that comes with it. This makes it possible for you to open a large can, take a small pouch of the food along on your outdoor excursion (or whatever), and store the rest for later. However, if you are looking for smaller amounts of a variety of foods, or if, perhaps, you are interested in sampling their wares before committing your money for a large supply of dehydrated food, Mountain House has a sampler you will probably want to order. It costs around $27.00 and contains 11 freeze-dried foods in foil pouches, two or more servings per pouch. Order it and you'll be dining on Pacific shrimp with cocktail sauce, chicken and rice, sausage patties, spaghetti with meat and sauce, turkey tetrazzini, tuna salad, green peas, eggs with butter, beef stroganoff, peaches, and pears. I tried this sampler and was pleasantly surprised by the appearance, taste, quantity, and overall quality of the food it held.

Meats in #10 cans include rib eye steaks, beef jerky, ground beef patties, cod fish fillets, pork chops, ham, sausage, shrimp, tuna, turkey, chicken, and bacon. Those I tried were remarkably fresh in taste.

Twenty-one-serving main course entrées in #10 cans range in price from around $10.35 for noodles with chicken to about $26.00 for shrimp creole. Priced in between those extremes are 16 more entrées, including beef almondine, vegetable stew with beef, rice and chicken, and potatoes with beef. Among the vegetables are carrots, corn, green beans, peas, and spinach, all priced at about $10.00 for 20 to 28 servings in a #10 can. About a dozen fruit varieties are on the list, including apples, banana chips, mixed fruit, strawberries, and pineapple. For dessert, you can choose from among chocolate, butterscotch, or banana cream pudding or select chocolate, strawberry, or vanilla ice cream.

A number of "survival packs" are offered, the least expensive costing about $55.00 and holding eight days' food for one adult, the largest holding 56 complete meals and selling for around $300.00. You could also put together your own stock of food against disaster and save money by ordering food by the case. Substantial discounts are given when you do this. Prices include shipping.

□

STOW-A-WAY INDUSTRIES
166 Cushing Highway
Cohasset, MA 02025
(800) 343–3803; within Masschusetts, call (617) 383–9116.
Free catalog. Accepts checks, money orders, Visa,
and MasterCard; no CODs.

"We ship throughout the world to groups and individuals who range from the highest mountains to the most dismal swamps!" says William White, president of this general backpacking store, which carries its own Stow-Lite brand foods, originally developed and formulated for the space flights under the supervision of the U.S. Army. Also available are other major brands of dehydrated and freeze-dried foods.

Rib Stickers is the name given by the company to its line of meals in a package. These are packaged in heavy-duty plastic containers that store easily and include all the essentials for four hungry people. Most packages weigh about 30 ounces.

Rib Sticker breakfasts range in price from $5.75 to $9.20 for the package of four complete meals. Typical of what you receive is a package priced at $6.95 that includes mixed fruit, oatmeal with milk and sugar, hash brown potatoes, salt and pepper, grape juice drink, and hot cocoa.

The lunches, which require no cooking, range in price from $4.40 to $5.80. The $5.80 choice gives you peanut butter, jelly, deviled meat, trail crackers, a fruit drink, and raisins.

Dinner for four ranges in price from $8.95 to $10.95. A typical choice includes beef soup, macaroni and cheese with ham flavor, crackers, salt and pepper, a fruit drink, and apple dessert. Like all other packages in this line, it comes with mixing pouches and vegetable shortening—everything but the water.

Stow-Lite is the brand name of the company's line of dehydrated foods put up in plastic pouches, four servings to the pouch. This line includes biscuit, cornbread, gingerbread, and brownie mixes, all priced at less than $1.75 per package; vegetables such as corn, beets, spinach, mixed peas and carrots, diced or mashed potatoes, mushrooms, rice, and sliced onions, all priced between $1.20 and $2.70; and desserts that range in price from 85 cents to $1.75 for choices such as butterscotch pudding, fruit-flavored gelatin, Apple Splendor, or Cherry Smash.

Average price for beverages is about $1.00 for four servings. Choices include tomato juice, orange or grapefruit juice, pink lemonade, coffee or cocoa, and even milk shakes in various flavors. Soups range in price from 60 cents for four servings of beef or chicken bouillon to about $1.75 for vegetable soup or minestrone.

About a dozen breakfast dishes are available, the most expensive being the Western omelet, which costs around $2.10 for four servings. Less costly items include French toast, scrambled eggs, and pancakes. Maple, raspberry, and blueberry are among the syrups you can pour over the pancakes, at about $1.00 per pouch.

About a dozen one-pot campfire meals complete the list of Stow-Lite dehydrated foods. In four-serving pouches, these include beef stroganoff, beef stew with gravy, chicken curry with rice, a meatless vegetable stew, and beef hash with potatoes and onions. Average weight of these pouches is about 6 ounces. Prices range from $1.70 to $5.50.

Stow-A-Way offers a unique service; a plan designed for those who plan extended backpacking or hiking trips along the Appalachian Trail or elsewhere. The plan provides for periodic resupply at pickup points along the trail. If you contact the company well in advance and give them your intended itinerary, they will work out a shipping schedule that allows you to pick up food supplies at designated post offices along your route. Free advice on planning your trip is also available from the company's specialists, and they carry a full line of camping, backpacking, and outdoor cooking equipment. Discounts are offered on volume orders, and most prices include the shipping charges.

□

COOKWARE AND ACCESSORIES

There was a time, I am told, when life was simple and cooking was a task. *The Fannie Farmer Cookbook* was the final authority on all things culinary, the ultimate sauce was white in color and that was its name, and a reference to cookware meant nothing but pots and pans. Everything was mixed and kneaded by hand, and nearly every utensil in the kitchen served a dozen purposes.

Today everything is different. We Americans have been introduced to—and learned to love—the cuisine of dozens of nations, added those to our own beloved regional cuisines, and made it nearly impossible to prepare our daily meals without a full battalion of specialized utensils.

But even as our cooking has become more complex it has grown more enjoyable. Miracles such as the blender, food processor, microwave oven and electric carving knife have joined with Teflon, low-cost stainless-steel, copper, and aluminum cookware to ease the physical labor of cooking and help make it one of the most popular hobbies in America. Millions of Americans cook not only because it is necessary but also because it is what they enjoy most. That was always true to some extent, of course, but I believe it is also true that the improvements made in cookware and kitchen accessories have made cooking easier and more interesting than ever before and demonstrated that gourmet dining is for everyone, not just the fortunate few.

Many companies listed in other chapters of this book carry a few kitchen accessories or cooking utensils. Usually these are specialty items linked in some way to the type of food sold by the company. For example, steak knives and other cutlery are sold by many of the companies specializing in meat, coffee mills and coffee pots are available from most companies dealing in coffee and tea, and grain mills and yogurt makers are offered by a number of firms who specialize in natural foods. You will encounter many interesting but limited lines of cookware and accessories as you browse through the catalogs you receive from the mail-order food companies you choose to contact.

In this chapter, however, I have listed companies who make available some of the more varied, interesting, useful, and complete lines of cookware, kitchen accessories, and gadgets. They make available by mail the oldest cooking necessities and the newest kitchen innovations. The familiar and the unusual are there; the basic, alongside the kitchen luxuries. In addition to items needed in preparing meals, there are all the dishes and utensils needed for serving them in nearly any style you choose. The following companies, I believe, offer the finest in cookware and kitchen accessories.

□

THE CHEF'S CATALOG
3915 Commercial Avenue
Northbrook, IL 60062
(312) 480-9400
Catalog subscription: $1.00 per year; 4 issues.
Accepts checks, money orders, Visa, MasterCard,
American Express, and Diners Club. Full guarantee.

"America is a center of international activity and our foods reflect our international tastes," says Marshall Marcovitz, president of The Chef's Catalog, a company that offers a wide selection of professional cookware and countless hard-to-find ingredients for the home chef. "Today, America's melting pot contains the finest antipasto from Wisconsin, chili from Texas, and Oriental sauces from California."

The Chef's Catalog offers all those delectables, along with other gourmet favorites such as Vidalia onions, mountain pepper jellies, smoked barbecue peanuts, rich dessert sauces, shortbreads, fine oils and vinegars, cooking chocolate, and many more. But it is as a source of professional quality cookware and kitchen aids that this catalog has its greatest value, and if you are truly serious about your cooking, you will find the subscription price is a dollar well spent.

Specialized, one-purpose items abound. From France (for less than $15.00) comes a trio of stainless-steel blades used to separate melons into two neatly fluted halves. There are high-speed roasting pins (around $20.00) which speed the heat to the inside of a turkey or roast, thus reducing both shrinkage and cooking time. For less than $15.00, there is an attractive Lucite cheese mill that allows your table guests to grind their own Parmesan or Romano; and for around $13.00, you can own a set of cast aluminum rosette irons of the sort needed to turn out deep-fried Swedish pastry, so delicious when filled with custard, fruit, or jelly. And of course the catalog offers nearly every type of pie, cake, tart, and muffin pan imaginable.

It is not just gadgetry that you'll find here. There is top-quality cutlery, such as the Henckel line of high-carbon steel knives made in Solingren, Germany. These were on sale at a savings of about 30 percent when I checked; also on sale, at comparable savings, was the full line of Cuisinart food processors and accessories. Here, too, you will find famous brands such as Krups and Hamilton Beach, and always at prices that are competitive with the local markets. Brand name or not, everything that goes into The Chef's Catalog is pretested by a staff of experts, and on every item your satisfaction is guaranteed with no questions asked.

□

COLONIAL GARDEN KITCHENS
270 West Merrick Road
Valley Stream, NY 11582
(800) 228–5656
Free catalog. Accepts checks, money orders, Visa,
MasterCard, and American Express. Full guarantee.

Discounts ranging from 15 to as much as 54 percent off the suggested retail price help make this company one of the most attractive among those specializing in cookware and accessories. That and their guarantee of full satisfaction or your money refunded with absolutely no questions asked.

In addition to a few pages of snack items and imported specialty foods such as Welsh rarebit, Irish beef pies, Dutch scrapple, maple syrup, and French escargots, the illustrated catalog shows nearly every tool for the kitchen and dining room one could need or imagine. It is likely to be found here if it is to be found at all.

When you get serious in the kitchen you might want to don a professional chef's apron. Made of 100 percent white cotton duck and obtained from a leading restaurant supply house, these come in a set of three for around $13.00. With the apron on and tied, you can start turning out pizza, bread, pasta, and pastry dough on the 14-by-24-inch marble slab (about $55.00) using the 16-inch rolling pin (under $20.00) that every chef needs. Meanwhile, sauces and such can be started in the stainless-steel, copper-bottomed double boiler that comes with a steamer insert and sells for under $50.00.

In the course of preparing any meal, one almost always encounters the need for specialized tools. Those are found in abundance here. Need a pineapple peeler? For around $5.75, you will find one that cores the fruit and cuts it into perfect slices. Is the ice cream frozen too hard to scoop? Then you should have ordered one of the scoopers that sell for around $15.00 for baller and spade and have inside them a permanent defrosting fluid that makes scooping easy, no matter how hard the ice cream or sherbet. For making deep-dish pizza, pita bread, omelets, and quiche there is a 12-inch cast-iron pan-skillet specially designed to help ensure success; the price is less than $40.00. For baking, broiling, serving, or even for use as pastry molds, authentic deep-sea scallop shells are offered at around $5.98 for a set of six. For more general use, and a real bargain in my opinion, there is a seven-piece copper cookware set that sells for about $35.00. The set includes a 1-quart covered saucepan, a 2-quart covered saucepan, a 3-quart Dutch oven, and an 8-inch skillet, all with brass-plated handles and trim.

For carving in the kitchen or at the dining room table, you'll probably want to have on hand a set of Wilkinson Sword self-sharpening stainless-steel knives. Each time you remove one of these knives from its sharpener-sheath, it is automatically honed to a razor edge. The knives have molded handles for a better grip, and can be wall mounted. The knives are priced between $12.00 and $16.00 each.

Here, too, you will find nearly every type of tableware you might imagine. These include such items as a beautiful salt and pepper set crafted of copper with brass trim (around $21.95), a rustic black candleholder modeled after those found in French wine cellars (about $5.98), a seven-compartment "salad bar" mounted on a lazy Susan (about $13.50), and silver-plated servers for every purpose, as well as glassware and china.

In addition to those items, you will find many novelties that might help brighten your dining hours. For example, there is a set of disposable "sterling" wine goblets that look as if they were crafted from the real thing, 24 of the plastic goblets of 5-ounce capacity for about $25.00. These would make even the most casual meal a little more impressive. To summon your guests to the table, there is a brass dinner bell, crafted in the shape of a windmill, for about $13.00; to impress those who imbibe, there is a clay wine cooler, imported from Italy, that uses no ice and costs around $6.50. Shipping charges are extra.

□

FIGI'S, INC.
Marshfield, WI 54449
(800) 826–8541; within Wisconsin, call collect (715) 387–1771.
Free catalog; request Figi's "Collection for Cooking" catalog. Accepts checks, money orders, Visa, MasterCard, and American Express. Full guarantee.

Serious cooking equipment: professional-quality cookware, practical, durable tools, distinctive serving accessories—from the smallest garnishing utensil to massive restaurant ranges, Figi's has brought it all together in their Collection for Cooking.

That restaurant range is made by Garland, a leader in the industry for more than 100 years. The impressive charcoal-gray stove features a highly sophisticated temperature control system to maintain precisely the temperature selected. Specially insulated double-wall construction provides better heat distribution and retention while saving energy. The cavernous oven and easy-to-clean design make this range the first choice of professional chefs. Call for full details, including price.

For smaller roasting and broiling chores, the Maxim convection oven (about $220.00) will be a welcome addition to the kitchen. The oven features a big, easy-to-see temperature control and a 4-hour timer with buzzer signal. A silent fan inside circulates air continuously for quicker, more uniform baking, broiling, or roasting, and the oven is entirely self-cleaning. A convection-oven cookbook, with more than 200 recipes, is available for $8.95.

With perhaps the exception of a favorite copper pot, nothing is traditionally as close to the heart of a gourmet chef as the butcher-block table. This very functional piece of equipment is the creative heart of the kitchen. Figi's offers such a table, crafted of solid hard-rock maple in the traditional design. The top, 4 inches thick, offers 324 inches of working surface above a handy utensil drawer. The table has adjustable leveling guides to ensure stability, and the price is around $275.00. Less traditional in design, but even more functional is the food-processor cart that sells for approximately $525.00. Constructed of solid hard-rock maple with a generous cutting surface 2½ inches thick, the cart features a removable chopping board that covers a deep stainless-steel dry sink, and along the back of the cart is a completely enclosed knife rack that will accommodate seven knives plus sharpening steel. Beneath the work surface is a wealth of storage space—a utensil drawer, a large, heavy wire vegetable bin, a tray to hold food processor blades, a large, slatted storage shelf, and four wooden pegs for linen and towels. The cart measures 24 by 36 by 36 inches high.

If you have no copper cookware to vie with the butcher-block table for your affection, you will surely be tempted to change that situation after browsing through this catalog. Nothing says "gourmet" as beautifully or traditionally as the soft, warm glow of handcrafted copper cookware, and Figi's has that in abundance. Preferred by great chefs because of its exceptional heat sensitivity, copper provides not only beauty but unequaled temperature control. All copperware sold by Figi's is handcrafted and hand polished.

For around $115.00, there is a set that includes a 2-quart saucepan with cover, a 4-quart stock pot with cover, an 8-inch omelet pan, a 10-inch sauté pan, and a 19-inch brass pot rack. With that rack filled and hanging on the kitchen wall, you may want to begin adding other copperware pieces with more specialized uses. To create velvet-smooth sauces, gravies, and custards you will want the elegant double boiler and 1½-quart ceramic insert that sells for about $49.50; and for the production of perfect au gratin dishes, the 10-by-7-inch oval casserole that costs approximately $37.50 is a must. For beauty as well as utility, there are matching 1-pint oil and vinegar decanters, and to complete your copperware collection, there is a wall rack that comes with a 16-inch fork, soup ladle, spatula, and skimmer (around $39.50 for the set).

If for some reason copper is not your choice in cookware, Figi's also offers a full line of anodized aluminum cookware. Said to be virtually stick-free and nonreactive to foods, the ware has a charcoal-gray satin outer finish that is impervious to chipping or scratching. An eight-piece set sells for approximately $139.50. The set includes a 1½-quart saucepan with cover, a 2½-quart saucepan with cover, an 8-inch omelet pan, a 10-inch sauté pan, and a 6-quart Dutch oven with cover. Pieces may be ordered individually, of course.

For specialty dishes, there are many useful items in this catalog. For example, there is a wok set (around $29.50) that includes a 14-inch, 14-gauge steel wok with aluminum cover, a reversible ring base, wooden steaming rack, chopsticks, and cook booklet. For use in preparing other Oriental-style dishes there is a bamboo steamer with aluminum base that sells for about $33.50. When fish is more tempting to the palate, you will want to break out the 18-inch stainless-steel fish poacher with removable poaching rack that sells for about $62.50, or the fish-shaped stainless-steel fish griller that costs about $18.75 and has adjustable legs so it can be used with any gas or charcoal grill. When your taste runs to the Italian, your hunger will be more easily satisfied if you own the Pastamatic that Figi's sells for around $240.00. All you need do then is place your ingredients in the workbowl. After 5 minutes of machine kneading, the dough will begin to extrude in your choice of eight different pasta shapes from basic spaghetti, noodles, and lasagna to hollow macaronis, bread sticks, cookies, or pizza dough. A step-by-step cookbook comes with this Italian machine.

Crystal, china, fine cutlery, and serving accessories of every kind flesh out this catalog, in such variety that to describe them here is impossible. My own eye was caught, however, by the Alt Amsterdam porcelain serving pieces that are so beautifully illustrated in the catalog. Designed by Villeroy & Boch, the serving pieces include a 13-inch platter (about $60.00) that would certainly be a fitting tribute to your finest crown roast or perfectly browned holiday bird, a 3½-quart tureen (around $125.00) so beautiful it would turn any soup or chowder into a dining celebration, and an 11-inch buffet server (approximately $55.00) you will surely reserve for your most special dinner parties. The pieces are hand-painted in a flowered pattern that reflects the color and charm of their European origins, trimmed with 24K gold plate, and will add a colorful and graceful accent to even the most formal dinner table. Prices do not include shipping.

□

MAID OF SCANDINAVIA COMPANY
3244 Raleigh Avenue
Minneapolis, MN 55416
(800) 228-6722
Free catalog. Accepts checks, money orders, Visa,
and MasterCard. Full guarantee.

Established nearly 40 years ago, Maid of Scandinavia serves as a supply house for hundreds of small commercial bakeries and catering services across the country. Their specialty, as described on the cover of the catalog, is "unusual housewares and cake decorating equipment," and they seem to have located virtually every source of equipment within that scope—enough to fill more than 100 pages of catalog.

For those with little or no experience at decorating cakes, there are dozens of books on the subject; for those who are skilled in this area, the catalog even offers books on how to do it for profit. Once you've decided to try out your hand at something fancy, the catalog has hundreds of cake-decorating tools, including packaged kits for turning out cakes of a specific design. For example, there is a kit that is used to turn out a cake in the shape of a grand piano. For $11.95 or so, you receive two 9-by-18-inch aluminum cake pans of the required shape, a plastic cake base, four snap-on piano legs, a gold-embossed piano lid with a propping stick to hold it up, a bench, pedals, music board, keyboard, and even two miniature candelabra. Dozens of designs such as this are available.

Of course, to produce most of them properly you'll need decorating tubes and bags, cake dummies, decorating combs, cake levelers, markers, food colors, edible glitter, and all the other tools of the cake decorator's art. I don't believe they have left one such tool out of this fascinating catalog.

If you want to turn out original cakes quite unlike all others, a Kopyright projector is the tool you need. This is an opaque projector that will project any flat, nontransparent picture or object onto any surface. You simply project the desired design onto the surface of the cake, outline the design, fill in the details with icing, and you have created a masterpiece. The Kopyright device sells for around $335.00.

For those who choose to cheat a little, there are candy roses, daisies, tulips, baby booties, initials, and other trim in the catalog, nearly all priced at less than $3.00 per dozen. Nonedible cake decorating props to fit every theme are also found here, and there are candy molds and cookie cutters in every shape imaginable. Prices do not include shipping.

□

PFAELZER BROTHERS
4501 West District Boulevard
Chicago, IL 60632
(800) 621–0226; within Illinois, call collect (312) 927–7100.
*Free catalog. Accepts checks, money orders, Visa,
MasterCard, American Express, and Diners Club.
Credit applications available. Full guarantee.*

With Cuisine Vu, "the ultimate cooking guide," you can store the entire contents of 100 cookbooks and then project every recipe on a large, bright screen. Each file card that comes with the set holds up to 98 pages of recipes and cooking advice. Included are nine classic cookbooks, such as *Mrs. Beeton's Book of Household Management* (1861), and books by James Beard, Julia Child, Joyce Chen, and others. The Cuisine Vu sells for around $260.00 and is just one reason every gourmet cook should have the Pfaelzer Brothers catalog.

Also from Cuisinart, and considered essential by many chefs, is the DLC-7E food processor, the most advanced model produced by that firm. With greatly increased bowl capacity, a much stronger motor, new safety features, and a new feed tube large enough to accept whole tomatoes, it is very reasonably priced at about $200.00. For heavier slicing, the company offers Krups' newest electric food slicer. Priced at about $95.00, the slicer comes with serrated stainless-steel blades that can be adjusted to cut meats, cheeses, breads, fruits, and vegetables wafer thin or as much as ¾-inch thick. The slicer folds away for easy storage.

To extract fresh, delicious, vitamin-rich juice from almost any fruit or vegetable, there is Krups' deluxe Biomaster model fruit and vegetable juicer. Priced at about $95.00, the handsome, stream-lined machine drains juice out immediately, preserving vitamins many juicers lose. Minimal moving parts make it easy to use, easier to clean. A special citrus press, also made by Krups, is priced at about $45.00.

The famous Krups line is further represented in the catalog by its electric coffee mill (under $30.00), deep-brew coffee and tea maker (around $150.00), and electric espresso and cappuccino maker (about $425.00). The espresso maker is said to use the same filter and filter holder found on machines costing thousands of dollars, has pushbutton controls, and will produce two cups of cappuccino or espresso every 30 seconds. It comes with four 2-cup stainless-steel baskets for holding the coffee.

From Taylor & Ng, there is an ingenious one-pan gourmet breakfast set that features a cast-iron press to hold bacon straight and flat on the 12-inch carbon-steel griddle. Two special corrals in the griddle help give shape and evenness to the eggs. The set sells for about $22.50, or you can spend just under $60.00 and receive with it 5 pounds of smoked, delicately spiced Canadian bacon.

For cooking some of the fine food you may order from

Pfaelzer and other companies listed in this book, you could do worse than use the famous Mirro cookware featured in this catalog. Made from extremely heavy-gauge, professional-weight aluminum, the Mirro line features a handsome charcoal finish that is bonded by a special electrochemical process. It is easy to clean, virtually scratchproof, and stick-free. A nine-piece set sells for about $140.00, a savings of 17 percent over the same pieces bought individually. The set includes a 1-liter saucepan with lid, a 2-liter saucepan with lid, a 5-liter stockpot with lid, a 10-inch frying pan with lid, and an 8-inch sauté pan. Available only by itself, at a cost of $35.95 or so, is a 12-inch frypan.

For those who like to more fully observe their food as it cooks, the glass cookware by Corning will be preferable to metal pots and pans. Extremely durable and virtually shatterproof, the five-piece LeClaire set is priced at about $75.00. It includes a 1.7-liter glass saucepan, a 1.5-liter glass casserole with cover, and a 2.5-liter glass casserole with cover. The pieces are attractive enough to double as serving dishes.

The copperware offered by Pfaelzer Brothers is so beautiful it will be admired almost as much as it is used. Artisans from France hand-hammered cold sheets of copper to produce this beautiful cookware, and the gleaming results will turn the dreariest kitchen into a place of real beauty. The complete seven-piece set sells for around $590.00, a savings of about $120.00 over the same pieces ordered individually. It includes a 2½-quart saucepan with lid, a 1-quart saucepan with lid, a 9½ inch frypan, a 2-quart *sauteuse*, and an omelet pan with an extra long handle. Not included in the set and available only individually is a beautiful, efficient, hand-hammered copper sauce and butter warmer (approximately $25.00). You simply place a candle inside, light it, and add an elegant gourmet touch to any meal. The gourmet flair can be heightened by using Pfaelzer's luxurious copper molds for appetizers and desserts. There are three 6½-inch molds in the set that sells for around $38.00, with sculpted designs of fruit, flowers, and lobster, an ideal gift for anyone who entertains with style and grace.

To add even more elegance to the dining table, Pfaelzer Brothers offers fine porcelain ware from Cordon Bleu. All this porcelain is tastefully decorated with Cordon Bleu's ever popular

Fontainebleau pattern. For under $60.00, there is a three-piece soufflé set that includes a 1-quart soufflé, a 1½-quart soufflé, and a 2-quart soufflé. Matching those, for just over $60.00, is a set of two casseroles, one of 1½-quart capacity, the other capable of holding 2 full quarts. In the same pattern, for about $25.00, is a cow-shaped creamer and matching sugar bowl.

For cutting into those fine steaks and roasts sold by Pfaelzer Brothers, tender as they may be, the finest cutlery is almost demanded. For that purpose, the firm offers Dreizack blades, imported from Europe. To make these, European craftsmen hand-forge carbon steel, molybdenum, and vanadium into blades of surgical quality. Unlike plain carbon-steel blades, these are stain resistant. For heavy cutting in the kitchen, the line features a finely-balanced, razor-sharp 8-inch cleaver with hardwood handle (about $23.00).

Then there is a seven-piece set (approximately $190.00) that includes all the professional-quality kitchen cutlery you are ever likely to need: a 10-inch carving knife, an 8-inch chef's knife, an 8-inch bread knife, a 3½-inch paring knife, a 5-inch boning knife, a sharpening steel, and a slanted knife block. Finally, for even more impressive serving of those delicious steaks, there is a set of six steak knives for under $55.00. Prices do not include shipping.

□

WILLIAMS–SONOMA
P.O. Box 7456
San Francisco, CA 94120
(415) 652–9007
Free catalog. Accepts checks, money orders, Visa, MasterCard, Diners Club, American Express, and Carte Blanche. Full guarantee.

Chuck Williams, president of Williams-Sonoma, has put together one of the finest, most complete collections of cookware and related items to be found anywhere. His full-color catalog features cookware and appliances by leading American manufacturers, as well as imports from all parts of the world. Kitchenaid, Pyrex, Hamilton Beach, Krups, and Cuisinart are just a few of the brand names customers will quickly recognize, while other goods are supplied by leading manufacturers in France, Italy, Belgium, Scandinavia, and even Brazil, to name just a few countries where Williams conducts his search for fine housewares.

From France, Williams brings a set of 10 tempered glass cooking bowls (around $20.00) that range from 2½ to 10 inches in diameter; a white porcelain *coeur à la crème* mold (about $15.00) for making the simple but classic dessert of cottage cheese, cream, and cream cheese; and dozens of other offerings, including a set of six shiny steel tartlet pans (under $10.00) that have removable bottoms so you can extract your pastries without breaking the edges. From England, he brings us a heart-shaped, tinned steel cake pan that measures 3¾ inches in height and 8¾ inches long (for less than $10.00) and has rolled edges to prevent warping, and from Italy, there is a 7½-by-6½-inch loaf pan specially designed for making panettone (about $7.00), the light and airy coffee cake of the Italians. From Brazil, he fetches some very fine porcelain, including a white porcelain coffee server that holds 40 ounces, is dishwasher safe, and sells for under $20.00.

If, during the course of some gray winter afternoon, you want to brighten life with tea and hot buttered crumpets, you will want to have on hand a set of crumpet rings. Made of aluminum and sold in a set of six, these rings are simplicity itself; you merely place them on a hot griddle or frying pan and spoon in the batter. The set sells for approximately $11.00. Brew your tea, then, in a stunning blue porcelain teapot with a removable porcelain infuser, 32-ounce capacity, imported from England and selling for approximately $15.00. But if coffee is your drink, you'll probably want to order, instead, the Krups coffee mill that mills the beans into flakes instead of cutting them into granules as most grinders do (about $20.00) and the Krups Coffee-time coffeemaker that maintains the ideal temperature of 203°F and has a timer that can be set up to 24 hours in advance to start brewing whenever you wish (about $130.00). If hot muffins sound better than crumpets, make them in a unique early American cast-iron muffin pan that turns out muffins in four shapes said to symbolize the four seasons, is hand-cast by Pennsylvania craftsmen, and sells for about $10.00. If you prefer waffles with your brew, produce those in a stove-top Belgian waffle iron made of cast aluminum with a nonstick coating, priced at around $35.00, and designed to produce waffles with extra deep pockets that will capture all the topping. One topping you might try is ice cream made in your own Minigel ice-cream maker. Priced at about $650.00, this professional-quality machine takes all the guesswork out of ice-cream making and will produce a quart of ice cream, sherbet, or fresh fruit *sorbet* in about 15 minutes.

Other appliances sold here include pasta makers, milk-shake mixers, juice extractors, bar mixers, and the complete Cuisinart line of food processors and accessories. Very frequently the company offers these appliances at greatly reduced prices. Shipping charges are extra on all orders.

□

Index

Abalone, 19, 23
Alfalfa seeds, 85
Almond(s), 129, 132, 134, 139–140,
    147, 149, 151
    paste, 69
Amaretti, 118
American cheese, 108, 109
Anchovies, 45
Anchovy sauce, 58
Anise, 52
    star, 203
Aniseed, 58
Antelope, 28
Antipasto, 232
Apple(s), butter, 67
    dried, 85, 86, 132, 152
    fresh, 131, 136, 138, 145, 146, 147
    organic, 131, 152
    schnitzel, 188
Apricots, 85, 130, 131, 132, 142, 145,
    150, 153, 155
Arrowroot, 51
Asparagus tips, 139
Avocados, 146

Babas, petit, 164
Bacon, 4, 5, 7, 10, 11, 14, 16, 18,
    23–24, 27, 29, 34, 166
Baked goods, 58. See also specific
    name; type
    natural, 77, 80, 82, 87
Baklava, 71, 117
Bamboo shoots, 58, 63
Banana(s), 85, 86

chips, 63, 132, 135
    flakes, 152–153
Bass, 44
Batter mix, 48
Bean(s), 50, 51, 52, 61, 63, 69, 152
    curd, 63
    curd cakes, 58
    green, 88, 145
    jelly, 63
    natural, 88
    sprouts, 63
Bear, 28
Beauty aids, natural, 76–77, 84
Bee pollen, 85
Beef, 6, 8, 10–11, 12, 16, 18, 21,
    22–23, 25, 27, 29–30, 31, 32, 34,
    96, 97
    corned, 70
    kosher, 70–71
    natural, 8, 81, 88
Beer cheese, 93
Beets, 65, 152
Beverages. See also specific name; type
    dehydrated, 223, 228
Biscuit(s), 117–118
    mixes, 123
    sourdough, 123
Blue cheese, 96, 100–101, 105
Blueberries, 153
Bluefish, 44
Bologna, 26–27, 32, 33–34, 70, 96
Bon Bree cheese, 104
Boursalt cheese, 91
Bowls, 242

Boysenberries, 141–142
Brazil nuts, 69, 130, 140, 149
Brazilian foods, 69
Bread(s), 19. *See also specific name*
  natural, 77, 125
  mixes, 125–126
Breading mix, 48
Breadsticks, 117
Breakfast, items, dehydrated, 222,
  223–224, 225, 228
  mixes, 121
Brick cheese, 93, 96, 99, 104, 107, 108,
  109, 110
Brie cheese, 91, 95, 99, 100, 108
Bruder basil cheese, 91
Brussels sprouts, 139
Bryndza cheese, 66
Buffalo, 6, 7, 25
Butcher-block tables, 235
Butter(s), 80
  cheese, 91
  dill-tarragon, 139
  fruit, 67, 69, 130, 137, 139, 188
  maple, 162
  nut, 153
Butterfish, 45

Cabbage, 59, 65
Cake(s), bird's nest, 71
  cheese. *See* Cheesecakes
  confection, 164
  cordial, 190
  decorating equipment, 237–238
  fruit. *See* Fruitcakes
  Italian, 118, 124
  Middle Eastern, 71
  mixes, 126
  natural, 80, 125
  nut, 119, 146, 149
  rye honey, 58
  sugar-free, 188
  tea, 125
Caldillo, 72–73
Camembert cheese, 91, 95, 100
Candied fruits, 69, 72, 118, 155
Candied rose petals, 69
Candies, 107, 164–165, 174, 180–181,
  189–190, 211. *See also*
  Chocolate(s)
  Cajun, 56
  fruit, 146, 175
  hard, 157, 158
  Italian, 118
  jelly, 157
  maple-sugar, 161, 162, 167
  Middle Eastern, 72
  mint, 155
  natural, 78, 86
  nut. *See* Nut(s), candies
  Oriental, 52, 53, 63
  yogurt-coated, 132
Cane syrup, 56
Capons, 18
Caraway cheese, 109

Carob, 78, 83, 85, 132
Carp, 47
Carrots, 145, 152
  natural, 86, 88
Cashews, 81, 85, 130, 132, 135, 140,
  149, 153
Catalogs, ix–x
Catfish, 47
Caviar, 18, 37–38, 45, 62
Cereals, natural, 76, 88
Cheddar cheese, 83, 86, 91, 93, 96, 98,
  99, 102–104, 105, 106, 107, 109,
  110, 124
Cheese(s), 9, 11, 15, 19, 26, 32, 58,
  90–110, 166. *See also specific
  name*
  balls, 78, 80, 83, 86
  curds, 48
  fondues, 91
  logs, 91, 95, 97, 98, 108
  mills, 232
  natural, 78, 80, 83, 86
  spreads, 91, 93, 95, 96–97, 100, 101,
  105, 108–109
  sticks, 80, 121
Cheesecakes, 116, 118, 119, 122–123
Cherries, 146
  brandied, 145, 164
Chestnuts, 62, 53, 186
Chia seeds, 85, 87
Chicken, 7, 8, 13, 23, 24, 25, 28, 30,
  71
Chick-peas, 59
Chicory, 55
Chili, 67–68, 72, 232
Chilies, 73, 203
  jelly, 186
Chinese foods, 52–53, 57–58, 202–204
Chocolate(s), 58, 118, 167–169,
  171–173, 176, 178–179, 192. *See
  also specific item*
  cakes, 117
  cooking, 164, 232
  dessert shells, 156
  Dutch, 58
  filled, 155, 157, 158–159, 160, 161,
  164, 173, 181, 192
  ground, 185
  natural, 78
  sculpted, 58, 156, 164, 179, 183
Chow-chow, 67, 188
Chowders, 37, 88–89, 273
Chubs, lake, 47
Chutneys, 57, 187
Cider, apple, 163
  jelly, 139, 166
Clam(s), 40, 43, 45, 46, 47–48, 50, 65
  sauce, 59
Cockles, 50
Cocoa, hot, 185
Coconut, 57, 58
  candies, 86
  chips, 58, 132
  natural, 86

Cod, 44
-liver, 58
Coffee(s), 19, 53, 65, 72, 91, 92, 171,
    193–194, 197–198, 201–202,
    206–207, 209, 210, 212, 213, 215,
    216, 219
  additives, 213
  decaffeinated, 198, 202, 213
  equipment for making, 199, 210,
    239, 242
  flavored, 61, 209, 210
  substitutes, 200
Colby cheese, 83, 86, 91, 92, 96, 106,
    108, 109, 110
Cold cuts, 26–27
Condiments, 11, 19, 55, 200. See also
    specific name; type
Cookbooks, 51, 66, 79, 238–239
Cookie(s), 113–114, 120, 121, 142
  chocolate chip, 115–116, 117, 119
  Danish, 112
  fortune, 53, 63
  Italian, 118
  mixes, 129
  natural, 77, 125
  wheat-free, glutenless, 82
Cookware. See specific item
Coriander, 52, 203
Corn, 152
  dried sweet, 54
Cornish game hens, 10, 17, 23, 25, 28,
    30, 71
Crab(s), 23, 43, 46, 48
  claws, 43
  legs, 19, 23, 43, 46
Crabmeat, 39, 40, 41, 42, 43
Crackers, 19, 113, 114
Cream, maple, 167
Creole foods, 55–56, 160–161
Croustilles, 117
Cultures, dairy, 79, 83–84
Currants, dried, 130
Curry powder, 52
Cutlery, 232, 233–234, 237, 241

Dairy cultures, 79, 83–84
Date(s), 72, 132, 135, 150
  natural, 86, 130
  products, 86, 136
Deer, 17, 28
Dehydrated foods, 220–229. See also
    specific item
Dessert(s). See also specific name; type
  dehydrated, 222, 223, 225, 227, 228
  toppings, 62, 131, 179–180
Dill-tarragon butter, 139
Dips, 219
Dog food, vegetarian, 89
Dough, 69, 71
Doughnut mix, 55
Dressings, salad, 188, 218
Ducks, 10, 17, 18, 25, 28, 58, 71
Dumplings, pike, 62
  veal, 62

Eastern European pastry, 71, 116–117
Edam cheese, 58, 91, 93, 108, 109, 110
Edel-Swiss cheese, 109
Eel, 19
Egg(s), drops, 69
  quail, 20
  substitutes, 82
Eggplant, 63
Emmenthal cheese, 93
Endive, 145
Entrées, dehydrated, 222, 223, 224,
    225, 226, 227, 228–229
Escargots, 61, 233
Ethnic foods. See specific ethnic group

Fat, chicken, 71
Fertilizer, 83
Feta cheese, 71, 100
Fiddleheads, 139
Fig(s), 72, 85, 131, 132, 150
  bars, 80
Filbert nuts, 81, 130, 132, 140
Finnan haddie, 44
Fish. See also specific name
  dried, 57, 58
  griller, 236
  poacher, 236
Flageolets, 62, 69
Flavorings, Oriental, 203
Flax seeds, 85
Flounder, 44, 48
Flour(s), 9, 50, 63, 67, 69
  mill, 81
  natural, 78, 83, 87, 88, 125
Foie gras, 18, 62, 65
Food coloring, 69
Food processors, 232, 239, 243
  cart for, 235
Française cheese, 109
Freeze-dried foods, 196, 221–222, 223.
    See also Dehydrated foods
French foods, 61–62
Frogs' legs, 47, 48
Fromage de Coeur, 109
Fruit(s). See also specific name; prod-
    uct
  brandied, 145, 164, 186–187
  candied, 69, 72, 118, 155
  canned, 153
  dehydrated, 222, 223, 224, 225, 227
  dried, 69, 72. See also specific name
  fresh, 116, 117. See also specific
    name
  juices, 72, 78
  pickled, 139
  pies, 141
  relish, 145
  spreads, 139
Fruitcakes, 62, 114–115, 116,
    118–119, 121, 125, 143, 146, 148,
    149, 177–178
Fudge, 157, 161, 185

Game. See specific name

Garlic, 73, 152, 208
Gelatins, natural, 78
Ginger, candied, 155
Glutenless baked products, 82
Goat, 28
Goose, 18, 27
Gouda cheese, 58, 91, 96, 108
Grains, natural, 81, 84, 85, 87, 88
Granola, 88
Granular curd cheese, 101–102
Grapefruit(s), 128, 132, 136, 145, 146,
    147, 148, 149, 151
  natural, 131, 144
Grapes, 136, 146, 159–160
Green Mountain Bleu cheese, 105–106
Green Mountain Jack cheese, 105
Griddle, 239
Grinders, food, 76, 81
Gruyère cheese, 93

Haddock, 44
Halabiyey cheese, 71
Halibut, 44, 47
Hams, 3–4, 5, 7, 9, 10, 13–14, 15, 16,
    17, 18, 21–22, 23–24, 25, 27,
    28–29, 34, 50, 55–56, 65, 166
  natural, 9
Havarti cheese, 93, 96
Hawaiian bread, 124
Hazelnuts, 69, 147, 149
Health aids, 76–77, 195
Health foods. *See specific name; type*
Herb(s), 52, 61, 65, 69, 194, 196, 199,
    203, 207, 208, 209, 211, 212, 217.
    See also specific name
  freeze-dried, 196
  medicinal, 195
  natural, 81
  plants, 200–201, 208
  tablets and capsules, 195
  teas. *See* Tea(s), herbal
Herring, 44, 45, 47
Hibachi, electric, 109–110
Hispanic foods, 50, 72–74
Hollander cheese, 109
Honey, 9, 76, 80, 83, 86, 135, 137,
    144, 147, 160, 162, 171, 184, 190
  cakes, 58, 71

Ice-cream maker, 243
Indonesian foods, 56–58, 63, 69
Italian foods, 58–59, 96, 105, 117–118,
    124

Jams, 9, 26, 69, 137, 139, 141, 142,
    148, 171, 184, 188, 190
  sugar-free, 188
Japanese foods, 51–52
Jarlsberg cheese, 93, 105
Jelly, 9, 26, 56, 58, 60
  bean, 63
  chili, 186
  cider, 139, 166

fruit, 88, 137, 139, 141, 142, 148,
    160, 188, 190
  natural, 88
  pepper, 60, 73, 232
  shrimp, 58
  sugar-free, 188
  tarragon, 139
Juicers, 76, 239
Juices, 72, 78

Kefir grains, 84
Kelp, sea, 83
Kishke, 70
Kitchen accessories and gadgets, 79,
    211, 232, 233
Kiwi fruit, 136, 146
Korv-Ost, 109
Kosher foods, 23, 69–71
Kümin cheese, 58, 109

Lamb, 12–13, 16, 18, 23, 26, 27, 30, 71
  kosher, 71
  natural, 9, 81
Leeks, 208
Lentils, 69, 85, 145, 152
Leyden cheese, 91
Limburger cheese, 91, 104
Liver, 8, 13, 18, 33, 58, 65
Llama, 28
Lobster, 23, 43, 45, 47, 50
  tails, 23, 47
Lox, 45
Lychees, 58

Macadamia nuts, 81, 85, 131, 140, 151,
    170–171
Mackerel, 44
Mallards, 18, 25
Mangoes, 58
Maple-sugar candies, 161, 162, 167
Maple syrup, 15, 78, 83, 102, 137, 138,
    161–162, 166–167, 173, 188–189,
    233
  cream, 167
Marmalade, 11, 142, 148
Meal, 9, 48, 125
Meat(s). *See also specific name; type*
  dehydrated, 223, 227
  kosher, 69–71
  substitutes, 78
Mexican-American foods, 72–74
Middle Eastern foods, 63, 71–72, 123,
    124–125
Milk substitutes, 80, 82
Mills, 76, 81, 232
Mints, candy, 155
Mix(es)
  batter, 48
  biscuit, 123
  bread, 125–126
  breading, 48
  cake, 126
  dehydrated, baking, 223
  doughnut, 55

Mixes *(continued)*
  macaroon, 129
  muffin, 126
  pancake, 123, 126
  wheat-free, 82
Mixers, bar, 243
  milk-shake, 243
Molasses, 76, 78, 80, 86, 163, 187–188
Molds, 242
Monastery cheese, 66
Monkfish, 44
Monterey Jack cheese, 91, 99, 110
Mousse, salmon, 38
Mozzarella cheese, 96
Muenster cheese, 93, 96, 104
Mushrooms, 19, 48, 52–53, 62, 63,
  65
Mussels, 43, 45, 50, 58
Mustard(s), 187, 218–219
  powder, 203–204
  sauces, 218–219

Natural foods, 8–9, 75–89, 118–119,
  125–126, 129–131, 134–135,
  143–144, 152–153, 188–189,
  214–215
Nectarines, 136, 146
Noodles, 53, 63, 69
Nut(s), 133, 135, 136, 153. *See also*
  specific type
  butters, 153
  cake, 119, 146, 149
  candies, 56, 61, 134, 140, 143,
    149–150, 158–159, 160, 161, 164,
    168–169, 171, 172, 173, 174, 175,
    176, 177, 178, 181, 185, 186, 192
  natural, 76, 80–81, 85, 86, 130, 131
  paste, 69
  pies, 117
  spreads, 171
  yogurt-coated, 132

Octopus, 43, 50
Oils, 50, 51, 83, 129, 187, 232
Old Heidelberg cheese, 100
Olives, 83, 145
Onions, 152, 232
Oranges, 56, 128, 132, 136, 146,
  147–148, 149, 151
  natural, 86, 131, 144
Order, receiving, xxi–xxiii
Ordering, x–xi
Oriental foods, 51–53, 56–58, 63, 69.
  See also specific country
Ostyepka cheese, 66
Oven, convection, 235
Oysters, 42, 43, 46, 50, 65

Paella, 50
Palm, hearts of, 62
Pancake mixes, 123, 126
Panettone, 118, 124
Panforte, 118
Pans, 61, 232, 233, 235–236, 240, 242

Papaya, 85, 130
  brandied, 145
Paprika, 64, 69, 211, 212
Parmesan cheese, 96
Parsley, 52, 203
Partridges, 18, 28
Pasta(s), 59
  makers, 243
  natural, 78
  wheat-free, 82
Pastes, 57, 69
Pastry. *See also specific type*
  Danish, 121
  Eastern European, 71, 116–117
  French, 117
Pâté, 18, 38, 39, 62
Payment methods, xxi
Peaches, brandied, 187
  canned, 153
  dried, 85, 130, 132, 145
  fresh, 136
Peanuts, 80, 85, 131, 135, 140–141,
  143, 153, 232
Pears, canned, 153
  dried, 86, 131, 142, 145
  fresh, 136, 146–147, 151
Peas, 69, 85, 139, 152
Pecan(s), 80–81, 85, 130, 143,
  148–149, 151, 174, 181
  pie, 117
Pennsylvania Dutch foods, 53–54,
  66–67, 187–188, 233
Pepper(s), 50, 59, 73, 139, 152. *See
  also specific type*
  jellies, 60, 232
Peppercorns, 52, 203
Pepperoni, 96
Perch, 44, 47
Petit-fours, 169, 178–179, 191
Pheasant, 10, 15, 17, 18, 25, 28
Pickled foods, 58, 62, 63, 65, 139, 163
Pickles, 138
Pies, 117, 141
Pig, suckling, 25, 27
Pike, 47
  dumplings, 62
Pine nuts, 81, 153, 186
Pineapples, 85, 132, 136, 153
Pistachio nuts, 80, 130, 132, 133–134,
  140, 151
Pita bread, 123, 124–125
Plum(s), 51, 146
  pudding, 121
Pollock, 44, 47
Pont l'Evêque cheese, 91
Popcorn, 54, 138, 182–183
  poppers, 183
Poppy seeds, 69
Pork, 13, 17, 23, 25, 26, 32, 65. *See
  also specific type*
  natural, 9, 81
Port Salut cheese, 93, 107, 109
Potatoes, 152
Pots, 61, 233, 235–236, 240

Poultry. *See also specific type*
    kosher, 71
    natural, 81, 88
Pralines, 56, 61
Prepared foods, 13, 24–25, 29, 30, 51,
    59, 63, 65, 71, 72–73, 78, 88, 203.
    See also Dehydrated foods
Preserves, 56, 72, 76, 136, 137, 139,
    141, 142, 145, 160, 162, 170, 187
Press, cast-iron, 239
Pretzels, 120–121, 161
Prosciutto, 18
Provolone cheese, 96, 105
Puddings, 121, 166
Pumpkin, 152
    seeds, 85

Quail, 6, 23
    eggs, 20

Raisins, 72, 130, 135
    carob-coated, 132
Range, restaurant, 234–235
Red snapper, 44
Relishes, 19, 138, 145, 162–163
Rexoli cheese, 100
Rice, 51, 61, 63
    cakes, 63
    wafers, 80
Rolls, sourdough, 123
Rondelé cheese, 93
Rose hips, 88
Rose petals, candied, 69
Rosebuds, brandied, 145
Rosette irons, 232
Rye bread, 50, 58

Salami, 6–7, 24, 27, 32, 50, 70, 96
Salmon, 15, 19, 23, 38, 40–41, 42,
    44–45, 46, 47
    natural, 88
Salsify, 145
Salt(s), 205
    sea, 83
    substitutes, 214, 215, 217
Salt-free products, 214–215, 217,
    218–219
Sandwich kits, 60–61
Sardines, 45, 50, 65
Sauces, Creole, 55, 60
    dessert, 56, 160, 186, 232
    Hispanic, 50, 73
    Indonesian, 57, 58
    mustard, 218–219
    Oriental, 51, 63, 203, 232
    seafood, 48, 58, 59
Sauerkraut, 65, 152
Sausage(s), 4–5, 9–10, 11–12, 14, 18,
    27, 31–32, 34, 50, 65, 96, 97, 106
    kosher, 70
    natural, 9
Scallop(s), 23, 43, 48
    shells, 233
Scrapple, 66–67, 233

Scrod, 23, 44
Seafood, 18–19, 23. *See also specific
    name; type*
Seasonings, 61, 200, 216, 217–218
    salt-free, 214–215, 217
Seaweed, 51
Seeds, 61. *See also specific names*
    natural, 76, 83, 85
Sesame seeds, 85
Shad roe, 45, 65
Shallots, 138, 208
Shark, mako, 44
Shipping, xi–xiii
Shortbread, 232
Shrimp, 23, 40, 42, 43, 45, 46, 47, 48,
    53, 57
    jelly, 58
Silver hake, 44
Smelt, 44, 47
Snacks, dehydrated, 222
Sno-Belle cheese, 100
Sole, 44
Sonoma Jack cheese, 124
Sorghum, 163
Soup(s), 19, 55, 59, 60, 61, 63
    bases, 218
    dehydrated, 78, 222, 223, 224
    natural, 76, 78
Sourdough products, 123, 126, 185
Soy products, 80
Spices, 19, 52, 55, 59, 65, 69, 194, 196,
    200, 203–204, 205, 207, 208,
    211–212, 216, 217, 218. *See also
    specific name*
Sprats, 45
Spreads, 139
    cheese. *See* Cheese(s), spreads
    dehydrated, 222
    sugar-free, 188
Squab, 17, 28
Squash, 152
Squid, 50
Steamers, 61, 236
Stollen, 121
Sturgeon, 40, 41, 45, 46
Sugar crystals, 69
Sugar-free products, 188
Sunflower seeds, 76, 83, 85, 132
Survival packs, dehydrated, 225–226,
    227
Sweetbreads, 8
Swiss cheese, 86, 91, 96, 104, 107,
    108, 109
Swordfish, 44, 47
Syrups, 11, 56, 72, 137, 138–139, 160,
    163–164. *See also* Maple syrup

Tableware, 52, 61, 110, 234, 237,
    240–241, 242
Tahini, 153
Tarragon jelly, 139
Tea, 19, 51, 65, 193, 194, 198,
    202–203, 204, 206, 207, 209, 210,

Tea *(continued)*
    211, 212, 213–214, 215, 216,
    219–220
  decaffeinated, 198, 216
  flavored, 198–199, 205, 210, 212,
    214, 220
  herbal, 72, 76, 88, 195, 199–200,
    205, 208, 210, 215
Thermometer, dairy, 79
Tiger Milk, 80
Tomatoes, 152
Toppings, dessert, 62, 131, 179–180
Tortes, 117, 170, 179, 191
Trout, 9, 23
  brook, 45
  lake, 47
  rainbow, 44
  sea, 44
Truffles, 62
  chocolate, 155, 173, 181
Tuna, 45
  albacore, 40, 41, 42, 46
  yellowfin, 44
Turkey, 6, 7–8, 10, 13, 15, 18, 24, 25,
    27–28, 34, 55, 71
Tuscany cheese, 109

Veal, 13, 17, 23, 26, 27, 30, 32–33
  dumplings, 62
  kosher, 71
  natural, 8
Vegetables, 19. *See also specific name*
  canned, 144–145, 152

dehydrated, 222, 223, 224, 225, 227,
    228
  natural, 152
  prepared, 71
Venison, 17, 28
Vine leaves, 62, 63, 71
Vinegar, 51, 187, 232
Vitamins, 76, 81

Wafers, 57, 80
Waffle(s), 58
  iron, 242, 243
Walnuts, 62, 69, 85, 131, 149
Water cracker, 113
Wensleydale cheese, 91
Wheat-free baked products, 81–82
Wheat germ, 83
Whey, 80
Whitefish, 44, 45, 47
Whiting, 47
Wine, 184
  coolers, 234
Wok set, 236

Yogurt
  beauty aids, 84
  -coated nuts and candies, 132
  cultures, 79, 83–84
  maker, 81, 84
  tablets, 84

Zucchini, 152